MARTIN ERBSTÖSSER

The Crusades

MARTIN ERBSTÖSSER

The Crusades

UNIVERSE BOOKS
New York

Translated from the German by C. S. V. Salt

Published in the United States of America in 1979
by Universe Books
381 Park Avenue South, New York, N.Y. 10016

Copyright © 1978 by Edition Leipzig

Library of Congress Catalog Card Number 78-60641
ISBN 0-87663-331-9

Designed by Volker Küster, Leipzig
Line drawings by Lutz-Erich Müller
Maps by Renate Gatza
Ground plans by Inge Brüx

Printed in the German Democratic Republic

CONTENTS

Introduction

The Crusades by the knights and princes of Western and Central Europe to the Near East were events which, although they happened between seven and nine centuries ago, still attract the attention of readers with an interest in history. This is perhaps not so much because of the alien nature of the concepts, happenings and customs of this age but rather because questions are implied which go far beyond the immediate historical process.

The people of the time initially regarded the crusade movement as a confrontation between Christendom and Islam and the "liberation of the Holy Sepulchre from the hands of the Infidels" as the principal purpose of all warlike actions. The historian sees this era from a somewhat different point of view, however.

In its very nature, the penetration of the Mediterranean area by knights from Western Europe was not simply just expansion but also represents a collision between the very different mediaeval feudal societies of Islam, Byzantium and Western Europe. Although the principal classes were similar in each case, there were fundamental differences in important details, particularly in respect of the material and intellectual level of society as a whole. The feudal society of Arab Islamism with its almost unique heritage in the historical sense of the civilizations of Classical Antiquity and the ancient Asiatic cultures had already reached its heyday before the Crusades; the feudal order of Europe could in no way be compared to this. Most of the Mediterranean area as far as Spain was included in this development. The Byzantine feudal system covered Asia Minor, South-Eastern Europe and Southern Italy. Its material and intellectual standards were of a similar order. On the eve of the Crusades, the Arab Caliphate and the Byzantine Empire were the centres of feudal civilization. In comparison to these, Western and Central Europe were at the periphery of world history.

This rough assessment outlines a state and says nothing about the social dynamics which existed within the feudal order of society in the territories in question. On the contrary, the orientation of the European feudal societies in the countryside, on estates and within small territories ultimately led to what was for mediaeval conditions a very continuous development of all feudal relations, covering the whole countryside and not just concentrated in certain centres such as Byzantium and the Arab Caliphate. The break with the city/countryside relationship of Antiquity was complete in Europe but only partial in the Orient and the territory of the former Eastern Roman Empire.

The movements of conquest emanating from Europe and extending to the Mediterranean area were thus not merely events of a politico-military nature but represented a confrontation with the more highly developed civilizations which already existed there. That phenomenon is not unique. This kind of tension accompanied expansion in almost every century of mediaeval history but it always appeared in very specific forms. The present book sets out to examine this confrontation as its main purpose and this naturally includes the description of the feudal forces of Europe concerned in this expansion. The attack was launched with energy and determination. Within two centuries, tens of thousands of knights plus the peasants, merchants and artisans accompanying them invaded the Orient. There were seven major Crusades by European armies of knights, numerous smaller military expeditions as well, a Peasants' Crusade and a Children's Crusade, without counting the constant stream of pilgrims. Four Crusader states were founded in present-day Syria and Palestine and a Latin Empire at the Bosporus. The main aspect to be investigated here is not so much the political details but rather the question of the motivation and the economic, social and intellectual reasons which produced this mass movement.

Although the Crusades were instruments of expansion used by European feudal lords against the Islamic states and the Byzantine Empire, an examination of the results of the expansion must also take account, if only in passing, of the commercial expansion carried on by the merchants of Northern Italy which was associated with the Crusades and of the conquest of Sicily and Southern Italy by the Normans and the advance of Europeans into Moorish Spain since this likewise concerns the question of the confrontation with the more advanced civilization of the subjugated peoples.

The author is aware that such an approach goes beyond the usual scope of descriptions of the Crusades but the formulation of the question justifies a different layout of the material. The first section reviews the material and intellectual structure of the Arab Islamic, Byzantine and Western European civilizations and the feudal societies to the extent necessary for understanding this expansion and its related aspects. The emergence and development of the ideology of the Crusades and the characterization of those who took part in the first Crusade then follow, supplemented by an outline of the Peasants' Crusade. The following sections concentrate on the problems of the confrontation with Arab Islamic and Byzantine society and its civilization in the regions where expansion took place and on the development of the ideology of the Crusades in Europe. The Crusader states are reviewed in detail, together with the commercial expansion of the Italian merchants, and a brief comparison is made with the Norman empire and the Reconquista. An examination of the content and forms of Oriental and Byzantine culture as adopted by European feudal society during the time of the Crusades completes the book.

The intention of the author is thus to present the history of the Crusades from the viewpoint of the history of civilization. The material and intellectual standard of living is always at the centre of the presentation, the aim of this being to give a more profound historical understanding of the political problems as a whole.

The book is written for the reader who is interested in history, i.e., it is intended as an introduction. This is why many details, controversial views and polemics have not been included and it is hoped that this has made it easier to gain an understanding of events as a whole.

THE ARABIAN CALIPHATE

In economic, cultural and political respects, the dominant power in the Mediterranean area on the eve of the Crusades was the Islamic feudal society of the Orient. In a mighty triumphal advance in the 7th and 8th centuries, the successors of Mohammed from the Arabian Peninsula had changed the political map of Central Asia, the Orient and large areas around the Mediterranean. Syria, Palestine, Egypt, North Africa, Spain and Sicily had been conquered and, together with Iraq, Persia, Transcaucasia and important parts of Central Asia, formed the Arabian Caliphate.

This conquest had far-reaching consequences for these territories and their populations. They found themselves confronted with fundamentally different economic, intellectual and political conditions. Mediterranean society from the Pyrenees to Syria was characterized by the Oriental form of feudalism. The contrast to Europe, the other part of the former Roman Empire, had become so complete within a few centuries that on the eve of the Crusades relations between Moorish Spain and the eastern parts of the Arabian Caliphate in almost all spheres of social life were closer than with Christian Europe. It was not so much religion that formed the demarcation line although this admittedly played an important role. The different forms of the feudal order and the resultant gradients in material and intellectual level had a much more profound effect than the frontier line.

Like other early feudal empires, the Arabian Caliphate was initially a very loose heterogenous configuration. The Arab conquerors were no more than a minority of the total population. Whereas the Arab aristocracy ruled the empire from the cities of the conquered territory, the ordinary Bedouin warriors stayed in self-contained military settlements dispersed throughout the empire. As a result of expansion and despite war losses, the number of Moslems and their influence in the conquered territories increased considerably in some cases. This was primarily due to the waging of the jihad or Holy War for the spread of Islam by force. This practice, originally employed for the Islamization of the tribes of the Arabian Peninsula, was in the main, however, only used

against the Arabs and related tribes. Christians of other ethnic origins and Jews were treated with tolerance. This resulted in a very uneven distribution of the Islamic Arab population throughout the empire as a whole. There were notable concentrations of this group of the population in Iraq, Palestine, Syria, Egypt and North Africa where the Berber tribes had readily adopted the Islamic religion and subsequently took an active part in the conquest of Spain and Sicily in particular. In other areas, the Arab population remained small in numbers, especially in Iran, Central Asia and Transcaucasia. The native population of the Mediterranean territories remained unmolested, too. The real problem with which the conquerors were confronted and which had a major influence on the general structure of the Caliphate was the shaping of the relationship with the subjugated cultural centres and their population. At the time they were conquered, Syria, Egypt, Persia, Transcaucasia and Central Asia in particular were regarded as territories with a high level of culture and advanced material standards. The old social structure based on slave ownership had already disintegrated, it is true, or was in the process of disintegrating but the economic level had not really been affected by this. There still existed important cities with a marked division of labour where crafts and commerce flourished and the science and culture of the Old World continued to be cultivated.

The Arab conquerors were able to profit from this urban civilization and to utilize it for the development of their empire. As early as 661, they transferred the residence of the Caliphate from Medina to Damascus. This was more than merely relocating it from the periphery to the centre of the empire. The real motivation for this action was to give more attention to the developed parts of the empire, to exploit the wealth of these territories to the full and to take the offensive in the confrontation with the old civilizations. The dynasty of the Omayyads, who initiated this process, made little headway, however. During their rule, the Arab aristocracy was not prepared to share its power with the nobility of the subjugated population and influential positions in the State were occupied solely by Arab aristocrats. The adoption of the Islamic religion, which would have meant participation in the system of privileges, was strictly prohibited since it would also have endangered the principle of conquest on which their rule was based. The entire territory belonged to the Caliph as the overlord. All tributes, taxes and duties from agriculture, production and trade were paid directly to him. They were then distributed in the most diverse forms to the conquerors or the distribution was made under the supervision of the Caliph. Revenues came mostly from the non-Moslem population, both from the peasants and artisans and from the nobility. The Moslems paid only a very low rate of tax.

The time of the Omayyad dynasty is considered to have been the most complete form of the rule of the Arab desert aristocracy. This development did not mean the end of economic prosperity. From Damascus and the provincial cities, the leading circles of the conquerors not only dominated the empire in a political and military sense but also put the entire production of the subjugated population, the highly specialized crafts, commerce and cultural achievements at the disposal of their State. The Arab aristocracy was primarily an urban one and this will be discussed in more detail below. This meant that the aristocracy moved towards the material level of the subjugated population, especially that of the ruling class which still existed, while on the other hand material and intellectual life in the cultural centres became Islamized.

The decisive change took place only when the dynasty of the Abbasids (750–1258) came to power. The social basis of the power of the Omayyads had become very small towards the end of their period of rule. The excessive tax burden and particularly the head-tax for non-Moslems aroused the anger of the subjugated population and resistance was apparent everywhere. The simple Bedouins were dissatisfied with the concentration of wealth in the hands of the aristocracy and they clearly sensed the process of social differentiation which was taking place among the conquerors. The native aristocracy and above all the Persian nobility was no longer prepared to be on the outside of political power. Uprisings which started in the east of the empire led to a change of dynasty which was very much more than a simple replacement. This is already evident from the transfer of the residence from Damascus to Baghdad. Persian influence on the Cali-

1 The climatic conditions in the Orient caused the peasants to pay particular attention to irrigation systems in agriculture as long ago as Antiquity. The Arab Caliphate continued this tradition and new systems were constructed in all parts of the empire. This water-wheel on the Orontes River in Syria was built about 1000 and, with its diameter of 25 metres, is still one of the largest in existence. The water from the canal is conveyed by the scoops to the viaduct and is then passed to the fields.

phate became dominant and from this time onwards influential counsellors at the court were recruited from the Persian nobility and held important State offices. This process was also favoured by the fact that Islam was now open to the subjugated population and no longer represented the privilege of the conquerors. Similar changes took place in the other parts of the empire.

The importance attached to the East by the Caliphate had political consequences for the Islamic world of the Mediterranean. Rapid progress was made by the individual provinces in achieving independence. Spain had already become an independent emirate in 756. Morocco, Tunis and Algiers followed and Egypt became independent in the 9th century. Minor realms emerged in Syria. This political development did not result in any negative consequences for the social, economic and cultural processes. On the contrary, this period was the real heyday of Arab feudal society and also included the Islamic states of the Mediterranean. It reached its climax between the 8th and 10th centuries but continued to dominate cultural life even during the time of the Crusades since it was not followed by a decline.

Two factors in particular left their mark: the inclusion of the subjugated population in the feudal society and to a certain extent the resultant emergence of a flourishing early feudal urban civilization. The division of labour between town and country was thus not just adopted but developed further. In many parts of the Caliphate, the producers—peasants and artisans—still largely came from the subjugated population. This was especially true of Central Asia, Persia and the Mediterranean territories,. too. In Spain, for instance, up to the end of the Caliphate, the peasants and artisans were Christians. The subjugated population was not driven out in the other territories, either. On the other hand, settlements of Islamic peasants were being established all the time, for example in Spain, Sicily, Egypt, Palestine and Iraq, as already mentioned. In culture and civilization as a whole, it was the Islamic element which became the dominant influence. Even the middle strata, the merchants, scholars and artists, became increasingly integrated in Islamic society, irrespective of their religious allegiance. Jews, Syrians, Persians and Egyp-

tians not only made a contribution to intellectual life but were also employed as minor State officials and occasionally as counsellors at Court. Thus the Jews, for instance, after the decline of the Caliphate of Damascus in Spain, played an outstanding part in the development of the culture of the Caliphate of Cordova.

The non-Arab population also contributed their cultural heritage to the society of the Caliphate. Above all, the traditions of the ancient Persian, Central Asiatic and Indian societies and Greco-Roman civilization exercised a direct influence on Islamic society. This will be discussed in detail below. On the other hand, this heritage did not remain an alien factor since the material and intellectual conditions of life in the Caliphate were successfully Islamized and even Arabized to an increasing extent. Exactly what the term "Islamic Arab culture" means and what the original character of the subjugated population was is a subject on which there is a difference of opinion at the present time. This problem is of exceptional importance with reference to the national history of the individual peoples. From our viewpoint, however, it should be stressed to begin with that the integrating elements, at least for the golden age from the 8th to the 10th centuries, were so powerful that there was similarity and even a certain uniformity in economic, social and cultural development, despite the political decline in all parts of the Caliphate.

However, this symbiosis was only effective for the specific relationship between town and country in the Arab Caliphate. Although agriculture predominated with reference to society as a whole, it was the towns that set the tone in cultural and material affairs. The fact that the Arab aristocracy first settled in the conquered towns was not a transitional phenomenon of the early stage of expansion. The ruling feudal class lived largely in the towns, it was here that the palaces and residences of the nobility were to be found and it was from the towns that the country was governed. They were the religious centres and possessed enormous economic and cultural influence. The towns were the real links in the mighty territorial complex. As will be shown later in detail, they did not exist in isolation from each other but usually maintained close relations in all spheres of economic, social and intellectual life. Changes and innovations spread relatively rapidly throughout the entire state and did not remain restricted to a small territory. Unlike European towns, which were distinguished by privileges and other decrees and by their social customs from the villages where most of the nobility lived and from where they dominated the society of the time, this differentiation did not exist in the Orient. The towns were the real centres of economic, social and political power in the Caliphate.

Despite their importance, little is known now about the populations of these towns. Baghdad, which was founded by the Abbasid dynasty, is reputed to have had about 300,000 inhabitants in the 9th century. Without doubt, it was much larger than all the other towns. In size, however, even the provincial capitals were already several times bigger than any mediaeval city of Europe.

The economic basis of the town was artisan production for the needs of the population. In addition to this, craftsmen supplied their products to all parts of the Caliphate and beyond its frontiers to Asia and even to Europe, although this was on a very limited scale. A high level of skill and ability plus specialization to an exceptional extent made this possible. Without doubt, textile production was the major sphere of activity. Fabrics of wool, cotton, linen, and silk were produced by artisans in almost all the territories of the Oriental world. The carpet weavers of Persia, Azerbaidzhan and Buchara, with their characteristic designs, were renowned far and wide. The cotton and silk products of Persia and Central Asia were world-famous.

This development of production also influenced the Islamic territories in the Mediterranean. Egypt, in particular, already known as the centre of weaving in Antiquity, achieved fame with its products at the time of the Arab Caliphate. Very delicate and almost transparent cloths for turbans were woven in Damiette and Tunis. It is reported that a cloth for a turban had to be up to 50 metres in length. Egyptian weavers produced printed linen and cloths worked with gold threads. The Moslems took the art of silk and gold embroidery to Sicily and not a few of the fabrics now preserved in European museums originated from there since this craft continued to exist after the conquest of Southern Italy by the Normans. Important centres for the weaving of cotton emerged during the time of the Arab Caliphate in Spain and North Africa.

The art of metalworking achieved a high standard. Gold had been discovered in Nubia and in the Sudan, and silver and copper in various parts of Central Asia. Iron was also extracted here and subsequently in North Africa and Sicily as well. Pearls and precious stones were imported from India, in particular. Metalworkers produced the most diverse objects from the precious metals and others. A very large number of vases, dishes and other vessels of fine workmanship, and decorated with precious stones, has survived. By the Middle Ages, the Arabs were past masters in the art of applying silver to copper and gold to silver in the process known as inlay work. They were also familiar with the technique of forging strips of metal twisted together. With this technique, they not only obtained steel of exceptional hardness but were also able to produce flame or flower patterns on the steel. This process, which originated in Persia, became so popular that one of the principal centres in the Arab Caliphate, Damascus, where it was employed, lent its name to the term "damascening" which, of course, is still in use.

A highly instructive insight into the high standards of artisan production is provided by the mechanical products of the metalworkers. Moving figures and time-pieces, the mechanical wonders of the time, are evidence of this. Complicated clocks with elaborate ornamentation which indicated the hour by pleasant chimes and contributed to the entertainment of their possessors were famous. However, these and similar masterpieces were really only secondary products of a craft which had developed in association with the natural sciences. Precision balances, astrolabes, maps of the heavens, telescopes and even complete observatories of which every large town possessed at least one were just as much examples of their skill as the making of high-quality technical equipment in which mastery of glass and ceramics was blended with a knowledge of science.

Glass and ceramics production was a major activity not only in Persia but also in Syria and Egypt in particular. Not only were simple vessels made for domestic use but also fine vases and dishes. This craft also produced industrial goods such as retorts, distilling flasks, test-tubes and large receptacles for the storage of liquids. Egyptian crystal glass won special renown.

Specialized production was not possible without trade on an extensive scale. Overland trade played the major role in this. Caravan routes linked all parts of the Caliphate, and even political decline did not interrupt it. At the beginning, privileges were granted to Arab merchants but by the 8th century other groups of the population certainly enjoyed equal rights. Jews and Syrians in particular were to be found with their caravans in all parts of the Arab world. The relations between the different territories must have been quite close. Apart from commerce as such, it is to be seen time and again that especially teachers and students, but also members of the upper classes, moved from one town to another for a fairly long time for professional reasons or for a visit.

Sea-trade was not of very great importance in the early stages. The Arabs were not familiar with shipbuilding and were no seamen. However, they very rapidly made use of the shipyards found above all in the Syrian and Egyptian ports, firstly for the construction of a fleet of warships and later on for mercantile purposes as well. Their mariners were chiefly Egyptians and Syrians.

In comparison with the urban economy, the countryside remained relatively backward. This was mainly because it was not possible to overcome the discrepancy between the highly developed cultural centres and the vast desert and steppe areas with their nomadic herdsmen. As a rule, the implements of the peasants were very simple but their long experience and extensive knowledge of the irrigation of the countryside was not lost. In the fertile areas, all this was utilized in the most diverse forms such as canal systems, locks, waterwheels and so on. This meant a considerable increase in yields not only from the orchards and market gardens catering primarily for the large towns but also in a series of field crops. The real level of agriculture was determined, however, by the variety of crops cultivated. In addition to the main cereal crops of wheat and barley, a wide range of fruit and vegetables was grown. Silk and wool production was typical of many districts. There was a relatively rapid increase in the cultivation of certain useful plants in the Caliphate and it was the Mediterranean countries that profited from this in particular. Thus, for instance, cotton became an established crop in Egypt, North Africa, Spain and Sicily and the same applied to sugar-cane which was much in demand. Date palms, among other things, were brought to Sicily and Southern Spain by Arab settlers.

For Europeans, both artisan and agricultural products represented fabulous wealth beyond their reach. It would nevertheless be incorrect to assume from these remarks that there was a general prosperity in the Orient. The artisans and peasants as the producers profited little or not at all from it. High taxation in gold and kind plus forced labour meant that it was impossible for them to achieve prosperity. Wealth flowed into the pockets of the landowners, officials, warriors, priests, merchants and usurers. The dependence of the ordinary people was of two kinds. The overwhelming majority paid taxes directly to the State which then used it to pay the feudal lords occupying the highest positions in the State. In addition, the peasants had to perform compulsory labour for the government authorities in the most diverse forms, such as the construction of irrigation systems or road building. At the same time, there was also an increase in the private ownership of land in a variety of ways, associated also with directly dependent peasants.

The high degree of the social division of labour, particularly the existence of large towns, concealed however the crass class differences. A large middle-class emerged, consisting of scholars, doctors, artists and highly specialized artisans, since this was a necessity for society. They were nonetheless in the service of the nobility but obtained a larger share of social wealth than the ordinary population. This middle class was responsible for mighty cultural achievements, especially during the rule of the Abbasids, and these achievements are now part of the common heritage of humanity. The population of the Islamic Mediterranean territories also played a part in this.

It was primarily Syrian Christians who translated the works of the Ancient Greek philosophers and scientists into the written Arabic language. There were regular schools of translators in Syrian cities and their repertoire included such authors as Galen, Hippocrates, Ptolemy, Euclid, Archimedes, Aristotle, Plato and many others. In the same manner, Persian scholars translated works from the time of Ancient Iran and native scholars in the Central Asiatic centres of Buchara, Samarkand and Khiva likewise provided access to the concepts of ancient civilizations. Knowledge of Indian and Chinese sciences also represented an enrichment of the culture of the Caliphate.

As a result of the excellent system of communications available, familiarity with this heritage was not restricted to a specific territorial area but was rapidly disseminated throughout the entire Caliphate, including all the countries of the Mediterranean.

It was this intellectual basis, in association with the advanced level of the division of labour, which made possible a golden age of science, covering practically all disciplines: philosophy, mathematics, physics, chemistry, biology, astronomy, history and geography being only the principal fields of activity. It is impossible even to give an outline of the most prominent scholars and their achievements, since the wealth of knowledge accumulated appears inexhaustible. A very few examples must be taken as representative of the whole:

Al-Khwarizmi, a native of Chorasmia (780–850), introduced the Indian system of numerals, wrote several works on algebra and calculated the distances and movements of the stars.

The physician and philosopher Ibn Sina (Lat. Avicenna, 980–1037) wrote down the whole of medical knowledge in a "Canon of Medicine". He was one of the most illustrious physicians of his time. As a philosopher, he held the view that matter is eternal and he linked this hypothesis with the idea of an absolute principle (God.)

Ibn al-Haitam (died 1059) composed scientific treatises about the eye.

Al-Biruni (973–1050) acquired knowledge on an encyclopaedic scale and was a native of Central Asia. Together with other astronomers, he drew up calendar calculations which in accuracy surpassed the later Gregorian calendar.

Al-Razi of Persia was a physician, chemist and philosopher who wrote renowned treatises on infectious diseases on the basis of accurate clinical examinations.

These examples could be continued. In the sphere of chemistry, the principal forms of experimentation were pioneered which are still usual today. Accurate observation of chemical processes and the use of distillation, filtering and other techniques were customary among scholars. The making of silver nitrate, soda, caustic solutions, blue vitriol and many other chemical compounds was possible and hundreds of drugs were produced. It is not by chance that many of our chemical terms in particular are derived directly from Arabic, such as "drug", "alum", "amalgam", "anilin", "arrack", "soda", "talcum" and so on.

In medicine, it was possible to treat complicated diseases. Anaesthetics were employed for operations and physicians had special medical equipment at their disposal.

The Mediterranean countries of the Arab Islamic world were not excluded from this development. Numerous scholars emerged here, too. The Caliphate of Cordova in particular was noted for its support of science.

Al-Zarawi, one of the leading physicians of the Spanish Caliphate, wrote a series of medical and pharmacological textbooks.

Ibn al-Baitar of Malaga was the author of treatises on medicinal herbs and medicaments in which 1400 drugs were listed. The geographer and cartographer Al-Idrisi, who was born in Ceuta, wrote a geographical description of the then known world.

Mention must also be made of the illustrious physician and philosopher Ibn Rushd (Averroes, 1126–1198), born in Cordova, who developed an original philosophical system known as Averroism which had a great influence on later European philosophy.

Of course, the outline sketched here of the crafts, of scientific, artistic and philosophic achievements should not obscure the narrow social limits of this activity. Although it is quite certain on the one hand that this creative work has become a permanent part of world culture, it is nevertheless true, on the other, that the ordinary people of the Arab empire did

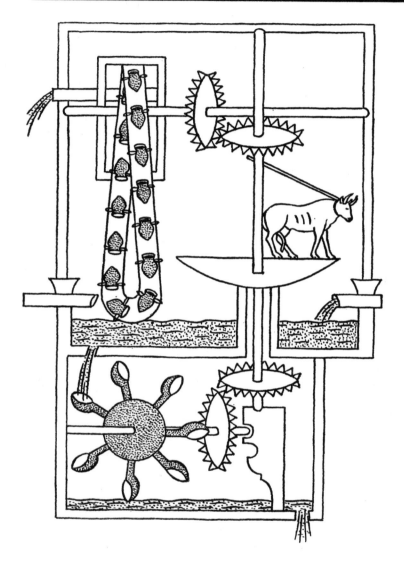

2 *Great ingenuity was used by the craftsmen of the Arab Caliphate in the design of automatons such as time-keeping devices and water-powered mechanisms. It seems that the animal is moving the bucket chain but in fact the mechanism is driven by a scoop wheel arrangement. (From a manuscript in the Metropolitan Museum of Art, New York.)*

not benefit from it to any marked extent and that science and art could only exist because they were in the service of the feudal oligarchy. The ruling personages had an interest in promoting them because they increased their fame and renown. The rewards were stupendous when one was of direct usefulness to the ruling class. A personal physician of the Caliph in the first half of the 10th century could accumulate wealth by drawing blood from his patient twice a year and performing a clyster with the same regularity. It was a similar story with other branches of learning. Court astrology was a prosperous business for many astronomers.

Cultural life was concentrated in the great cities of the Caliphate and the states which succeeded it. It was here that the ruling class lived and governed and it was they who controlled the use to which social wealth was put. This was reflected in personal luxury, such as the collection of treasures, elaborate court life with all the pleasures available within the country, the construction of magnificent palaces and in general the shaping of cities as centres of power in which appropriate expression was given to the totality of material and itellectual culture. This upswing was concentrated during the first period chiefly in the capitals of the Caliphate—Damascus during the rule of the Omayyads—and Baghdad as the centre of power of the Abbasids. After the political disintegration of the empire, all the rulers of the states which succeeded it competed with each other in the development of their residences and of all the cities in their territory, every city in the Mediterranean area being included.

The pronounced division of labour called for a certain level of education for the urban population. The wealthy and middle classes at least were given a five-year course in the study of the Koran, reading, writing, history, poetry and arithmetic in general schools. The range and continuity of this education are not known exactly, however. There must have been general approval in other parts of the Arab Islamic world for the founding of twenty-seven schools for the poor in Cordova in 965. Unfortunately, no record has survived of the practical implementation of this measure. Every large town had a "medresa" which corresponded more or less to a grammar school in its basic objectives. The subjects taught included the study of the Koran, language, and literature, geography, ethnology, astronomy, mathematics, chemistry, music and geometry. The reputation of each school was determined by the quality of the teaching staff and the size of its library.

The most important of these developed into institutions with a university character. Baghdad had the best reputation up to the 13th century and Alexandria, Cairo and Cordova were highly respected, the latter possessing a library of 400,000 volumes already by the 10th century.

The towns also possessed other research and educational establishments apart from the medresas and universities. Observatories which regularly carried out surveys of the heavenly bodies were no rarity in the Arab Islamic world. There were libraries not only in schools but also at the courts and in mosques. Their size was an indication of the fame and reputation of the local ruler.

The ruling class itself was influenced by the atmosphere of education. Initially and in its relationship with the common people it was no less feudal than its European equivalent, for instance. However, the Oriental feudal lord considered the possession of a vast library to be essential for his reputation and it was in libraries such as this that records were first kept of new scientific findings. There are even examples of rulers themselves pursuing studies. Many scholars earned their living as private teachers in the households of the various ruling families. The Caliphs of Cordova, to which repeated reference has already been made, attracted many Syrians and Jews to their court, for example, and in this way encouraged the development of culture in Moorish Spain.

Similar reasons applied to the promotion of architecture and literature. The Omayyads undertook the development of Damascus, and castles, palaces and magnificent mosques were built in the other capital cities as well. In Cordova, richly ornamented mosques and other edifices bore witness to the power of the local emirs and caliphs. The great mosque of this city, completed in the 10th century, was an amalgam of artistic elements from all parts of the Arab Islamic world. In Cairo, the famous Al Azhar mosque was built by the Fatimids around 970.

A special event of no small interest was experienced by Jerusalem in this respect during the time of the Omayyad dynasty. Their residence was at Damascus and they endeavoured to develop Jerusalem as a religious centre. There was a political motivation for this; a major role played the enmity between the Omayyads and the rulers of Mecca. Jerusalem was intended to compete with Mecca. The Dome of the Rock was built in the city between 687 and 691 and named after the holy rock in the square of the Temple. The building is characteristic of Omayyad architecture, its principal feature being a dome supported by sixteen columns. The inner walls are ornamented with fine mosaics while the outer ones are lined with marble. Byzantine influence is unmistakable both in the general design and in the details and corresponds to the role already mentioned of Greeks and Syrians in the development of Islamic Arab culture. Shortly before this, the Al Aqsa mosque had already been built in the square of the Temple so that the whole ensemble constituted a religious centre which was a popular place of Moslem pilgrimage not only for the people of that time but also in the following centuries. This was also true at the time when the Crusaders established their kingdom here.

Concepts such as this were naturally not in the minds of the local rulers when they erected their buildings but the attraction of every Islamic city, and thus the renown of the ruling dynasty, was measured not least by the splendour of the mosques in their capitals.

All other spheres of material civilization and daily life in the Mediterranean territories were likewise influenced by the general trend in the Caliphate, as was particularly apparent in the cities. There is evidence almost everywhere of vast parks and gardens around the palaces in particular. Most of the cities had drainage systems and public baths and Damascus is said to have had a hundred of the latter. Every city possessed hospitals in which trained physicians tended the sick. Here, again, these are just a few of the many examples possible.

The general structure of the Caliphate had a considerable influence on the development of Islam. It was no less religious than any other and covered the entire life and thinking of the Faithful. Many had to answer for opinions which were

2　The mosque of Cordova (Spain), built between 833 and 844, is one of the most significant edifices of Islamic architecture in the Iberian Peninsula. It proclaimed the prosperity of the politically independent Caliphate of Cordova. It was constantly extended and rebuilt in the following centuries. The outer wall of brick and stone encloses a complex of richly decorated courtyards, towers and rooms. The heart of the mosque is a hall of 1290 marble columns. A great deal of the building materials required (marble, porphyry, alabaster) was taken from ancient ruins.

3　The Ibn Tulun Mosque in Cairo, built between 876 and 879, was regarded as a symbol of the rule of the Tulunids who, as governors of Egypt, gained practical independence in c. 868. It covers a total area of 140×116 metres and its spacious courtyard measures 90×90 metres.

On the following pages:

4 It was in the Islamic "medresas" that the children of the upper class received their general education. Many scholars earned their living here by teaching.
Bibliothèque Nationale, Paris

5 The classrooms were either in the direct vicinity of the mosque or part of the mosque itself.
Bibliothèque Nationale, Paris

في حلقة ويتخـيّرون المركز للاستماع الهـ... ولم يزل من تمس بـدخلون في دين الله أفواجـاً ويـردّون
فرادى وأزواجـاً حتى إذا اكتـظ الجامع بحفلـه واطـل السـادي الشخص وظله برز الخطيب في أهبتـه

منـها ديباج خلف قـضتـه وارتقى في منـبـر الدعوة الى الذروة بالزرد ... فسـلّم مشـيراً باليمين
ثم قعد حتى خـتم نظر المـؤذّنين ثم قام وقـال ٥ الحمد لله المطلع الاسماء

6　The Al Azhar Mosque in Cairo was one of the most important of the Islamic world and proclaimed the power of the Fatimid dynasty. As a training centre, it was here that Shiite missionaries received their training.

7　The Dome of the Rock at Jerusalem (691) is the oldest building still surviving from the time of the Omayyad dynasty. Greek craftsmen were responsible for much of this mosque which, erected on the site of the "holy rock", was intended to be part of a new Islamic religious centre and thus to overshadow Mecca in importance.

وتحل القفص والجمالة والفنس والآلة انها لفظت علي بالنز فأضاعت نفض من زجها

نفسد من زجها لما دانني وقنت بالرقعة درهما وقطعة وقلت لها ان رغبت فالمشتوى المعلم

واشرن الي الدرهم فوقي بالنز المدهم وان ابنت ان ترجي تخذي القطعة وابرزن

قالن الي استنقاض البدر النز والأبلج الهم وقالن دع جدلك وبناع ابد لك فاقنط

طلع الشيخ وبلده والثغر وابيج برده فقالن ان الشيخ من أهل ترخ وهو الذي وثني

8   Military bands were regarded as a
small but important attribute of court life.
The possession of such a band for use on
solemn occasions, was a matter of prestige
for almost every ruler in all parts of the
Caliphate. It is therefore not by chance that
this subject frequently appears in illustrations in manuscripts and also in the designs
of fountains.
Bibliothèque Nationale, Paris

9   Agricultural implements were very
simple in the Arab Caliphate, too. Sickles,
spades, harrows and hooked ploughs were
in general use and donkeys and oxen as
beasts of burden and draught animals
helped to make the peasants' work easier.
The upper half of the illustration demonstrates the influence of medicine on agricultural production. A physician is checking
the crop of medicinal plants.
Bibliothèque Nationale, Paris

10/11 Mechanical devices such as this elephant timepiece or the water-raising machine were particularly popular with the rulers of the Arab Caliphate and the leading court dignitaries. The clocks were installed either in the private rooms or on the outer walls of stately buildings. A complicated mechanism, driven by water power, caused the figures to move in an hourly or daily cycle. Metropolitan Museum of Art, New York

12 The principal difference in warfare between the Islamic and the European armies was the use by the former of larger units of mounted archers who, with their relatively heavy arrows, were capable of inflicting heavy losses from a safe distance on the enemy cavalry and, of course, on the baggage train, too. British Museum, London

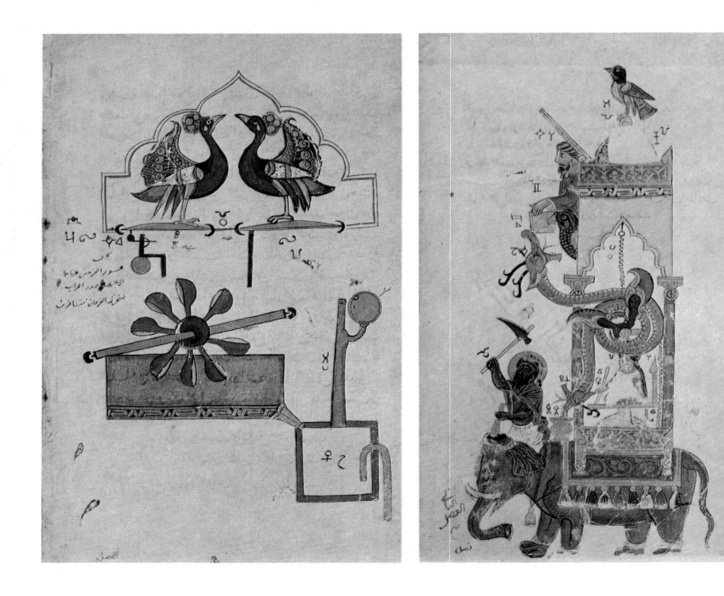

13   The city walls of Constantinople
(partial view) were built from 379 to 395.
The systematic fortification of Byzantine
and Oriental cities was customary even
during Antiquity. For protection against
attackers and especially the periodic raids
by Barbarian and nomadic tribes, these
fortifications had to be constantly renewed
and extended even during the Middle Ages.
The principal wall was about 5 metres
thick and was built of ashlar and bricks.
Towers and battlements facilitated an active defence.

14   The plundering of Constantinople
by the Crusaders during the fourth Crusade
affected not only the palaces but also the
churches from which precious treasures
and especially relics were stolen. The Hagia
Sophia as the principal church of the Byzantine capital had a particularly large treasure-
house.
Lithograph by Louis Haghe (1806–1885);
26.9×37.4 cm.

15   The Hagia Sophia was the most monumental church of Constantinople during
the Middle Ages. Its foundations date back
to the time of Emperor Constantine.

16   On account of repeated destruction
and plundering, little now remains of
mediaeval Constantinople. The ground
plan of the city of 1420 conveys a vivid

impression of the imposing size of the
Byzantine capital for the people of that
time.

Bibliothèque Nationale, Paris

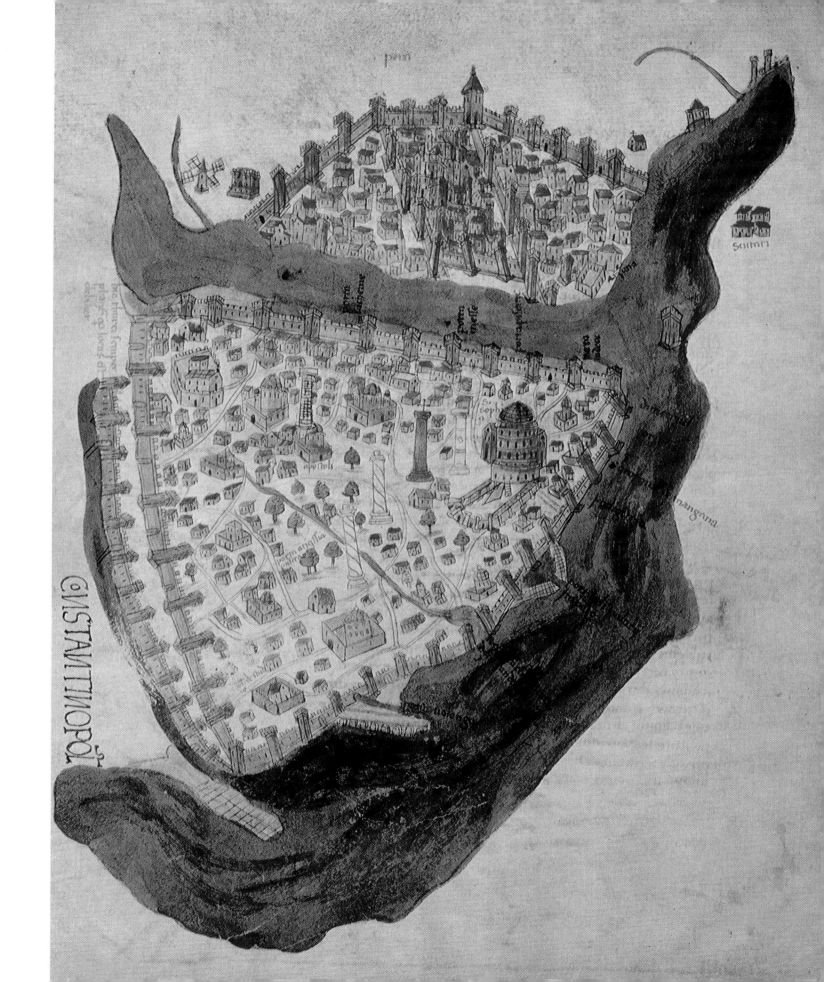

17   The production of luxury goods
was primarily intended for the ruling class.
In addition to splendid palaces with the
appropriate furnishings, the Arab nobility
attached great importance to expensive
and richly decorated clothes.
Bibliothèque Nationale, Paris

33

not in agreement with the doctrine of the Koran and its interpretations. Nevertheless, Islam, under the new conditions of the Caliphate, developed differently, say, from the Catholic Church in the Middle Ages. It was at the centre of a complex society. The mosque was not simply a holy place but a religious, intellectual and social centre. The area of a mosque included a spacious courtyard of square layout, lined by flat buildings with open columned halls. The muezzin called the Faithful to their daily prayers from a minaret, a high tower. People came to the mosque, which owed its rich furnishings to the gifts of the local rulers, not just for religious services but also for instruction and academic work, for playing chess and listening to storytellers.

Of special interest in connection with the emergence of the ideology of the Crusades is the relationship of Islam to Christianity.

It has already repeatedly been mentioned that the development of Arab Islamic society in its early feudal stage would have been impossible without the constructive collaboration of the subjugated population in the traditional manner. Christians and Jews played an outstanding part in this but few of them adopted the Islamic creed. The intellectual basis for their inclusion in Islamic society was the constant religious tolerance of the Moslems towards people of other faiths. Jerusalem fell into the hands of the Arabs in 637, Caliph Omar himself taking possession of the city. This in no way implied the beginning of a period of darkness for the Christians of the Orient. Islam did not have their conversion in mind. It was above all economic factors which determined attitudes in the early stages. Moslems were required to make only a small contribution whereas all others were obliged to pay a very high head-tax. This material basis would have suffered if too many had embraced Islam. It was against this background that the tolerance of the Moslems towards Christians and Jews developed as a basic intellectual attitude. Admittedly, there was initially some friction before harmony was achieved and many churches were turned into mosques. In Jerusalem, this also affected the vestibule of the Church of the Holy Sepulchre since it was here that Caliph Omar is said to have prayed. However, these changes did not reflect an anti-Christian attitude but rather the need for places of prayer since the percentage of Moslems in the total population of Syria and Palestine was relatively high from the very start. In any case, the conversion of churches into mosques and vice-versa was usual in the Orient when a change in political power took place.

Under Islamic rule, Christians were able to practise their faith without hindrance. There were only brief periods of persecution and these were more for political than religious reasons. This occurred in Syria and Palestine in the middle of the 8th century when local feudal forces confiscated churches and subsequently allowed the Christians to redeem them; further at the beginning of the 11th century when Caliph Hakim issued decrees against Christians, confiscated Church property, allowed churches to be plundered and ordered the destruction of the Church of the Holy Sepulchre in 1009. These actions caused great dismay in Europe. But they were only episodes in the long history of the Christians in the Orient.

For the numerous sectarian Christian churches and religious movements of the Orient, Islamic rule was even an advantage since through this they escaped suppression by the Byzantine state. Many an anthem in praise of Islam still bears witness to this today.

The Church of the Holy Sepulchre, which after its destruction by Caliph Hakim was rebuilt again by the Byzantine emperor in the middle of the 11th century, continued to be a religious centre for the Christians. There was a constant stream of pilgrims to Jerusalem from all parts of the Christian world in the centuries before the Crusades. The picture we have of all this is relatively clear. A few centuries were enough to bring about a profound political and cultural change in the Mediterranean world of Antiquity. A prosperous feudal society had developed in the Mediterranean area between the Pyrenees and Syria which became Islamic and Arab in character. It was this which determined the level of intellectual and material culture, a level which was characterized not solely by its excellence but even more by the stability of the symbiosis resulting from several component parts.

The other factor which exercised a major influence in the Mediterranean area in the centuries before the Crusades was the feudal society of Byzantium.

THE BYZANTINE EMPIRE

The Islamic Arab states in the West had emerged primarily at the expense of the Byzantine Empire since practically all the Mediterranean territories conquered by the Moslems in the 6th century had either directly belonged to Eastern Rome or had been regarded by it as part of its sphere of political influence. In the centuries up to the eve of the Crusades, Byzantium had been in constant conflict with the Islamic Arab states. Wars of defence and aggression alternated with each other, interrupted by periods of peaceful coexistence in which trade and diplomatic contacts flourished.

When the European Crusaders set off on their first campaign in the Orient, Byzantine society already possessed centuries of experience in bellicose confrontation. There had been no sign of a crusading spirit, no union of a "Christian world against an Islamic one". Nor was there ever any question of cultural or social symbiosis in a closer sense on the agenda of history. A close look at the internal history of Byzantium will facilitate an understanding of this development and also of the emergence of the Crusade movement in Western Europe.

The specific features of feudal development in the Byzantine Empire—the transitional period extends from about the 7th century to the 10th—resulted from the fact that the process of transformation followed directly from Antiquity with the continued existence of a central State apparatus. Despite all the external influences, it was therefore primarily a process of inner confrontations. The territorial losses of the Eastern Roman Empire, in comparison with the period of Emperor Justinian (527–565), were indeed considerable but the major territories, as they existed on the eve of the Crusades, Asia Minor, the Greek islands and parts of the Balkans remained as a centrally governed state. Only Southern Italy was lost to the Normans in the 11th century. The consequence of this was that the confrontation with the remaining Antique aspects in economic, social, political and intellectual life had to be waged in a far more intensive manner and that many major elements of the old order were adopted by feudalism and influenced the character of society.

The impetus for the development of feudalism in the empire had come from the countryside. The change began with the form of the army under Emperor Heraclius I (610–641) who granted country estates to soldiers for their military services. This replaced their pay, which was not available anyway, and at the same time ensured the defence of the empire since at the beginning it was primarily a question of land in the exposed frontier provinces. Organized in "themes" or military districts, this meant that new social forces emerged in the form of "stratiotes" or peasant-warriors. Their military leaders, the aristocracy of the themes, were soon given civil administrative functions as well. However, subsequent developments did not give the countryside priority over the cities. In the shelter of effective military defence, the cities and especially the capital, Constantinople, rapidly began to flourish.

A strange phenomenon was that, although the new element basically came from the countryside while the cities in the social and political respect represented the conservative element, the material and intellectual level of this transitional society was nevertheless shaped by the cities. Though the slave-owning order had disappeared from the social scene, the remaining strata of the Antique system were able to maintain their class positions. This was not only in the shape of the large State and urban bureaucracy, clergy and intelligentsia but also included political concepts, ideas and customs, i.e., the entire heritage of Antiquity was carried over into feudalism. The transition was far less abrupt than in the West. During the transitional period, there existed two ruling classes in fact, the themes aristocracy, which was developing as the feudal class, and the urban aristocracy which was still ruling according to the Antique pattern. A centuries-long struggle for power in the empire, for decisive influence at the Imperial Court, marked Byzantine history during this time, in both internal and foreign affairs. This contradiction in development was apparent in the specific relationship between town and country.

Constantinople, the capital of the empire, remained the outstanding political, economic, intellectual and religious centre during the whole of the transitional period to feudalism and this is how it also appeared to the Crusaders from Western Europe. It was both a magnet and a source of influence for not only the whole of the empire but also for the Orient and Western Europe as well. The leaders of the ruling class, centred around the Imperial Court, the great State and urban bureaucracy and the dignitaries of the Church, the bishops and abbots, had their residence here and, despite all the changes in the countryside, determined the fundamental policies and intellectual views. There must have been a large number of splendid palaces, churches and other edifices but few of them have survived the destruction wrought by later centuries. It is nevertheless quite certain that the centre of the city was dominated by prestige buildings. The emperor alone possessed a whole series of palaces and pleasure seats. The "Great Palace", the principal residence, was set apart from the rest of the city. Together with other palaces in the locality, it possessed its own water main, baths, sports grounds and gardens. Every kind of rare building material was used, being richly ornamented with precious metals. The emperor's table in the banqueting hall was made from solid gold. The rulers had a large number of philosophers, astronomers, physicians, philologists, theologists and artists at their command. They were dedicated above all to the preservation and cultivation of Antique culture. Trade and a variety of crafts in the tradition of Antiquity provided the economic backbone.

For mediaeval concepts, Constantinople remained a gigantic city. Its population in the 6th century was about 400,000 people and it could not have been much less than this in the centuries leading up to the Crusades. Mighty walls protected the vast assemblage of buildings on the land and sea sides. On the land side alone the fortifications stretched for six kilometres. There were three systems of ramparts, consisting of a parapet, an outer wall and the principal wall, which was about five metres thick. Ninety-six towers reinforced its defensive capability. Its outer appearance alone, which was unique in European eyes and was even comparable with other gigantic fortifications of the Orient, made a tremendous impression. Behind the walls, the busy activities of a great city flourished. This was the centre for the trades and crafts of the empire. All the essential trades were well established here, the city being also famed for its production of luxury articles. Fine silk fabrics were woven here and jewellers, goldsmiths, ivory carvers and other craftsmen produced work of artistic perfection. Architecture had achieved the same high level as painting and the production of exquisitely decorated glassware. These objects in the exceptionally large number of palaces, churches and cloisters of the city always excited the admiration of even those visitors to the city who were familiar with such objets d'art. Every single one of these buildings seemed to be a treasure house.

3 The implements for the tilling of the soil remained very simple in Byzantium, too. The wooden plough only scratched the surface of the soil. (From a miniature dating from the end of the 11th century, Bibliothèque Nationale, Paris.)

Constantinople was the trade centre of Eastern Europe. Goods arrived here from Eastern Europe, the Orient, Asia (along the "silk road" which led to China), Africa and Western Europe. Merchants from all over the world, Orientals, Jews, Russians, Venetians and Genoese bought and sold their goods here. In the centuries before the Crusades, the commerce of Byzantium had become largely stagnant and there was a constant flow of gold away from the empire. Despite this, the rulers of Byzantium still believed that they could afford this inactivity in foreign trade. Indeed, it had little effect on the life of luxury they led.

In addition to Constantinople, there existed other centres of trade and craft in all parts of the country, especially Thessalonica and Smyrna which were famous for their craft products. Their wares will be referred to again in connection with Venetian commerce. None of these trade centres could be compared with the capital, however.

Constantinople preserved many of the scientific and cultural traditions of Antiquity. There were educational institutions uniting scholars from various disciplines. Craft production played a dominant role but in contrast to Western Europe the corporate associations of craftsmen, as in the guilds, were only of subordinate importance. Self-administration was not very highly developed in Byzantium. An efficient system of State control by government officials plus taxation and service for the State made the producers dependent. Although a number of artisans and merchants enjoyed certain privileges, their subordinate position under the coercive bureaucratic apparatus inherited from Antiquity was largely continued. The artisans and small merchants retained little of the wealth they produced. Although they were better off in the material sense than the peasants, it was considered that — with few exceptions—the urban population lived in poverty. The same chronists who admired the magnificent edifices write of narrow filthy streets lined with small dwellings, admittedly built of stone for the most part, although adobe structures were found in many towns. Self-indulgence and hunger, splendour and misery, wealth and penury, these are the contradictions which must have been unusually crass in Constantinople. They caught the attention of almost every traveller and indicate from a specific side how the leading figures of the feudal state were mostly to be found here and how they endeavoured to keep under their control not just the production of the city but that of the whole country as well.

In comparison with the crafts of the towns, agriculture was backward. In the villages there were scarcely any of the advantages which in the crafts resulted from an advanced division of labour and professional specialization. Implements remained primitive and wooden ploughs without wheels only scratched the surface of the soil. Oxen were generally used as draught animals by the peasants and stony soil was worked with the hoe. Reaping was done with the sickle. Threshing was carried out with the threshing sled commonly used in Antiquity, this being dragged to and fro across the cereal crop by oxen. Wheat and barley, a variety of fruits and vegetables and oil-seeds were the principal crops. Viticulture was carried on in almost all the territories of the Byzantine Empire. Irrigation was not unusual, especially in horticulture, but large-scale irrigation systems did not exist. Although no exact data have survived, yields were probably higher than in Western Europe during the Middle Ages. Sheep-raising was a speciality of the peasants in certain districts.

In comparison with this relatively average level by mediaeval standards, the social structure of the village community was very interesting, however, and profound changes had been taking place here since the 7th century. In addition to the stratiotes, it was mainly Slav peasants who took possession of the land. They first of all settled the Balkans and pushed forward to the gates of Constantinople. Subsequently, after the military order of the Byzantine Empire had become stabilized, they brought new social features to the villages of Asia Minor as a result of systematic resettlement. The countryside was now dominated by free peasants who, as a result of their migrations, still followed many of the practices of primitive society. Private ownership of land had not yet fully materialized. It was restricted by such factors as the priority rights of relatives and neighbours in the purchasing of land and by the direct responsibility of the peasant for his neighbour in economic and social matters. Woods, meadows and pastures were used by the villagers in common and much of the work which had to be performed in and around the village, such as the building of bridges or roads, was carried out on the same joint basis. These elements of communal co-operation were far more persistent in the Byzantine Empire than in Western Europe. They influenced social development in the countryside up to the eve of the Crusades.

Agricultural production in Byzantium was largely on a small scale up to the 10th century. The existence of cities facilitated market production so that the villages, too, were included in the commodity/money relationship. Under these conditions, large estates were only able to develop at a very slow rate and it took a long time for the themes aristocracy to establish their own economic basis.

In addition to these communal links, it was the relations between town and countryside which hampered the emergence of large estates. The theme legislation had indeed given the themes aristocracy not only military powers but also important civil functions, such as jurisdiction and the collection of taxes and the stronghold of a strategist could certainly represent a force in power politics. Nevertheless, it was not possible for it ever to become anything more than a provincial administration. The themes aristocracy remained in relatively strict dependence on the central government and the urban aristocracy took very good care that the countryside did not become too powerful. It was to the State that peasants paid their various taxes, i.e., to Constantinople. In short, it was a question of two alternatives in the process of feudalization in Byzantium: dependence of the peasants on the State or on the themes nobility. It was a hard-fought struggle. A climax was reached with the revolt under Thomas the Slav (821) in which the peasants and themes aristocracy marched together from Asia Minor to Constantinople to take action against the increase in the burden of State taxation. It is true that the two groups had different class interests but they were united, initially at least, in the face of the common enemy. Further unrest followed in the 10th century, this time on the part of the peasants against the growth of the big estates.

Both groups, the urban and the rural aristocracy, increasingly made use of the emperor to further their interests. As a result, the actions of the central authority were often contradictory. Concessions to the themes aristocracy such as the allocation of landed property and taxation privileges were followed by decisions to the contrary, for example a demand that land should be returned to the peasants. Despite all the contradictions which occurred, the outgoing 9th century and then the 10th brought visible historical progress. The landed property of the themes aristocracy had increased substantially. The mass of the peasants were dependent either on a landowner or on the State, with the exception of the stratiotes who, as warriors, enjoyed special protection against feudalism and were themselves becoming small landowners. In the themes of Asia Minor, in particular, but also in the Balkans, these changes resulted in the emergence of a social and military force which could be used for massive expansion.

It was only in the second half of the 11th century that the great landowners became the decisive element in the countryside as far as the agrarian structure was concerned. A significant decline had taken place in the numbers of peasants who were dependent on the State. Throughout the empire, a powerful stratum of great rural landowners had appeared on the scene and it was this stratum which controlled the peasants. This process was accentuated by the fact that an increasing number of State peasants were made dependent on the nobility by imperial decree. Either their land came into the hands of the great landowners or the nobility was allowed to collect and utilize the taxes owed to the State. It was not only the themes aristocracy that obtained landed property in this way; the aristocracy of the towns, the monasteries and the emperor himself also became landowners. Under the influence of Antiquity, a class of feudal landowners thus came into being at a relatively late stage. However, even now they did not abandon their links with the towns but for the most part continued to reside there. Of perhaps even more significance was the circumstance that now even the mass of the stratiotes fell into a state of feudal dependence. This marked the disintegration of a decisive military institution of the Byzantine Empire which, bearing in mind the preference of the great landowners for city life, could only be replaced to a limited extent by the establishment of a feudal force. It was not long before efforts succeeded in placing the army on a mercenary basis again.

This principle had indeed never been entirely abandoned in the preceding centuries. Normans, in particular, but also Slavs, Armenians, Flemings and warriors of other ethnic origin served as contingents in the Byzantine army of the 11th century. It was intended to raise the army for the Crusades in a similar manner.

The picture of Byzantine society presented at the eve of the Crusades was shaped to a not unimportant extent by the dispute about religious images and its consequences. All the contradictions of the specific development, such as the development of the relations between State and Church, town and country and also the problems of the absorption of the Antique heritage, played a part in the conflicts which lasted for more than a century. In 730, Emperor Leo III banned the worshipping of holy images in the churches. At this time, the veneration of icons had assumed an unprecedented importance. The common people, in particular, associated it with the expectation of definite assistance against poverty, natural catastrophes and personal misfortune. The iconoclasts, the destroyers of images, rejected the view that icons could act as mediators between God and Man. At the back of this theological dispute, there was the proclamation of the Imperial right to issue decrees affecting the faith, following precisely the same practice as that which had existed under Justinian. The iconodules, the venerators of images, disputed this right while the iconoclasts confirmed that the emperor possessed such authority. The intention of all this was to restrict the authority of the Church which was beginning to develop as an independent political power. The dispute was linked specifically with practical measures such as the confiscation of ecclesiastical treasures to the advantage of the central Imperial authority. The sides in the dispute about religious images reflected the process of social development. Whereas the urban population, led by the clergy and the intelligentsia, mostly took the part of the iconodules, the iconoclasts had their most stable social basis, disregarding the immediate retinue of the emperor, in the countryside among the themes aristocracy and the stratiotes.

At a synod in Constantinople in 843, the venerators of images carried the day but this did not mean that the old relations were restored nor was the Church able to achieve an independent political position within the State.

The veneration of images and the relic cult experienced a revival. Constantinople possessed an exceptional profusion of religious relics and consequently had the impact of a religious centre on the ordinary members of the Church.

Up to the 13th century, there was no other Christian city which had such a profusion of relics. Practically everything was represented here, from parts of the bodies of all the saints to splinters from the Cross and fragments from Christ's crown of thorns, the appropriate effect being achieved. Many pilgrims also from Western Europe came to adore the relics. Nevertheless, everything, including the position of the Church in the State, was subordinated to State authority. It was the emperor who had won the political victory and the relationship between State and Church already established by Justinian continued to be maintained in its essentials. Although there was never any marked caesaropapism in Byzantium, the Imperial power nevertheless clearly outranked the Church. Spiritual authority was de facto subordinate to temporal power. The emperor presided over the synods and selected the patriarch from the list of three candidates submitted to him. This position resulted not so much from the political balance of power but from the Byzantine view of Imperial authority which had been inherited from Late Antiquity. The elected emperor was regarded as a sacred personage. Even his clothing and palace were sacred. A profusion of ceremonies and symbols emphasized his sublimity. However, this reverence of the emperor was not centred around his person but rather the Imperial institution as such. Many emperors achieved very little political power and dynasties were very short-lived. For a long period, the position of emperor was an elected office and the son only had a chance of being his successor when he had already been declared as co-regent during the lifetime of his father. The more profound significance of the emperor cult resulted from the prevailing conviction that Byzantium was the heir and continuator of Antiquity. The Imperial throne was regarded as the principal symbol of this tradition. All other peoples and states were despised as barbarians, no matter whether they were Western Europeans,

Slavs or Arabs. None of them was really regarded as an equal. Individual concessions may have been made in practical negotiations but fundamentally this attitude was never abandoned. This gave a specific direction to all the military, political and intellectual confrontations which affected Byzantium during the transitional period up to the 11th century.

It was not by chance that the 9th and even more the 10th century was regarded as the golden age of Byzantium in its early feudal stage. The exceptional economic upswing in the cities was associated with the increase in power of the great rural landowners, with the army of stratiotes which was still intact and up to this time had been largely unaffected by feudalization and the uniting bond of a powerful central authority. The political scene was dominated by the implementation of foreign policies.

It was significant that most attention was paid to the northern and particularly the eastern frontiers. Admittedly, the conversion of the Bulgarians by force (after 865) and their subsequent subjugation (1018) could not effect a fundamental change in the situation along the northern frontier —the desire of the Bulgarians for independence was far too strong for this—but their temporary successes may well have appeared to the Byzantines as confirmation of the correctness of their political concept. The mission to the Rus, which was initiated with the baptism of Vladimir (988) probably had the same effect. Of more importance from our standpoint, however, were the happenings on the eastern frontier. After eventful battles during the 9th century, the second half of the 10th century was marked by the beginning of the great offensive under the emperors Nicephorus II Phocas (963–969), John I Tzimisces (969–976) and Basil II (976–1025). Cilicia, the eastern part of Asia Minor up to the Caucasus and, above all, Syria were conquered by the Byzantine army of stratiotes and incorporated in the empire. All this presented an impressive balance. In the east, the frontier had advanced to the Araxes while Northern Syria with Antioch constituted the frontier district (theme). For a time, Byzantine garrisons were maintained along the Mediterranean coast as far as Caesarea. The island of Cyprus had been conquered and a number of Islamic princes, including the lords of Aleppo

and Damascus, had recognized Byzantine sovereignty. In this way, Byzantium had clearly indicated its very special interest in the territories which were conquered by the Crusaders of Western Europe some eighty years later. The motivation of the conquests was not at all religious, however, or at least not primarily. There was some talk of a holy war against the heathens and of proclaiming those killed as martyrs. Nevertheless, the dominating idea was the memory of the ancient Roman Empire and in Byzantine thinking these territories were never abandoned.

The links with the Christians living in the Orient had never been allowed to lapse completely. In the theological sphere, there were admittedly formal religious disputes with the sectarian churches existing in the Orient, particularly with the Nestorians, but on the other hand this clearly demonstrates the interest of the Byzantine Church in the overall development of Christianity in the Orient as well. There were close contacts with the Orthodox Christians of Syria and Palestine. Favoured by the religious tolerance of Islam, these contacts were even maintained in times of war. Leading theologians, especially those of Antioch, were able to influence the general policy of the Church time and again. In fact, from the overall trend, it was obvious that the patriarchs of Alexandria, Jerusalem and Antioch would opt for Byzantium when the division into the Eastern and Western Church took place in 1054.

The relations of the Byzantine Empire with Western Europe followed a somewhat different pattern. Only in Italy did Constantinople have any territorial interests, which will be examined later in another connection. It was with particular attention that the Byzantines observed the development of politico-State and ecclesiastical relations. There was no question of abandoning claims which derived from the Antique tradition. This was made quite clear in 968 in respect of the Imperial title. The German King Otto I had been crowned as emperor in Rome in 962, had conquered almost the whole of Italy and was now seeking for his son the hand in marriage of the sister of the Byzantine emperor. Scorn and indignation was the reaction of Byzantium to this proposal. It was considered that Otto was not an emperor but a Barbarian king and that there could be no question of a marriage with a princess who had been born to the Imperial purple. A clear distinction was drawn at this time between the children of the Imperial family who had been born in the Imperial palace of porphyry and the others. Only the first group, the porphyrogenetes or those born to the purple, enjoyed the Imperial privilege. A marriage with foreign rulers would have implied equality of birth with Byzantium. The envoys were humiliated. It is true that Byzantium acceded to the proposal in 972 but the union of Otto II with Theophano did not result in the title of the Western emperor being accepted as equal to that of Byzantium.

The differences in development between Western Europe and Byzantium are most clearly demonstrated by the split in the Church. There had already been divergent opinions in theological matters between the individual Sees since Late Antiquity. Sectarian churches, such as the Nestorians or the Monophysites, had long been in existence in the Orient. Despite serious differences regarding dogma and liturgy, the form of ecclesiastical unity had nevertheless been preserved between Byzantium and Western Europe until the 11th century. The real background of the actual split was not characterized by theological questions, however, but rather by the increasing differences in the cultural and ethnic respect. These constantly growing differences had their roots in the overall social development in Eastern and Western Europe which was indeed following quite contrary directions, as will be shown in detail in the next chapter. Totally divergent views on the relationship of State and Church were a part of this. After a difficult beginning, Papacy had become a political and intellectual power in 11th-century Europe with a programme of reform which prescribed the primacy of spiritual authority over temporal power. The Byzantine Church, subordinated to the State but subscribing to the concept of the specific mission

4 *The Byzantine army was still relatively very well equipped in the transitional period to feudalism. The mounted warriors had an iron helmet, scale armour, a round shield, bow and arrow, a lance (about 3.60 metres long), a battle-axe and a sword. Stirrups had been added to the saddle in the 6th century and were a revolutionary innovation, giving the rider a much firmer seat in combat. The archers were usually organized in specialist military units. (From an 11th century ivory box. Cathedral Treasure of Troyes.)*

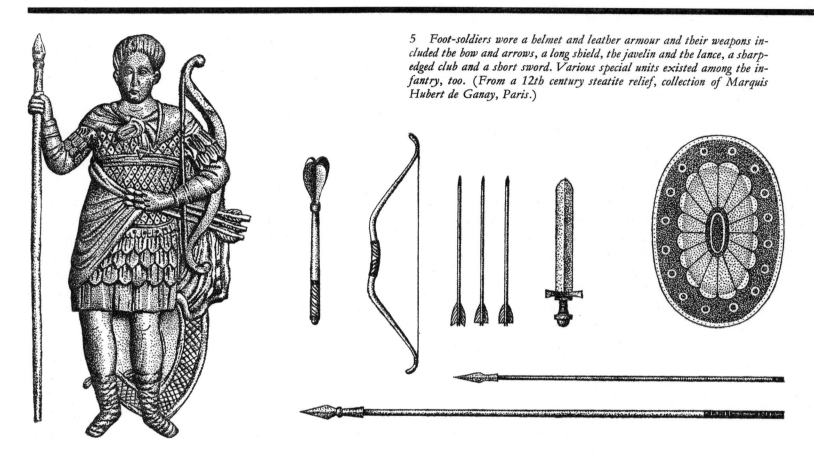

5 Foot-soldiers wore a helmet and leather armour and their weapons included the bow and arrows, a long shield, the javelin and the lance, a sharp-edged club and a short sword. Various special units existed among the infantry, too. (From a 12th century steatite relief, collection of Marquis Hubert de Ganay, Paris.)

of the Byzantines, likewise insisted on the exclusivity of its authority, although taking a different position. It had long been apparent that two Churches would develop which would be independent of each other even in the formal sense. Schisms had occurred already in the preceding centuries but a compromise formula had been found time and again, not so much from an appreciation of the opposing standpoint as from the wish still to be able to dominate the other side.

In the middle of the 11th century, the arguments between the militant clerics again flared up. Rome expressed the belief that the Holy Ghost emanated not only from the Father but also from the Son; the Eastern Church rejected the "filioque" formula, likewise the Roman fasting on the Sabbath and the enforced celibacy of priests. Since this was a subject which was understandable for the ordinary people, the dispute was dominated by the question of whether leavened bread, as in the East, should be used for Holy Communion or unleavened bread. None of the matters of contention was new but they now led to the splitting of the Church.

In 1054, the Roman Cardinal Humbert da Silva Candida travelled to Byzantium and placed the Papal bull of excommunication on the altar of the Hagia Sophia. Byzantium took revenge for that. The fact that this was no more than a formal act despite all the drama associated with it is indirectly confirmed by Western European contemporaries who were present at church services in the East and thought that they were in an alien church. Great differences had developed in the ritual. The liturgy in the Eastern churches was longer and occupied a much more important position, the language of the Church was Greek or Slavic in the Rus whereas everywhere in the West it was Latin. The clergy had different hairstyles and wore different robes. In short, the total sum of minor details made the split apparent even to the layman. Nevertheless, even within the ranks of the reformed Papacy, there were still important personages who hoped at the beginning of the Crusades that it would still be possible to heal the schism—naturally under the primacy of the Holy See.

At first, this development seemed to be solely a loss of prestige for Constantinople and of no significance in practical politics. However, in the 11th century as a whole, Byzantium no longer was the power which it had been even a century before. This was not so evident in the West as along the eastern frontier. A fundamental change had taken place in the balance of power in the Orient. The impetus came from a Turkish nomadic people, the tribal association of the Oghuz, who originally came from the Tarim Basin and the steppes as far as Lake Balkhash. They adopted Islamism as early as the 10th century and founded an early feudal state, the centre of which was in Transoxania. They rapidly absorbed Islamic culture. In the middle of the 11th century, groups led by the tribal leader Seljuk advanced westwards and in a whirlwind campaign overran the states which had succeeded the Arab Caliphate in Central Asia. Baghdad fell to them in 1055. Henceforth the Caliphs of Baghdad were no more than religious leaders and in this function led only a background existence. Political power was in the hands of the Seljuk sultans. Around 1070, led by Alp Arslan, they conquered Syria and took possession of Jerusalem.

But it was not these events which led to the Crusade movement for saving the Holy Sepulchre but rather the threat to the Byzantine Empire. A Seljuk army pushed forward to Anatolia and destroyed the Byzantine forces in the battle of Manzikert in 1071 where the emperor was taken prisoner. The Seljuks then established the Sultanate of Rum in the eastern part of present-day Turkey. Even after this defeat, the military situation for Byzantium was not particularly critical. There was apparently no need to fear that the Seljuks would advance still further. And yet the Byzantine emperor appealed to Western Europe for military assistance. The reasons for this were connected with changes in the internal structure of Byzantium. The organization of the themes and the stratiote forces were in the process of disintegration. The emperor had been obliged to fight the battle of Manzikert with a motley army which had been hastily put together from mostly mercenaries. New units of mercenaries were urgently needed since at the same time the Normans were advancing into Southern Italy and were extending their raids to the Balkans. The Bulgarians, Serbs and Croats were also engaged in fighting Constantinople. When the first Crusade was being prepared, the situation in the Orient had already quietened down again. The Seljuks were in no position to build a great empire for a fairly long period of time. Individual sultanates had already been set up in 1092—in Syria and Palestine, particularly in Aleppo and Damascus. This breakaway process became even more marked in the following years. Each fairly large town had its own ruler. The more dangerous antagonists of these small Seljuk potentates were the Fatimids of Egypt, a force which the Crusader states were also to profit from for more than a century. For Byzantium, the reaction of Europe to its appeal for help marked the beginning of the end of its claim to hegemony within the Christian world.

WESTERN EUROPE

The feudal society of Western and Central Europe at the eve of the Crusades presented quite a different picture. Economic life was dominated by the bartering system, while commodity production played a subordinate role. The reasons for this are associated with the emergence of feudalism. Only a few cities had survived the collapse of Antiquity; it was only in Italy that they were of any economic importance. As a whole, they did not constitute any of the points of crystallization shaping society, as in the Arab Caliphate or Byzantium for instance. This is why feudalism in Europe was based on the countryside from the start. The cities with their privileges and civil liberties developed only at a later date. In the legal and social sense they were quite distinct from the countryside and retained this special character for centuries.

Agriculture was marked by low productivity. It has been calculated that as a rule harvest yields did not exceed three or four times the quantity of seed planted. The tilling of the soil was done with the most primitive implements. Wooden ploughs were used to prepare the soil while harvesting was done with sickles. The three-field system was that most commonly used, i.e., summer and winter cereals were planted alternately after which the land lay fallow for a year. Manure, marl and ashes were used as fertilizers.

The peasants themselves made nearly all the important things they needed in their daily life. This applied not only to their agricultural implements but also to their dwellings—simple huts of clay, wood and straw—and clothing. Their standard of living was low by any standard. They had little furniture in their huts. They slept on straw and their tables were usually rough-hewn boards placed on trestles. The majority possessed only one set of clothes and often had to go barefoot even in winter.

This material basis also determined the standard of living of the feudal lords, more or less. The economic and social unit was the feudal ownership of the land. It united the dependent peasants, bondsmen, serfs and copyholders under the control of a feudal lord. The nobleman, the Church or the monastery received the surplus product of the peasants in the form of tithes or socage. Thus even the lord only had a limited selection of goods at his disposal on his own territory. Socage craftsmen at court made only a slight contribution to the range available. Crafts specialization only became more important in the 11th century and later.

In the 10th and 11th centuries, cities as the future centres of specialized craft production and exchange of commodities, sprung up in almost all parts of Europe. Trade routes over land and water linked the territories of Central and Western Europe and reached as far as the Orient and Byzantium. The Rhône and the Rhine were arteries in the trade routes linking England, Flanders, Northern and Southern France, Northern Italy and Rome. Overland routes led from both Flanders and the Rhône Valley to Cordova in Islamic Spain. During the 11th century, the routes eastwards via Regensburg, Prague and Cracow to Kiev and the Danube waterway via Regensburg and Niš to Constantinople became increasingly important. Trading towns flourished along these routes from the 11th century onwards and economic centres developed which were outside the control of the landowners.

Via these trade routes, which terminated at the Northern Italian ports of Venice, Genoa and Pisa, knowledge of the Orient and Byzantium spread north of the Alps. Fine fabrics, spices, ornaments, wine and other goods of Byzantine and Oriental origin were brought to Europe by foreign merchants. To be sure, in the 11th century it was not yet a stream of goods. Only the leading circles of society could afford such goods and even then only seldom. Apart from commodities, these trade routes also brought information about the Orient to Europe. They were used not only by pilgrims but also by couriers, envoys and not least soldiers. By the 11th century, they were already in such general use that it was quite natural that the crusading armies should use them to reach the Orient.

A low level of production, a low standard of living and, despite the developing social division of labour between town and country, the generally slight degree of exchange made European feudal society exceptionally vulnerable to natural catastrophes and plagues even in the 11th century. Contemporary accounts contain reports almost every year of famine and epidemics in the most diverse regions of Europe. Large numbers of peasants left their villages and wandered across the country, begging for food. The great religious houses were often their last hope of obtaining a few alms. Starvation frequently led to horrifying consequences. The chronist Raoul Glaber writes of the years 1032/1033 in France as follows: "Travellers are carried off by those stronger than they, their limbs cut off, cooked and eaten ... Many showed children a piece of fruit or an egg, enticed them in this way to a lonely place where they killed and ate them. In other places, corpses are dug up to satisfy the pangs of hunger."

Despite its narrow economic basis—in comparison with the Orient—European feudal society was not weak and did not stagnate either. Feudalism primarily means development of society from the position of the countryside.

It was characteristic for Europe that the dynamics of development emanated from relatively small territorial units, from the village and the manorial estate. Further development meant closer economic and class relations within this narrow framework. The result of this was that the feudal divisions, i.e., the powerlessness of the central authority and the relative independence of local feudal lords, as was quite characteristic for France from the 9th century on, did not represent a wrong path of development but was rather the expression of a natural process. From the 11th century, new factors appeared with the emergence of more clearly defined feudal class relations and the development of the two principal classes. They explain the objective reasons for the Crusade movement and will consequently be set out in some detail.

The sum of all the new processes and phenomena can be designated by the term "national development" which is to be primarily understood as the development of all the economic, social and political relations from the manorial estate upwards but still within a narrow territorial sphere. All classes and strata of society were involved in this.

Because of the marked increase in population but even more because of the impossibility of ceaselessly dividing up the tilled land, the peasants began to use woodland and wasteland for agricultural purposes. This was done not only in the immediate vicinity of existing villages but also in remote mountainous districts and great forests. Considering the prim-

itive implements at their disposal, this was exceptionally tedious work, it is true. As a rule, the trees and undergrowth were burnt off and the roots pulled up by hand so as not to damage their implements. To begin with, yields were very poor and many plots of land, won from nature by hard toil, were again abandoned. The land had to be worked for years before all the trees and roots had been cleared to a reasonable extent. Despite all this, the attractions were relatively great. For the most part, the new areas of land lay outside the manorial estates and the peasants were not subject to villeinage. Initially they paid few or no taxes. With the new settlements on cleared land, new groups of the peasant class emerged outside the territory of the feudal lords and the prevailing type of production by villeinage was supplemented by a new form. The area of new land cleared was considerable. This movement, which began in the 11th century and continued to about the 13th, largely established the present limits of cultivated land. Even today, many place-names still recall the founding of settlements during this period (e. g., the endings -rode, -rade, -ingerode, -roth, -reuth and -rieth in German).

Other peasants moved to artisan settlements or into the towns that had grown up, and in this way likewise strengthened the sphere outside manorial rule.

As regards the feudal lords, the economic trends provided them with new opportunities to extend their power. In France, in particular, violent feudal quarrels determined the political situation from the 9th century onwards. When exploitation was concentrated to locally restricted estates, the struggle to extend these estates became the dominant feature of politics. The feudal lords sought to extend their possessions at the expense of others either by military confrontations or by various political measures. The devastation of the countryside and the plundering of villages were the consequence of this. The ecclesiastical estates, which had less military protection, and the manorial estates consisting of scattered holdings, were at a particular disadvantage. The answer to the worst forms of feudal anarchy was offered by the concentration of power in the hands of a few great feudal lords within a restricted area who relied, in addition to their landed estates, on the most diverse privileges which existed in the area and which they appropriated. With the establishment of settlements on cleared land and the emergence of towns from the 11th century onwards, important economic positions had been established which favoured the consolidation of a central authority within a definite territory since these positions strengthened the power of the great feudal lord as the actual or legal town governor or master of the peasants on the cleared land within the territory and outside his own manorial estate.

Both the constant warfare and the exercise of the new functions resulting from national development demanded the establishment of new feudal forces. A group of feudal lords came into being who, though numerous, were endowed with only a minimum of landed property.

Specialization in military service was the second tendency which became evident. Contemporaries regarded society as being divided into three groups. These were the knights as the warriors of this society, the clergy and the peasants. The structure was naturally much more complex than a simple division into temporal and spiritual feudal nobility. The feudal pyramid provided for the most diverse grades. Apart from the great liege-lords, who had received their possessions directly from the monarch and, as counts, potential territorial lords, dukes, bishops and abbots of great monasteries, represented the most powerful stratum, there were also numerous small vassals with only small estates.

There were narrow limits set to the material and cultural standard of living of the ruling class. Thus it is known that Henry IV of Germany, when he stayed in the Harz Mountains with his numerous retinue around 1170 for more often than was his wont, was obliged to hear on a number of occasions the justified complaints of the administrators of the royal victual stores that nothing more could be supplied from the cellars and barns until the next harvest.

This affected the minor vassals with only small estates to an even greater extent. Above all, it was the division of inherited land that was a threat to feudal existence since his share of the land was no longer able to supply the feudal lord with what he needed. Old French accounts report that knights had to return to the plough. Even in this respect the dividing line between peasants and lesser nobility was very vague. It thus appears to be of general significance that among the minor feudal lords of the 10th and 11th century in France new customs were developed for safeguarding the feudal possessions of the family. In the north, the practice of the first-born inheriting everything became widespread which obliged the other children to seek a new feudal existence within the Church or in the military service of a powerful feudal lord. A different solution was found in Southern France and Italy. As a reaction to the constant division of the family heritage, the development of the confrerie emerged, whereby all the members of the large knightly family in their totality had a share in the family estate. The members of the family had to submit to a measure of discipline which was sometimes so strict that the approval of the family was needed for marriage since a further increase in the size of the family was a serious affair. Despite this, privations had to be endured in many cases to ensure that at least one member of the family could be equipped from their own resources as a mounted knight in the accustomed style. The younger members of the family had to look for another means of support in keeping with their standing. Entering the service of a feudal lord was one possibility but for many there was no alternative but the Church.

Another special stratum which made its appearance from the 11th century onwards were the ministerials. At this point of time, they were still emerging from the peasant class, some of them still being serfs. They owed their emergence to the expansion of the authority of the State in the territories where they were employed for specific services in the feudal administration such as the collection of taxes, jurisdiction or in the administration of castles. The great feudal lords also needed people such as these for similar purposes.

The small-scale feudal war for the safeguarding or expansion of landed estates or area of authority determined the life-style and habits of the nobility and its followers. A relatively large part of the surplus product was expended on military equipment and war. A complete set of equipment included a coat of mail, an iron helmet and a great shield. The principal offensive weapons used were the sword and the lance, the latter replacing the spear.

The noble warrior was mounted, used stirrups and saddles and wore spurs at his heels. This is how he is shown in contemporary illustrations. It is equally well known, however, that a complete set of equipment was very expensive and almost beyond the reach of the minor vassals. It is reported that a suit of armour cost as much as a farm of the size of a hide (60–100 acres). It is to be assumed that the other articles of equipment cost just as much. Only the wealthiest feudal lords could afford a complete set of equipment without difficulty. The minor vassals and followers often received a part of their equipment from their lord or were not fully equipped. This explains why there were often only a few mounted combatants in the cut-and-thrust feudal confrontations. Many examples can be quoted of where followers of noble birth had to fight as foot soldiers. Even in the 12th century, the mounted German knights displayed remarkably little prowess in the fighting in the Crusader states.

Of at least equal significance to military equipment was the safeguarding of feudal power by the construction of castles from the 11th century onward. These had a double function: to assert the lord's power over the peasants and to provide protection against possible foes. It was the general custom of feudal lords to construct a system of fortifications in which the use of wood and earthen ramparts still dominated, although stone was slowly becoming the principal material for this purpose. Of the types which appeared on the scene, the "donjon" or keep of the Normans proved especially effective. This was a massive stone tower built of stone slabs which, situated at a prominent point, dominated the countryside around it. It was almost impregnable and provided sufficient room for storage chambers and the residential apartments of the lord and his retinue. It was first seen among the Normans in Southern Italy, Normandy and after 1066 in England. In related forms, it soon spread across the whole of Western and Central Europe. These castles had become established as the centres of social life even before the Crusades. It was here that courts were held, judgements pronounced and additional socage performed. Travelling merchants and artisans visited them, too, and acrobats and other entertainers found a grateful public there who were willing to pay for their amusement. Not a few of the most important castles became the centre of a city in the 11th and 12th centuries.

It was this specific situation which gave the European aristocracy of the 11th century its markedly aggressive character. The struggle for new possessions by the sons of minor vassals who had no right to share in the family estate or the urge to increase existing feudal property reflect the objective side of the causes. From this there resulted attitudes and social norms which attached particular importance to war. Prowess in knightly combat strengthened one's reputation and demonstrated his membership of the ruling class. For the lowest group in particular and for the ministerials emerging

6/7   The wheeled plough and the harrow, the horse-collar and the kummet were some of the major innovations in European agriculture. They permitted more intensive tillage of the land and more efficient use of animal traction. Unlike today, centuries passed before these improvements came into general use. (From a manuscript in the Bibliothèque Nationale, Paris)

from the peasant strata, this attitude provided a stimulus for expansion. These social norms and customs attained their final form only in the 12th and 13th century but they were already developing in the 11th. The main obstacle to the development of this trend in the 11th century was the lack of any political and intellectual power which could unite these urges to expand and move from small-scale confrontations to great military conquests. It was the Catholic Church and especially the reform papacy which sprang into the breech. In the intellectual sphere, a new phase of penetration of all areas of social life by Christian concepts and ideas had already been evident since the 10th century, becoming even more apparent in the 11th. This is generally characterized by the development of a feudal religious spirit, i.e., the feudalization of Christianity in Western Europe now attained its real climax. It was sponsored by various ecclesiastical institutions and was associated as a whole with monastical and ecclesiastical reform

As early as the beginning of the 10th century, a movement for the reformation of the monasteries had been started at the Abbey of Cluny in Western Burgundy and rapidly spread over the whole of Central and Western Europe to about two thousand religious houses by the end of the 11th century. The reorganization of monastic life with the aim of eliminating the disorderliness and loose living of the organized clergy was the internal aspect of this reform. It was considered that monastic life should attract laymen to the Church and not be a source of repulsion. The development of the liturgy and of piety seemed to be a suitable way of establishing Christianity more firmly in the minds of the common people. Many innovations were introduced for this purpose, such as a pompous cult of the Virgin, the cult of the Cross and others. The number of masses celebrated increased. Festive processions influenced the common people in the closer and wider vicinity of the monasteries. The Cluniac monasteries practised praying for the dead. Systematic attention was given to the display of religious emotion among the monks and also among the common people by the revision of Church ceremonies. Thus the preparation of the Host, for instance, became a solemn and special occasion. The wheat was selected and washed grain by grain, the mill-stones carefully cleaned and covered with cloths. The water for the dough could only be taken from the pitcher used for Mass. The monks sang psalms and hymns of praise while the dough was being prepared and during baking.

The actual background against which this exceptional degree of religiousness could be developed so effectively consisted of economic measures. As the result of efficient organization and concentration on intensive methods of production, the estates of the reformed monasteries became centres of advanced agriculture and the refuge of many peasants in times of devastation and famine. The Cluniac monasteries were effective media in the consolidation of religious ideas at

18 The type of residential tower (donjon) preferred by the Normans in particular spread relatively rapidly throughout the territories conquered by them and also to the neighbouring areas. The illustration shows a residential tower (castle Tonqué-doc at Lannion) built in Brittany.

all levels of feudal society and heralded the political and ideological advance of the Church as a whole, as manifested in the development of the reform papacy. The reformed monasteries soon achieved remarkable popularity. Under the protection of the monasteries, deserted villages and uncultivated fields prospered as never before. The great feudal lords gave the monasteries political support. They wanted economically strong ecclesiastical estates in the territories they ruled and, in the upswing of monastic agriculture, saw a way of overcoming the worst effects of the division of land. Through their ministerials, the aristocracy possessed political and legal influence since the monasteries needed powerful temporal protection. The peasants were eager to farm the estates of the black monks since their entire life was considerably more assured here.

The reform papacy emerged in the middle of the 11th century and by the beginning of the Crusades, i.e., within a very short time, had become the greatest political and intellectual influence in Central and Western Europe.

It began with the demand for the emancipation of the Church from feudal authority. Henceforth, no prince should have the right—as was customary hitherto—to influence the appointment of individual clergy as bishops, abbots and vicars. The Papal Election Law of 1059 set the precedent for the leading positions in the Church hierarchy: the Pope was to be elected by the cardinals. As the successor to St. Peter, he was regarded by the reformers as the supreme representative of God on Earth and as the Head of Christendom.

With this ideology, the Papacy followed two objectives. Within the Church, strict subordination was required. Only the Pope could appoint and dismiss bishops. Only the Bishop of Rome was legally designated as universal. This defined the attitude towards Byzantium and the churches of the Orient. The Patriarch of Constantinople was subordinate to the Bishop of Rome. This view was not abandoned even after the division of the Church in 1054 and had a not unimportant influence on relations with Byzantium during the time of the Crusades.

The other aspect of the new orientation concerned the relationship of Church and State which was defined in general as the relationship of head and limbs, of body and soul: as the representative of God on Earth, the Pope was the only person whose feet all princes were obliged to kiss. He had the authority to dismiss emperors. Here again the formulation does not only apply to the relations with the temporal power in Europe and specifically with the German emperor although the struggle for power took place in the second half of the 11th century during the investiture controversy.

The actual implementation of the objectives of the reformers seemed fairly limited. Resistance to simony and the investiture of laymen in the dispensing of clerical appointments and the observance of celibacy by the clergy were the principal slogans advocated by the popes and their followers in the investiture controversy. Nevertheless, these slogans were very sharp weapons since they were directed against important spheres of power of the great temporal lords and the German kings in particular. No feudal lord was to invest a newly appointed Church dignitary with the insignia of his office, the ring and the crosier, as was the usual practice hitherto; this was the exclusive privilege of the Church. It was asserted that the investiture of laymen was already a simony in fact, no matter whether money played a part in the purchase of appointment or not. Both the priest consecrated in this manner and the feudal lord had to be regarded as heretics, as the servants of Hell. This was the argument of Humbert da Silva Candida, better known as Cardinal Hildebrand, one of the leading exponents of the reformed papacy. However, the intention of the Papacy was not at all the establishment of a puritanical Church organization. This would have meant a rapid end to the ambition of a Papacy with universal authority. Rome skilfully exploited the upswing of a money economy and used every possible opportunity to strengthen its financial basis, even the purchase of official positions, although this was now in the hands of the reformed papacy.

The confrontation was still raging at this point. The reformers made use of all the movements of the time and were not squeamish in the choice made. They supported the communal movements against bishops loyal to the Emperor, favoured the travelling preachers in France who proclaimed the ideal of an impoverished primitive Church to the com-

19 The donjon built in South Italy in 1090 was modernized in the year 1230 for Frederick II. A number of these buildings which were erected in the 11th and 12th century were subsequently extended and turned into castles.

20 The Abbey Church at Cluny was built at the beginning of the 10th century. The Abbey of Cluny achieved fame from the reform of the monasteries which started here in the 10th and 11th centuries and spread over the whole of Western and Central Europe. Pope Urban II paid a visit to the Abbey shortly before the Council of Clermont.

21/22 St Bernard of Clairvaux, the advocate of the second Crusade, addressed a passionate appeal from the pulpit of Speyer Cathedral in 1146 to the German King Conrad III in particular and persuaded him to take the Cross here. The Cathedral, an outstanding example of Western European architecture of the 11th and 12th centuries, dates back to 1030, alterations taking place about 1100 and in the second half of the 12th century.

23   The Normans were some of the most active warriors and conquerors of 11th century Europe. Small groups settled in Southern Italy while the majority concentrated their efforts on the conquest of England. The Anglo-Saxons were defeated in 1066 at the Battle of Hastings. The Bayeux tapestry commemorating this battle (70 × 0.50 metres) shows the weapons used by the Normans: Norman helmet, coat of mail, lance, sword and stirrups. Bayeux Museum

REX ROGAT ABBATEM MAThILDIM SUPPLICAT ATQ;

24 The confrontation in the investiture controversy forced Henry IV of Germany to come in penance to Canossa in 1077 to persuade the Pope to lift the excommunication imposed on him. The fortress to which Gregory VII had retired belonged to Matilda, Margravine of Tuscany. According to legend, it was she who persuaded the Pope to receive Henry IV and absolve him. Vatican Library, Rome

25 The political history of Western Europe before and during the time of the Crusades was dominated by feuds fought by the nobility. The illustration from the chronicle by Otto of Freising, second half of 12th century, depicts the confrontation between the followers of Emperor Henry IV and his son Henry V. University Library, Jena

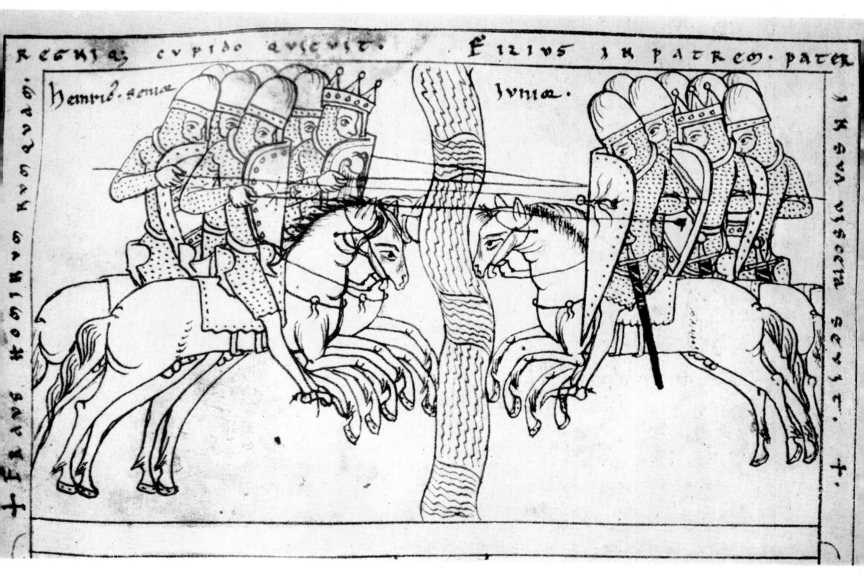

29 Almost all the crafts of the Orient were capable of producing objects of great luxury. Beautifully cut vessels richly ornamented with gold and silver and precious stones were outstanding examples of their art. The vessel shown is made of rock crystal. It is now in St Mark's Cathedral, Venice.

30 This magnificent goblet from the Imperial Court of Constantinople is testimony to the skill of Byzantine craftsmen. Numerous other objects of such value were taken from Byzantium by the knights of the fourth Crusade. This goblet is now part of the Cathedral Treasure of St Mark's, Venice.

31 Scientific knowledge was also applied
in the development of navigation. The
treatise of magnetism by Petrus Peregrinus,
based on the studies made by the author
in the Orient, provides a clear insight
into this and, in the associated drawings,
an idea of how the compass was constructed and used. Austrian National
Library, Vienna

32 With the astrolabe, an instrument
which was already in general use during
the early period of the Arab Caliphate, it
was possible to measure the positions of
the celestial bodies, to record their movements and to carry out astronomical
calculations. Library of the Deutsche
Morgenländische Gesellschaft, Halle

33 The Arsenal of the city of Venice in
the Middle Ages was the greatest municipal shipyard for the construction of mercantile and naval vessels. It was here that
the municipal authorities checked the sea-
worthiness and equipment of the ships
which were assembled as escorts for the
Crusades. Painting by Antonio Natale,
18th century, 78 × 103 cm, Museo Correr,
Venice.

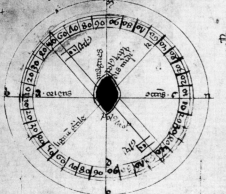

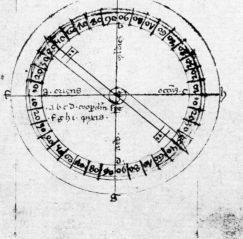

On the following pages:

34   The bronze horses brought back in triumph by the Venetians in 1204 from Constantinople were part of the principal spoils and were set up in front of St Mark's Cathedral.

35   St Mark's Cathedral (San Marco) of Venice, named after the patron saint of the city, was the most important church of this Northern Italian seaport. Building started in 823 and continued during the following centuries. The original archi-tecture, particularly the interior, displays Byzantine influence throughout. The Cathedral has a treasure chamber in which numerous Byzantine objets d'art are kept which came to Venice during the Middle Ages in various ways—as gifts, through trade or by theft.

36 These reliefs are some of the details
of St Mark's which reveal Byzantine influence.

65

mon people and encouraged the opposition of the princes to Henry IV. The anti-Papal party did not remain inactive. On the one hand it supported the Imperial assertion that the Emperor was the head of the Church and had received his authority from God alone and, on the other, sharply criticized the Reformers. Above all, the hunger for power and the greed for money were the targets of biting satire. It was said that two new saints, Albinus and Rufinus (gold and silver) had made their appearance in Rome and that their bones could open any door.

In comparison with the struggle against simony and the investiture of laymen, the demand of the reform popes for observance of celibacy was not of such topical importance. Priests had been urged time and again to remain unmarried since the end of Late Antiquity but this requirement had never been observed by all. On the contrary, many reports of priestly marriages have survived from the 9th and 10th centuries and it does not seem that they met with much opposition from the society of the time. Many contemporaries even approved of marriage since this had a favourable effect on the practice of concubinage. The reform popes proclaimed the importance of celibacy to counter the weakening of ecclesiastical estates—many clerics provided their children with Church land or prebends—and because in this way it was possible to mobilize the masses of the people against easygoing priests who were not totally and exclusively dedicated to the Church.

The investiture controversy affected the whole of Europe. Despite the complex nature of the struggle, it cannot be denied that the authority of the Papacy and the influence of religious ideas on the whole of society increased considerably during this short space of time. Numerous feudal princes, as followers of the Reformers, were subsequently bound to Rome. Some acknowledged the Pope as their liege-lord. Of more significance were the militant methods of the reform papacy. When necessary, the Reformers proceeded against their opponents by force of arms and mobilized feudal lords to fight for their interests. This change met with the particular approval of the feudal aristocracy. The intensification of Christian ideology and the propagation of warlike means to implement the ideas of the Reformers—these were essential conditions for the realization of the Papal claim to leadership of the aristocracy. The Catholic Church succeeded in combining the expansionist ambitions of the aristocracy with Christian ideology.

So far, attention has largely been concentrated on the situation in Europe north of the Alps. Some of the important economic and ideological features of the Crusade movement came from Italy. In the South, there was a great deal of Byzantine influence while the existence of relatively powerful trading cities lent a special character to the feudal society of Northern Italy.

Following the expansionist restoration policy of Justinian, Southern Italy and Sicily had come under Byzantine rule. It was only the advance of the Arabs and the conquests of the Normans that had changed this state of affairs. The association with Byzantium had brought about far-reaching cultural consequences for Southern Italy. The fighting men had been followed by craftsmen, merchants and peasants. Greek influence predominated in the cities, especially in Amalfi, Bari, Salerno and Naples. Close commercial links with the "mother country" accelerated the spread of Byzantine culture in Southern Italy. Artisans produced commodities in the style of Eastern Rome. Byzantine military colonists moved into the countryside. Here, too, it was largely Greek which was spoken and Byzantine culture predominated. The organization of the Church was subordinate to Constantinople. Byzantine monks founded a number of monasteries.

Until the beginning of the 11th century, the material and intellectual civilization of Southern Italy had a not inconsiderable influence on the areas to the north of it. Monasteries were established by Greek monks in many parts of Italy, even outside the Byzantine sphere of influence. A separate colony of Greek priests, merchants and craftsmen had come into existence in Rome. Byzantines helped to build a number of monasteries and churches even north of the Alps and their concepts of culture and art were reflected in the structures they built and the statues they carved.

This material and intellectual civilization of Southern Italy did indeed decline in influence following the Norman conquest and the independent development of Western Europe from the 11th century onwards but it remained a firm part of the economy and culture of the Norman empire up till the 13th century, as will be examined in more detail later.

Venice in Northern Italy enjoyed a similar intermediary position. Since the time of Justinian, the city had had political links, very loose though these may have been, with Byzantium. Admittedly, it was practically independent in actual fact —its advantageous geographical position in the lagoons prevented the local feudal powers from seizing it—but it allowed itself to be officially considered as a vassal of Byzantium. The advantages of this were obvious. The burdens which Venice had to bear and the duties it had to perform were slight and even these were mostly in the direct interests of Venice itself—such as aiding the Byzantine army, for example. On the other hand, Venetian merchants, like those of the South Italian cities, had practically unrestricted access to the Byzantine market. At the end of the 11th century, the city received the right by express charter to carry on trade throughout the whole of the Eastern Roman Empire with

the exception of the Black Sea areas. Exemption from customs duties and taxation was granted and permission given for the establishment of trading posts. Venetian merchants were regular visitors to Constantinople and other cities of the empire. There were regular ship-services operating between Venice and Byzantium, the routes usually following the coastline to avoid the dangers of the deep. In return for certain kinds of woollen cloth, weapons and timber, for which there was always a demand in Byzantium, the Venetians imported a varied range of Byzantine and Oriental commodities. Precious fabrics of cotton and silk, furs, apparel of sumptuous splendour, spices, perfumes and other products were distributed via Constantinople and Venice throughout the whole of Europe while the South Italian cities mainly supplied the South and Central Italian market. Venice naturally maintained trade relations with the Arab Islamic world as well, with Egypt, Syria and, since the 11th century, with Sicily, too. An incidental episode, not without interest in the history of civilization, regarding the link with Egypt, was the theft of St Mark in 828 from Alexandria who then became the pa-

8 In comparison to the Orient, the level of civilization of the ruling class of Europe was relatively low on the eve of the Crusades. Domestic furniture usually consisted of simple wooden tables and stools. It took a long time for knives and forks to come into use as everyday objects.
(From a contemporary manuscript, monastery archives of Monte Cassino.)

tron saint of the Lagoon City. However, it was Byzantium which took first place in Venetian trade, a unique state of affairs which applied to no other North Italian city.

What Venice had acquired with little effort, the other important mercantile cities of Northern Italy, Genoa and Pisa, had to fight for hard. Nevertheless, their merchants also appeared in Byzantium and achieved commercial success. In addition, they were also to be found in various parts of the Arab Islamic world, in Sicily, North Africa and Egypt. They traded in the same goods as the Venetians.

The relatively large-scale and continuous trade of the Italian cities led to the emergence of powerful mercantile and naval fleets. The protection of merchants from the attacks of pirates was a matter of primary importance. By the 11th century, the Italian cities had become so powerful that they were capable of waging wars with their fleets on their own account. The rapid expansion by force of the Mediterranean trade was now on the agenda, marking the interest of the feudal lords in military operations in this area.

Europe on the Way to the Crusades

The beginning of the Crusades in 1096 appeared to contemporaries as something new, as something without precedent. The mighty response which followed the appeal of Pope Urban II for a Crusade even makes an impact on the historian. And yet the Crusade movement did not owe its emergence to a sudden and contagious swing in mood but, in its major elements, to a slow process of development so that the actual appeal merely acted as the spark which set the whole thing going. Thus, just as the special economic situation of the ruling class created the general objective conditions for interest in expansion and the rise of the reform papacy, the general intellectual conditions for the links between the feudal aristocracy and the Church, the particular economic and ideological reasons which led to the Crusades had also been taking shape for some considerable time. There were signs of an approaching confrontation with the Orient and with Byzantium in three areas in particular: feudal military campaigns of conquest in the Mediterranean region, penetration of the Eastern Mediterranean by Italian merchants, the development of special militant elements in Christian ideology in the interests of the feudal lords. Taken singly, these tendencies are very complex and interlaced with each other but, considered as a whole, they culminate directly in the first Crusade.

Within the framework of the small-scale feudal wars fought for a variety of reasons, there was evidence, from the beginning of the 11th century especially, of a relatively continuous series of confrontations with the Islamic states of the Mediterranean which occurred with increasing regularity and ultimately turned against Byzantium as well. One of the principal areas of these military actions was the Iberian peninsula. Small Christian states in the north of Spain, remnants of the Carolingian empire, had been involved in constant fighting with the Arab Caliphate since the 9th century and, from the middle of the 11th century in particular when the Caliphate of Cordova had itself broken up into a number of small states, had been able to acquire considerable territory on their southern borders. These conquests, which have gone down in history as the Reconquista, were constantly nourished by the stream of French, Norman and Flemish knights who, in the service of others or on their own account, strove for feudal power. This military support, especially during the 11th century, was a decisive factor in this expansion. In 1085, Toledo was taken by force from Castile and in 1093 French and Spanish knights advanced as far as Lisbon. Although these areas had to be relinquished again a few years later, these thrusts heralded the expansion that was on the way.

Throughout the entire 11th century, Italy was at the centre of the confrontation with Islam and Byzantium. The Western Mediterranean—an area which directly concerned the small Arab Islamic states of North Africa and Spain—was made unsafe by the activities of corsairs who extended their raids to the coasts of Italy, their primary interest being the mercantile cities of the north. On several occasions they threatened regions in which Pisa and Genoa had direct interests. For the whole of this century, the fleets of the North Italian cities, headed by Pisa, Genoa and Venice and supported by the local feudal authorities of the Apennine peninsula, were in a constant state of violent warfare with the Arab Islamic corsairs. Interestingly enough, this was not just a question of defensive actions and it was rather the case that there was a steady increase in the radius of action of the war-fleets and in the sphere of operations of the North Italian merchants in the course of these struggles. The Saracens had been expelled from Sardinia already in the early years of the 11th century (1016). A little later, Corsica also passed under the influence of Genoa and Pisa. On the eve of the Crusade, the Western Mediterranean was controlled by the North Italian fleets. Pisa secured a foothold at Bono (North Africa) in 1034 and, in alliance with the Normans, took part in the conquest of Palermo in 1063. The great thrust forward to the Eastern coast of the Mediterranean, to the great ports of the Oriental world, appeared on the agenda at the end of the 11th century. The material conditions for this already existed in practically all the major Italian seaports. There was an economically powerful body of merchants with the ambition to expand their activities and fleets of adequate size had been built. Each city not only had merchant ships but also sufficient numbers of warships. Economic prosperity was accompanied by a simultaneous political upswing in the urban community. Venice, Genoa and Pisa were notable for the self-assurance of their citizens who, through their elected councils, pursued independent policies and negotiated with feudal authorities as independent partners with their own interests. By the 11th century, the major seaports of Northern Italy had already become city states and republics.

The Venetian merchants found themselves facing major worries in the second half of the 11th century. The trade with the Byzantine Empire had been affected by the repeated expulsion of Venetian merchants from Constantinople. The Normans threatened the dominating position of the Lagoon City in the Adriatic. And yet this period was one of exceptional activity for Venice; it endeavoured to extend its relations with Southern Italy and the Saracens as well.

The picture which European society had of Islam and the Oriental world before the Crusades was inaccurate and contradictory. Little was known about Mohammed and his religion. The information brought by pilgrims and merchants from the Orient was restricted to details and included not only miraculous legends but also tales of horror. It was impossible to obtain an overall picture of any kind from these accounts. At the focal points of the confrontations in Spain and Italy, the concept of a religious war did not play a major role in the military struggles, although religious antagonism was certainly present. The idea of war as a religious mission was alien to the knights until the eve of the Crusades.

In times of peace, the kings and counts of Northern Spain maintained good relations with the court of the Caliph of Cordova. In times of war after the disintegration of the Caliphate, alliances between Moslems and Christians against other Moslems or Christians were not unusual. The attitude of the Spanish noble Rodrigo Diaz of Vivar, better known by the name of "Cid" (died 1099) was typical. He served and fought for a succession of Christian and Moslem princes and, although he received the name by which he is best known (Cid=Master) from his Moslem followers, it was against the Almoravids advancing from North Africa that he last fought. Conquests were not always followed by religious persecution; tolerance predominated, although this was

marked by the fact that the majority of the peasants had remained Christians even during the time of the Caliphate in Spain. The policy of religious tolerance and cultural contacts survived in Spain even during the following centuries and despite repeated efforts in the other direction.

The situation on the Italian peninsula was characterized by similar tendencies. Despite the bitter struggles of the maritime cities in times of war, there was no change in their basic view of Arab Islamic merchants as trade partners. Their business acumen was already such that even in the 10th and 11th centuries it was possible for them, under certain circumstances, to supply Arab states with essential war materials for use against Christian rulers. It is known that Venice supplied a variety of Arab seaports with shipbuilding timber, a rare and consequently much sought after commodity in the Arab world—despite repeated Byzantine protests and even during hostilities. Religious differences played no part in business as far as the merchants of Northern Italy were concerned.

A subject of exceptional interest is the Norman empire in Southern Italy at the end of the 11th century. Normans returning from a pilgrimage to Jerusalem in 1016 apparently learnt by chance of unrest in the South Italian cities and, with the support of new arrivals from Normandy, established their feudal rule in Southern Italy. The process of conquest was a long one. Disputes among the Normans themselves about land and the best castles complicated the occupation of Southern Italy and Sicily. Greeks, Romans, Saracens, Jews and Normans, members of the Greek Orthodox, Roman Catholic, Jewish and Islamic faiths, were united in a single empire. This feudal society had a high standard of material and intellectual civilization. As a result of Islamic influence in Sicily and Byzantine influence in Southern Italy, the whole range of public and private life had little in common with the feudalism of Western Europe. From the very start, the Normans were not prepared to be forced into a religious war nor did they wish to suppress any national culture. They accepted the existing social and intellectual structure and built their system of government on this foundation, each religion having the same rights. It is true that Christians headed the administration in Sicily which was otherwise Islamic—the town governor of

Palermo had the Arab title of "emir"—but the rest of the civil administration was in the hands of Moslems. It was a similar situation in commerce and the crafts. The previous traditions in social life and cultural affairs were continued. Saracen units occupied an important position in the army. They had their own officers, having acquired the status of elite troops already by the 11th century. Thus a cultural upswing on the basis of different feudal civilizations had already begun to emerge in the Norman empire even before the Crusades, a development which continued in the following centuries as well. Perhaps the most apt example of the co-existence of different cultural backgrounds is provided by the development of the medical centre of Salerno. The traditions of this city as a place of healing date back to Antiquity and even in later centuries, when Southern Italy belonged to Byzantium, Salerno benefited from the importance attached to medicine in the Eastern Roman Empire. Its most illustrious period began in the 11th century when Constantinus Africanus of Carthage, a physician familiar with the Greek, Arabic and Latin tongues, settled in Southern Italy about 1075 and entered the service of the Normans. At first, he worked in Salerno but then retired to the monastery of Monte Cassino where he translated Arab, Classic Antique and Byzantine treatises on medicine into Latin. His tranlations included works by Galen and Hippocrates which, through this, became known in Western Europe. He indicated that some of the Arab works were his own. Even in the late Middle Ages, these translations were of eminent importance in the training of physicians throughout the whole of Western Europe and established for Salerno its reputation as an outstanding medical school and centre of healing. Those who came here for treatment included, among others, William the Conqueror, Robert Guiscard of Normandy and Hartmann von der Aue. Similar illustrations of cultural development could be quoted from other spheres and areas of the Norman empire as well.

To begin with, there was no significant hint of a religious war from the expansion in the Mediterranean area. It was only when the Catholic Church and above all the Papacy became involved in the conquests that the idea of a "Holy War" emerged which then led to the project for a Crusade.

As such, the approval of wars is incompatible with the words and spirit of the New Testament. The Early Church always maintained this opinion in fact, although it had practically no influence on the continued existence of warfare. This conflict with reality led to the development of the idea of a just and unjust war, as formulated by St Augustine in particular. According to this, wars for the defence and recovery of stolen possessions were permissible. For the Church of Western Europe in the early Middle Ages, this distinction was practical and adequate since the majority of the major military confrontations of the Christian feudal states were defensive struggles.

A new element in the definition of the attitude of the Church to war was contributed by the 10th century in the shape of the "truce of God" movement. The constant feuds during the period of feudal disintegration, when not only the peasants but also the ecclesiastical estates suffered greatly, led to the idea of the truce of God. Various Church institutions, within local boundaries, had succeeded in restricting these feuds. The agreements made with the aristocracy signified that the Church had to take specific action against breaches of the peace, not just by excommunication or similar measures but also by direct means. Expeditions to punish peace-breakers were carried out with the approval of the Church. Even though the idea of the "bellum justum" was underlined by this, it also meant that concepts of quite a new kind forced themselves upon the attention of the knights who were now no longer simply faced with the general view of the clergy that fighting was justified but with the prospect of special service for a principle of the Church.

The reform papacy of the 11th century went significantly further. In the efforts to centralize the Church and to endow it with intellectual and political authority in feudal society, its relationship to war was also defined. Pope Leo IX in 1053 personally led a campaign against the Normans in Southern Italy with the aim of strengthening the power of the Papacy in the Apennine peninsula. Those taking part in the campaign were promised immunity from punishment for their crimes and remission of penance. In retrospect, death in the decisive battle was recognized as Christian martyrdom. This honour

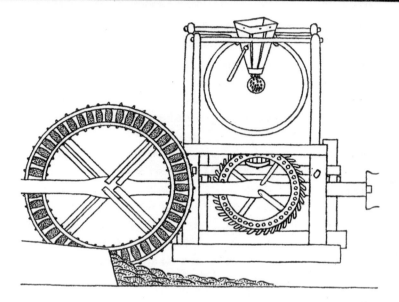

9 Water-power and the appropriate mechanical equipment was also in use in Europe during the time of the Crusades. This drawing from a 12th century manuscript is a functional representation of a corn mill. For the sake of clarity, the water-wheel, gear-wheel and millstone are not shown in the proper perspective.

caused a considerable stir among the people of the time. A new interpretation had appeared. In Spain, too, the Papacy endeavoured to stimulate a new attitude towards the nature of struggle between the Christian feudal lords and the Moors. About 1064, Pope Alexander II promised remission of penance to the knights fighting in Spain and proclaimed the war against the "heathens" to be a just war. It would seem that nobody had asked him to do this. The attempt to become involved here was not by chance, however. At the same time, the Spanish bishops announced a truce of God in the interests of safeguarding the hinterland. Alexander forbade persecutions of the Jews in Spain so as not to cause a division in the forces available. Cluny also made its contribution by engaging the forces of reform in Spain. Not only were the monasteries reorganized in the second half of the 11th century, Cluniacs also took over the major episcopates. In a systematic and skilful manner, Cluny publicized the idea of a pilgrimage to Santiago de Compostela throughout the whole of Europe. A marble coffin had been found here in the 9th century and was claimed to contain the bones of St James the apostle. The Cluniacs utilized this legend to encourage pilgrimages to

Compostela to such an extent that, after Rome, it became the most famous place of pilgrimage in all Europe. Thus a link was created between pilgrimage and participation in the Reconquista. Beginning in the 11th century, this movement continued in the following centuries as well.

All these activities, which influenced not only the Spanish knights but also the French, brought about a change in the attitude to war.

It thus appears completely logical that Hildebrand, who later became Pope Gregory VII, should have signed a treaty with the French count Ebolus of Roncy giving the land conquered in Spain to St Peter as liege-lord. The war against the heathens now appeared as something meritorious since it was waged on behalf of Rome otherwise Hildebrand would have rather forbidden the count to take part in the campaign.

The climax in this trend of the reform papacy was represented by the intentions of the aggressive Gregory VII who in 1074 conceived the plan of assisting Byzantium with an army of European feudal lords in its struggle against the Seljuks. However, he also hoped that the campaign would help at the same time to heal the division of the Church which had taken place in 1054 and that Byzantium would recognize the Pope as the Head of Christendom on Earth. It was only the investiture controversy that negated Gregory's plans.

This change of attitude towards war by the Church and specifically by the Papacy meant that a new foundation was given to the Pope's claim to leadership of the feudal lords and that Christian ideology was able to provide the necessary justification for expansionist trends. The basic conditions were created for uniting the feudal lords, who were eager for conquests, on a scale which went beyond the usual framework of society. At the same time, it would be wrong and without historical foundation to see the shaping of the relationship of the Church towards war in the 11th century as associated with individual persons by chance or as an aberration of the clergy. The roots go deeper than this. Christian ideology could only make a serious impression on the feudal aristocracy by concerning itself with the objective class interests and customs. In parallel with the emergence of the concept of the Holy War or of war in the interests of the Church, new elements of Christian ideology appeared in other spheres as well. These led to closer relations between Christendom and the ruling feudal class which may be termed the militarization of Christianity. There is a wide range of evidence in this connection. It includes the designation of patron saints for warriors. Although this was already a well-established practice in Byzantium, this process began—with certain exceptions—in the 11th century in Western Europe but reached a climax in the 12th, i.e., it was directly associated with the establishment of the feudal warrior as a standard-bearer in the Holy War. The holy martyrs Saints Mauritius, Sebastian and George became the patron saints of the fighting knight. New concepts of knightly piety were propagated. The basic question of whether the piety of feudal lords specializing in war had to be outside this area of activity was no longer always given a positive answer. Protection of ecclesiastical property, vengeance for raids on Church estates, protection of pilgrims and other people—these were the elements which began to expand the meaning of knightly piety. The consecration of swords in church and the dedication of banners increasingly lent a symbolic aura to this trend. A change also took place in the interpretation of

the term "militia christi". This had originally been used to refer to those Christians who, with peaceful means, endeavoured to further the cause of the Church in society and was mainly applied to the clergy. As an ideological reinforcement of the "truce of God" movement and of the overlordship of the Papacy, it now became associated with the concept of armed warriors for the Church.

Towards the end of the 11th century, there is an increase in the amount of contemporary evidence in which the struggle against the heathens is presented in a spirit of Christian militancy. In the French "Chanson de Roland", the final version of which was written down around 1100, the fight of Roland against the Moors at the time of Charlemagne is depicted as a just struggle. The Moslems were vanquished because they were in the wrong. In this epic, Charlemagne is directly influenced by God who helps him through the agency of his archangel. The time of the Crusades was to make its contribution to this concept, too.

Another factor which influenced the Crusade movement was that of pilgrimage. Those who took part in the Crusades are often described in contemporary sources as pilgrims or this was how they considered themselves. In Christian teaching, pilgrimages had long since been regarded as meritorious works and were an important form of earthly penance for sins committed. Apart from the places of pilgrimage in Europe, notably Rome and Santiago de Compostela, it was Jerusalem and Bethlehem which attracted Christians. The journeys to the holy shrines in the Orient were regarded as particularly effective. The journeys of the pilgrims were onerous if, as was usually the case, they took the overland route, even though well-protected roads led across the Byzantine Empire. As long as the pilgrims behaved with decorum, they could rely on the hospitality of the Byzantines. Following the loss of Asia Minor in the 11th century, there was indeed added danger, though not so much for religious reasons as from the spread of bands and robbers. With only a few exceptions, the Moslems of the Orient allowed the pilgrims to pass without any hindrance.

With the 11th century, there was an increase in the stream of pilgrims to the Orient. We know of a whole series of feudal lords who undertook the journey a number of times. It is reported that about 1064 Bishop Gunther of Bamberg journeyed to Jerusalem with a host of seven thousand people. The number quoted is doubtless exaggerated but it does give an indication of the growing popularity of pilgrimages.

The increase in pilgrimages must have stimulated the desire to acquire possession of the holy places of Christendom and not to have to rely on the hospitality of non-Christians. This could not be achieved by unarmed pilgrims but might be done by linking the idea of a Holy War with the journey to Jerusalem. It was the militant reform papacy which amalgamated these two ideas, as was first evident in 1089. Urban II had decided on the re-establishment of the Spanish archbishopric of Tarragona and called for the full support of the Christians of Catalonia for the implementation of this objective. He promised them the remission of penance on the same scale as would have been obtained by a pilgrimage to Jerusalem. Indeed, he even demanded that they should rather pilgrimage to Tarragona than to the Orient. Since this was in fact an appeal to resist the advance of the Moors, a Holy War was equated with the concept of pilgrimage. At the beginning of the first Crusade, he forbade the Catalonians to take part in it since their duty was to fight in Spain. Incidentally, the whole tone of the appeal for the Crusade in 1095 and the activities of Urban II in Southern France indicate that the Papacy had similar ideas for the advance into the Orient as for the repossession of Tarragona.

Influences of many kinds played a part in the emergence of the ideology of the Crusades. Expressed concisely as the "feudalization of Christianity", the foundations were broader than is subsequently apparent from the actual Crusade movement. It was the reform papacy which was responsible for this adjustment. It could do this because no other intellectual or political force of 11th century Europe was capable of organizing and leading the feudal powers impatient for expansion.

The Proclamation
of the Crusade

In November 1095, the Council of Clermont was held in Southern France to examine ecclesiastical questions in France. However, its actual importance in the history of the mediaeval Church does not come from the resolutions taken in connection with these but derives from the events which happened on the last day. On 27 November 1095, Pope Urban II preached the sermon which has gone down in history as the call for the first Crusade. This was no session of members of the Council held behind locked doors but an assembly which was designed from the start to achieve the maximum effect on the masses. It was on a large, open area before the gates of the city of Clermont that the Pope gave the starting signal for the Crusades.

The actual words used by Pope Urban in his speech, which was delivered in French, have not survived but his message was recorded by several contemporary chroniclers. Fulcher of Chartres, who was actually present, wrote down these words: "Beloved brethren! Impelled by the demands of this time, I, Urban, the wearer of the Papal Crown by the grace of God and the supreme priest of the whole world, have come here to you, the servants of God, so to speak as a messenger, to reveal the Divine Will to you... We cannot refuse to give our brethren in the Orient as speedily as possible the assistance which has so often been promised and is so urgently needed. The Turks and Arabs have attacked them and have advanced into Romania to that part of the Mediterranean which is called the Arm of St George; and by penetrating further and further into the country of these Christians have defeated them seven times in battle, have killed and taken captive a large number of them, have destroyed the churches and laid waste the land. If no resistance is offered to them now, the true servants of God in the Orient will no longer be able to withstand their assault.

I therefore urge and entreat you, and not I but the Lord urges and entreats you as the heralds of Christ, the poor and the rich, that you hasten to drive out this common vermin from the territories inhabited by your brothers and to bring speedy help to the worshippers of Christ. It is I that speak to those here and I will also proclaim it to those present but it is Christ that commands . . .

Should those who set out thither lose their life on the journey, on land, on the water or in the battle against the heathens, so will their sins at that moment be forgiven them, this I will grant by the power of God which has been conferred on me . . .

Let those who have previously been accustomed to fight private feuds in a criminal manner against members of our faith, battle with the infidels and wage the war to a victorious end, the war which should have been begun long ago; let those who were robbers up till now become soldiers . . . ; let those who were otherwise mercenaries for a filthy wage now fight for the eternal reward; let those who have exhausted their strength to the detriment of body and soul now strive for a twofold recompense . . . On the one side there will be the wretched, on the other the truly rich, here the friends of God, there his foes. Pledge yourselves without delay; let the warriors put their affairs in order and find what they need to pay for their expenses; when the winter ends and the spring comes, let them venture out in good spirit under the leadership of the Lord."

This was the formal response of Urban II to the request of the Byzantine emperor after the battle of Manzikert in 1071 for military assistance in his struggle. In actual fact, however, the sermon contained all the elements which had accumulated in the 11th century in the justification of the Holy War, the struggle under Church leadership against the heathens, and thus defined the objective for the disunited feudal forces eager for expansion. Even the choice of venue is of interest. The knights of Southern France were not caught unprepared by the demand to go to war. They had a tradition of fighting against the Moslems in Spain.

It is not certain whether Jerusalem was named in Clermont as the final objective of the Crusade but within a few weeks, as can be inferred from the actual preparations, this must have been quite clear to the clergy and the Crusaders since publicity was immediately concentrated on the Holy City. Asia Minor was regarded as stage on the way there.

The possibility of a poor response to the call for a Crusade had been excluded by the organizers. Urban, who had spent the summer of 1095 in France, had personally held discussions with bishops, established contact with feudal lords and first obtained the assent of a number of nobles who had had combat experience of the Moslems in Spain.

According to eye-witnesses, Urban's sermon in Clermont was received with great enthusiasm. When he had finished speaking, the first to step forward was Bishop Adhémar of Puy who asked the Pope to give him his blessing and permit him to take up the Cross. His action was of a symbolic character and was intended to demonstrate that the leadership of the Crusade was in the hands of the Church. Many of those present crowded forward, so it is related, and took the vow. Every promise was greeted with the shout "Deus le volt" (God wills it). Originating in Clermont, this slogan became the call to battle during the preparatory period of the Crusade in France.

As an outwardly visible sign, the future Crusaders attached crosses of red fabric to their clothing, symbolizing that they were in the service of Christ and enjoyed the protection of the Church.

The sources report that the spirit of the Crusade rapidly spread from Clermont to almost everywhere in Christendom. France was the main centre but the call was followed in Spain, Scotland, Denmark, Flanders and Italy as well. It is quite clear that three approaches were used in the preparations, the real core of which consisted in the skilful diplomatic negotiations of Urban with the powerful feudal lords. He addressed himself systematically to individuals whom he persuaded to take the Cross together with their vassals. In February, Urban wrote the following lines to the Count of Flanders: "We believe that your fraternity has already learnt from many reports how barbaric ravages have destroyed the churches of God in the Orient through unhappy devastation, even more, that the Holy City of Christ has been forced to endure intolerable servitude. For this reason we have come to France and have urged the princes and subjects of this land to liberate the churches of the Orient ... Should God inspire some of you to make this vow, let them know that they can join this departure with their following."

Actions such as these, together with personal negotiations, laid the foundations for the military array of the knights. It seems that almost all the important leaders of the first Crusade were approached individually in this matter. This policy corresponded with the view of Urban that a powerful army of knights under the leadership of the Church should be dispatched to the Orient. To support the expedition, the Genoese were requested to provide a fleet to ensure control of the Eastern Mediterranean. The planning and circumspection which became evident in the organization reveal the Crusade as a deliberate undertaking with well-defined political objectives.

Urban had probably not reckoned with such a mass-movement at the beginning but mass-enthusiasm was then aroused from the pulpit in support of the preparations for the Crusade. Sermons publicizing the Crusade were the order of the day in all churches and were primarily intended to back it up. Urban himself took a very active part in this. He remained in France until the August of the following year. In addition to political and organizational negotiations, he preached the cause of the Crusade wherever he could, as at Tours in the meadows at the gates of that city, in the cathedral of Limoges, in various dioceses of Provence, in Toulouse and other cities. The French clergy did the same. In this manner, the concept of the Crusade was popularized within a short time and the preparation of the knights for the campaign became a matter of public concern. There was a considerable increase in the prestige and authority of the Church in France in the few months from the Council of Clermont to the start of the Crusade, a phenomenon which was fully in accord with the aims of the reform papacy, particularly when it is remembered that at the same time in the German Empire events were dominated by the investiture controversy.

Few inhibitions were evident when it was a question of what arguments to use. In a letter to the count, Urban had already conjured up the atrocities of the barbarians in vivid colours and, as a result, together with sermons and the rumours that rapidly circulated, a horrifying picture emerged of the situation in the Orient. Details of alleged mistreatment were invented and were linked with distortions of Islam as a religion and of the Moslems as people. At the same time, there was no lack of dramatic descriptions of the riches of the

37 Pilgrimages in the Middle Ages were not always free from danger. As a rule, pilgrims travelled in groups for better protection against unforeseen difficulties. Pilgrim's hat, stave and bag (for alms) were the classic accessories of pilgrims' clothing. Musée de Monuments Français, Paris

Orient which could be acquired on the journey. Everywhere and in every phenomenon, divine omens were seen which were interpreted as urging people to take the Cross and promising them the support of God. In short, a mood developed which was close to ecstasy.

It was only gradually that instructions followed which enabled the individual organizational questions to be clarified, although there was little evidence of a systematic approach to this. Women, old men and newly-married husbands were advised not to take the Cross. The Pope instructed the bishops to watch over the families of the Crusaders and their possessions. It was only at a later stage that order appeared in these matters.

However, before the first Crusade of the European feudal lords had passed through the preparatory stage, another event occurred which caused a lot of discussion—the Peasants' Crusade. It was so far removed from the project of the first Crusade that it was not even included in the list of Crusades. Nevertheless, it throws a great deal of light on the mood of the people since it provides an interesting insight into the social situation both from the material and from the ideological viewpoint.

38 Pope Gregory VII, shown here in a stylized representation, was born in Tuscany, subsequently became a monk at Cluny and, as Pope (1073–1085), consistently supported the reform policy of the Curia. University Library, Leipzig

39 Louis IX (the Saint), King of France (1215–1270) is depicted as a Crusader together with his Queen, Margaret of Provence. Both figures are characterized by individual features. As a sign that he has taken the Cross, Louis holds a model of the Holy Sepulchre in his hand. There is an opening for the keeping of relics in the back of the head of this sculpture which was carved in oak by a Strasbourg master. Stiftung Preussischer Kulturbesitz, West Berlin

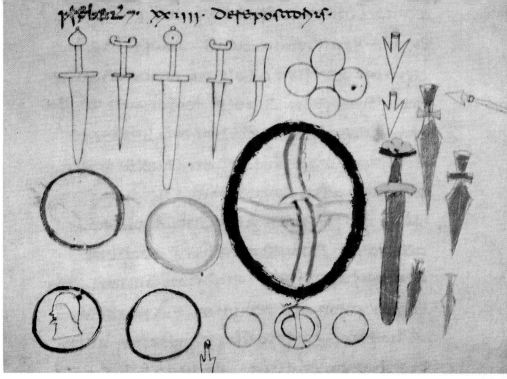

40   European knights on the march.
This illustration from a manuscript dating
from before the time of the Crusades
shows characteristic details of the knights'
arms and equipment: the lance as a weapon
of attack, stirrups and chain-mail cowls.
MS Hrabanus Maurus, Monte Cassino

41   The most important of a knight's
weapons: sword, lance, dagger and shield—
an illustration from a contemporary description. MS Hrabanus Maurus, Monte
Cassino

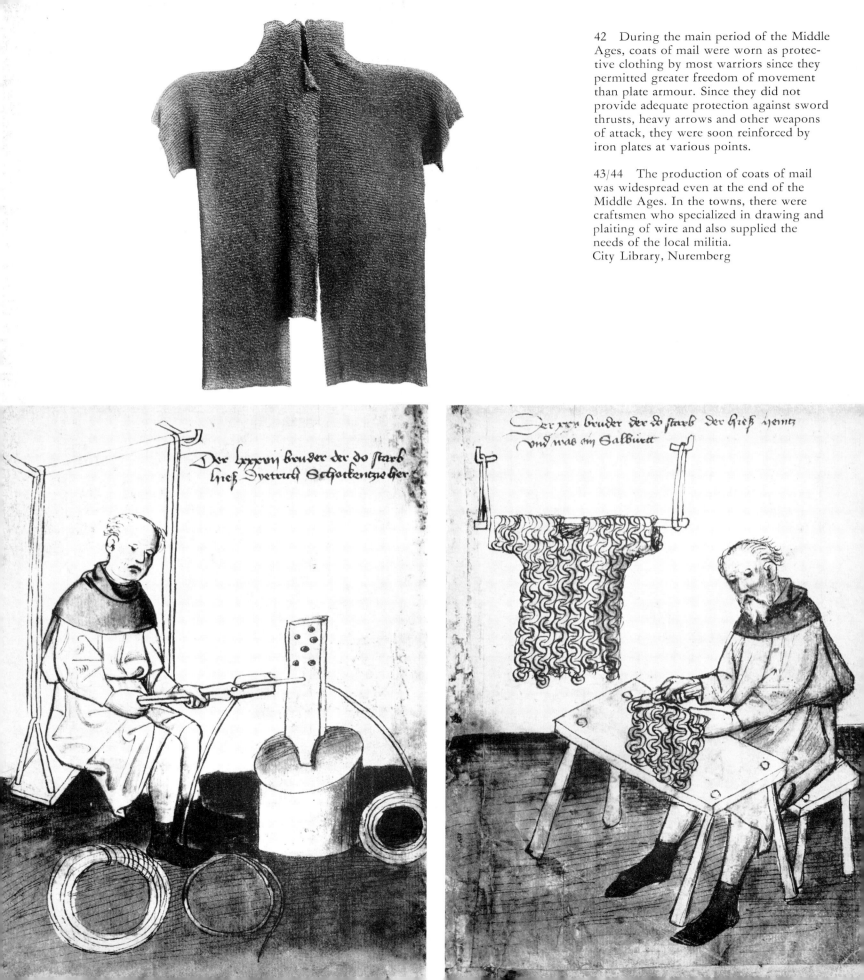

42 During the main period of the Middle Ages, coats of mail were worn as protective clothing by most warriors since they permitted greater freedom of movement than plate armour. Since they did not provide adequate protection against sword thrusts, heavy arrows and other weapons of attack, they were soon reinforced by iron plates at various points.

43/44 The production of coats of mail was widespread even at the end of the Middle Ages. In the towns, there were craftsmen who specialized in drawing and plaiting of wire and also supplied the needs of the local militia.
City Library, Nuremberg

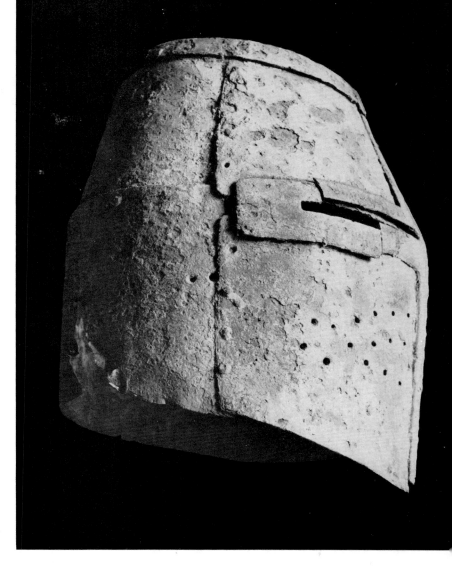

45   The Germanic type of helmet was
customary from the early Middle Ages to
about the eve of the Crusades when it began to be replaced by a chain-mail cowl
or the "Norman helmet". The Germanic
helmet illustrated is of gilded bronze and
dates from the 6th/7th century, being of
Ostrogothic origin. Formerly in the Zeughaus, Berlin

46   Heaume (13th century). This afforded
good protection for the face but had the
disadvantage of a limited view of the
wearer's surroundings. Formerly in the
Zeughaus, Berlin

On the following page:

47   Spurs and stirrups were two of the
most important innovations in the knight's
equipment since they gave him greater
control of his mount. St Mark's Cathedral,
Venice

It was not the clergy who laid the groundwork for the Peasants' Crusade and even the Pope had not thought of a direct mobilization of the common people, even though he would have probably welcomed the spirit that a general movement of this kind would have inspired. It was rather the case that the wave of agitation emanated from a particular group of preachers. Traditionally and to a certain extent in respect of some of the individually involved, too, it followed a socio-religious movement which had achieved a certain success in various regions of France in the last years of the 11th century. This was the movement of the "itinerant preachers". Priests and monks had retired to woods and other lonely spots and lived there in extreme poverty, in accordance with the precept that in this way they were closest to the ideals of Christ. In their sermons, they not only lauded this way of life but also violently attacked the wealthy Church which had moved away from the tenets of the Early Church in every respect. Their followers were peasants, charcoal burners and those who had lost their homes and sought refuge in the woods where they cleared the land and found a new life. The common people listened to the words of these itinerant preachers with enthusiasm. They respected these men since in their way of life and in what they preached they saw, above all, a kind of Christianity which was very close to their own miserable condition and contrasted with the material prosperity of the clergy. This movement was one form of opposition to the feudal Church among the ordinary people and, in a specific historical context, it supported the policy of the reform papacy against the wealthy priests with their worldly outlook.

It was from this band of itinerant preachers that the principal voice of the Peasants' Crusade came—Peter the Hermit. In all likelihood a member of a knightly family of Picardy, he was a well-known and beloved itinerant preacher even before the Crusade movement. In appearance he was an impressive sight. He was of small stature and his skin was dark brown in colour and covered with dirt. It was said that his face resembled that of the donkey on which he rode. Peter went barefoot, ate neither bread nor meat and apparently lived mainly on fish and wine. This is precisely the characteristic of the itinerant preacher living in poverty.

Peter's power of suggestion must have been tremendous. Chroniclers depict him as a passionate zealot of extraordinary eloquence. An abbot characterized his activities in the following words: "Of that which he received, he gave generously to the poor. He did not send wenches to their future husbands without a dowry. In feuds and quarrels he established peace everywhere with remarkable authority." All this endeared him to the peasants and explains the popularity of Peter. He was venerated as an apostle of peace and a saint and people crowded around him, trying to touch him or his donkey or to get hairs from his steed as relics.

Not very much is known of what he said in the sermons he held immediately after the Council of Clermont in Central France, to begin with, and then in Champagne and Lorraine. We may be sure that he spoke of a heavenly message which promised that the Christians, with divine help, would succeed in freeing Jerusalem from the heathens without difficulty. According to versions from other chroniclers in which he preached the same message, he related, as divine evidence, a vision which came to him at the Sepulchre of Christ on the occasion of his pilgrimage to Jerusalem. This reference to divine revelation as a reinforcement for ideas and demands was not uncommon in mediaeval history. This form of legitimation is frequently found and was employed to bolster both social and political views and demands. In general, this is an indication that the society in question was not yet able to formulate its aims in a manner making an ideological impact on the masses without referring to divine authority. However, it also follows from this that the gap between the actual social or political contradictions and the ideological forms of expression was very great.

The peasants who followed Peter the Hermit and the other Crusade preachers were attracted by the idea of the Crusade because the objective social circumstances had caused an exceptionally severe deterioration in their economic situation. Their material basis, which had been precarious enough before as already outlined, became significantly worse in 1095 in the centres of the Peasants' Crusade movement, this being due to floods, famine and epidemics. For economic reasons, the even more extreme impoverishment which followed made it easier for the peasants to leave the soil, which was not their property anyway. The result of years of famine such as these was that increasing numbers of peasants were to be found wandering around the country since they had lost their means of livelihood and had been obliged to leave the area where they had spent their lives. In this situation, they made their way to the towns, provided additional labour for clearing new land or wandered through the countryside as beggars. All this made the work of the Crusade preachers relatively easy. A chronicler revealed a very perceptive appreciation of these less obvious factors when he wrote: "The West Franks can be easily persuaded to abandon their land since Gaul has been plagued for some years by discord among the people, famine and many deaths."

The columns which followed the preachers accordingly did not resemble organized military detachments so much as a legitimate flight from misery. The few material possessions which the people could not take with them were hurriedly sold. Entire families set off with their domestic utensils and agricultural implements. "Poor people shoed their oxen with iron like horses, harnessed them to two-wheeled carts, loaded them with their few provisions and young children and walked behind them; and as soon as the young children caught sight of a castle or a town, they asked if this was Jerusalem." This is how the scene was recorded by a historian. Only a few of these peasants possessed weapons in the military sense or knew how to use them.

What the peasants on the move actually expected was of a highly imaginative character. They looked forward to the second coming of Jesus Christ who they hoped would put an end to the actual misery of the ordinary people on earth. Jerusalem was not simply regarded as a worthy place of pilgrimage but took on supernatural features. For many of the people of the time, the earthly and heavenly Jerusalem were the same place, the journey to this holy place was the beginning of the final period of the World and the return of the state of paradise on Earth was believed to be imminent. Many of Peter's flock believed that the journey to Jerusalem would take them to the land of milk and honey described in the Bible when the legions of the Anti-Christ had been vanquished.

All unusual phenomena of Nature such as locust plagues or the appearance of shooting stars were regarded not only by the participants but also by the general public as signs of God indicating that a Crusade should be undertaken. The chroniclers of the time report numerous interpretations of this kind, occasionally not without highly sarcastic comments.

The Peasants' Crusade was a spontaneous happening. Peter, the mainspring of it, travelled from village to village, from town to town, and his adherents followed him. It was a similar story with other preachers. In all, according to the unreliable statistics, some fifty to seventy thousand people took part in the Peasants' Crusade. They consisted of a number of groups which set out in the direction of Jerusalem from Central and Eastern France, the Netherlands and the Rhineland. The historical sources record that they included not only peasants and artisans but also beggars, thieves and tricksters. Apart from Peter the Hermit, their leaders are said to have been Walter the Penniless (Sans-Avoir), a French knight, a certain Gottschlak from the Rhineland, a man known as Volkmar and finally the knight Emicho of Leiningen. There will be further mention of the evil role played by the latter.

Peter the Hermit and Walter the Penniless were the leaders of the French groups while the others mainly looked after the people from the Rhineland although they, too, benefited from the rousing effect of the sermons that Peter had delivered in the cities of the Rhineland in support of the Crusade.

The departure of the individual contingents was associated with the first pogroms of the Jews in mediaeval Europe. Relatively large Jewish communities had become established in the flourishing trading cities. Not being allowed to work as artisans, they traded with the Orient and also handled money transactions, benefitting from the fact that Christians were not permitted to charge interest on loans. In addition, they had made a name for themselves in the thriving cities through their skills in the sphere of medicine where their abilities far surpassed the general standards in Europe. The Jews had no rights as citizens but they were respected and prosperous. They dwelt in separate districts of the cities and as communities led a very active intellectual and religious life. Of profound religious convictions, each community possessed a synagogue of its own. Close relations were maintained between the individual communities. Thus Metz in the 11th century was the intellectual centre of all the Jewish communities in the cities of the Rhineland and Lorraine.

Almost all the Jewish communities of the Rhineland cities in particular experienced trials and tribulations of a horrifying nature as the individual bands of peasants passed through. Extortion, plundering and mass-murder were the loathsome results. The Jewish colonies in Metz, Speyer, Worms, Mainz, Cologne, Neuss, Xanthen and Trier were exposed to this terror in one form or another. There is also evidence of a whole series of persecutions even in smaller places. Bamberg and Prague also suffered in the further course of the expedition. Contemporary reports of the situation in French cities are unclear. It is known for certain that the Jews of Rouen were subjected to extortion but there is no other information in the old accounts.

The general reasons for the persecutions of the Jews have already been identified. Recent research has shown that the encouragement for the Jewish pogroms came from the ranks of the Church reformers. The Jews enjoyed the special protection of the king or his representatives charged with the administration of the cities, i.e., they had to pay a relatively high tax to the king or his commissioners. The Church reformers attacked the king by disputing this right. Thus the Jewish communities became involved in the investiture controversy. The reformers did not hesitate to direct the anger of the people against the "murderers of Christ" and to stir up hatred. Time and again, we hear of preachers who adroitly aroused feelings against the Jews. In Rouen, words of the following tenor were used: "We have a long way to go against the enemies of God but his worst adversaries, the Jews, stand before us. Is it not precipitate to overlook them." It was a similar story in other cities. Seen from this aspect, it appears to be no accident that Pope Urban II did not speak out against such incitement although he was still in France at this time and consequently must have heard of these excesses soon after they happened. As a result, the general pattern was set of the events to come. The new findings are of critical importance since they have made it impossible to hold the view

that the people who took part in the Crusade were anti-Jewish from the start because of religious considerations. However, there were also other factors which became apparent in the course of the terror and plundering and caused a further deterioration in the state of affairs.

In the first phase, the Crusaders only indulged in extortion, as in Rouen and Trier where the peasants led by Peter the Hermit demanded money from the Jews, to buy equipment for their journey to the Orient. Indeed, the peasants were in no position to feed and arm themselves during the journey by legal means so that they were only too ready to heed the whisperings of the reformers. In Hungary and the Balkans, they made the same material demands on the Christian population and again underlined their demands by plundering. This method of enrichment rapidly became a habit. Peter showed the Jewish communities of the Rhineland a "letter of introduction" from French Jews in which they were urged to give the Crusaders material assistance on their journey. Peter had quickly learned to exploit the possibilities of extortion.

The deciding phase of the pogrom began with the organization of the "German contingents" and the groups led by Emicho of Leiningen in particular were notorious for their bestial cruelty. A vivid account of what happened in Mainz has survived. Emicho laid siege to the city and demanded a ransom from the Jews in return for sparing their lives. Having received the money, he nevertheless stormed the city. The archbishop, who happened to be a relative of Emicho, left the Jews who had sought refuge in his palace to their fate. It was a hopeless situation. The oldest people were first killed. At the same time, the Jews themselves now began to kill their own people in ritual form. Women killed their sons, husbands their wives and each neighbour killed the other. Only a few fell into the hands of their enemies. They were given the choice of baptism or death. The Jews of Mainz refused to be baptized and were murdered.

In the second phase of the pogrom, more importance was attached to the baptism of the Jews. Thus members of both the Trier and Bamberg congregations, for example, physically survived the second phase of the terror by allowing themselves to be converted, they nevertheless suffered severe financial losses. The desire, born from religious fanaticism, to convert the Jews by force was a consequence of the ideology of fighting against the enemies of Christ, against the Anti-Christ. However, this seems only to have been a front for the greed of especially those people around Emicho of Leiningen who is known to have considered the acquisition of personal wealth to be a matter of prime importance. He deliberately organized a series of pogroms under this pretext. For him, the heady sentiment of his followers was only a means to an end. The attitude of the majority of the Jews in preferring martyrdom to Christianity was the result of another religious factor. In the European Jewish communities of the 11th century, it was widely believed that the coming of the Messiah was about to take place and that he would lead the Jews who were dispersed throughout Europe back to Palestine. The persecution of the Jews was interpreted as an omen of this event and fortified the Jewish communities in their faith. Incidentally, it was not long after the pogroms that the forced conversion to Christianity was nullified again.

Some of the survivors emigrated, to Poland, Russia and Byzantium. In some cities, the Jewish communities were re-established but only for a short time. The preparation of the second Crusade was again accompanied by persecutions of the Jews in the Rhineland. Although this was not on the same scale as in the first Crusade, suffering was caused to the Jews in Speyer, Mainz, Worms, Cologne, Aschaffenburg, Würzburg and other cities in 1146/1147. There was a systematic propaganda campaign. Demands were made for the confiscation of Jewish property to pay for the expenses of the knights taking part in the Crusade. This was an attempt by the feudal lords to put their finances on a healthier basis. Others simply wanted to kill the Jews as enemies of the Christian faith. The principal preacher of the second Crusade, Bernard of Clairvaux, sharply criticized the persecution of the Jews since this led to forces being diverted from the aim of providing assistance for the Crusader states.

The peasant bands of the first Crusade marched upstream along the Rhine, the Neckar and the Danube in separate groups with the intention of reaching Constantinople via the Balkans. Only the first two groups, the French peasants under the leadership of Walter the Penniless and Peter the Hermit, succeeded in reaching this intermediate station after many difficulties. On the way there, plundering and violence had become a habit. What the Jews of the Rhineland had been forced to give was now taken from the Christian population. The inhabitants of the Hungarian villages were particularly hard-hit in this respect. Granaries were taken by storm, livestock driven from the fields and the population of the various regions mistreated. The news of the preparations in Europe had already reached Byzantium and the emperor, as a precaution, had stocks of food placed in readiness. Nevertheless, the population of the country were shocked at the sight of the hordes of peasants. The groups were escorted to Constantinople. Here, too, the bands of Walter and Peter began to plunder. Public buildings were ransacked and lead panels ripped from the roofs and sold. Without losing much time, the Byzantine emperor had the Crusaders taken over to Asia Minor in August 1096. The column did not get very far. Untrained in the handling of weapons and without experience in military tactics, they were totally at the mercy of the Seljuks. To begin with, one group was surrounded and cut off. Not possessing any reserves of water, they suffered such thirst that they opened the arteries of the donkeys and horses that they had brought with them. On 21 October, the main group was ambushed by the Seljuks at Civetot and killed to the last man. The knights of the first Crusade passed by the great piles of bones, the mortal remains of the first two groups. Peter the Hermit returned to Constantinople with a few followers and waited for the army of knights. He was still to play a not unimportant role in the first Crusade of the European feudal lords.

The bands of German peasants did not reach Constantinople at all. Some groups under the leadership of the knights contented themselves with persecuting Jews. The columns under Volkmar and Emicho got as far as Hungary. Plundering began already in the border districts with the result that Kolman, the Hungarian king, sent his army out to meet the bands of peasants who were defeated after a few skirmishes. The great majority of them were killed, while other members of the Peasants' Crusade had already turned back or found new homes en route.

And so the Peasants' Crusade ended long before it had even reached Jerusalem. It was doomed to failure from the start. Strictly speaking, it was not really part of the Crusade movement but should rather be classified in the broad stream of socio-religious movements, i.e., those movements which attempted to implement their wishes and demands, which resulted from social contradictions, with the aid of current religious ideas. The real objectives of such movements were consequently very obscure as a rule. As shown by history and not just from the example of the Peasants' Crusade, it was characteristic of such movements that they were easily diverted along paths which had nothing in common with their original aims. It would thus be wrong to see in the ranks of the Peasants' Crusade only people who had no morals from the very start. This was demonstrably true of some of the knights who led them but cannot be said at all of the mass of the peasants. The plundering can only be understood when it is realized that the peasants set out with totally inadequate supplies and equipment. At the outset of the journey, the alternative was death from starvation. Even the reports of the food that had been collected for them could not change this.

Within the scope of the movements of expansion of the Middle Ages, the peasant elements are mainly associated with the settling of new lands; for example, as part of the expansion in the East by the German feudal lords. These peasant settlers, too, had the same motivation as the Peasants' Crusade. For them, it was a "legitimized escape", though the consequences were of a considerably different nature. However, if the Reconquista is not included, when large groups of peasants from Southern France in particular moved across the Pyrenees into Spain, very few settlements were established as a result of the Crusades.

The Army of Knights on the First Crusade

In general, the first Crusade is regarded as the most typical undertaking of the wave of expansion as a whole since it incorporated all the social, economic and intellectual factors in their original form.

The feudal lords made careful preparations over a long period for the expedition. They were little affected by the hectic atmosphere and restlessness of the countryside. Most of the knights who had decided to set out for the Orient came from Normandy, Flanders, Lorraine, Southern France and the Norman possessions in Southern Italy. The majority were feudal lords of territories which had already demonstrated their appetite for conquest in past decades and possessed the appropriate experience. The organization of the expedition was in the hands of ruling families who also provided the military leaders. The assembly of the four parts of the army was not a spontaneous affair but rather in the form of feudal contingents.

They set out separately for Constantinople, the end of the first stage of the expedition. Godfrey of Bouillon set out in August 1096 with his knights of Lorraine and took the route through Hungary, Belgrade, Niš, Sofia, Philippopolis (Plovdiv), Adrianople and Constantinople where he arrived at the close of the year.

The Normans of Southern Italy under the leadership of Bohemund of Taranto crossed the Adriatic in ships and arrived at the end of April 1097 in the Byzantine capital.

Count Raymond of Toulouse and the knights of Provence turned southwards on reaching the Balkans and then followed the route taken by Bohemund. They reached Byzantium at about the same time as the latter.

Robert (Curthose) of Normandy with his followers from the North of France and the Flemish knights decided to take the route across the Alps. From Southern Italy, they crossed the Adriatic in small groups and joined the main body of the army at the Bosporus.

The campaign as such began in April 1097. The political situation with which the Crusaders were confronted was a favourable one for them. Through its division among a number of heirs in 1092, the vast Seljuk empire had disintegrated into a number of small states and even the approach of the

10　Siege towers for the storming of fortresses were some of the most complicated but also most effective technical constructions used for attacking castles and fortified towns. (From an engraving in the "Dictionnaire" of Viollet-le-Duc, 1854–1869.)

Crusaders had not caused them to unite their forces. In Asia Minor, through which the Crusaders passed relatively rapidly, they defeated the army of Kilij Arslan, the Sultan of Iconium, at Dorylaeum. By October 1097, the Crusaders had reached Antioch. The city really belonged to the Seljuk ruler of Aleppo but the feudal disintegration in Syria and Palestine had reached such a stage that in actual fact there was an independent state around every fairly large city. Nevertheless, the Crusaders suffered heavy losses in a long siege before they were able to storm the city in June 1098 when they were immediately besieged themselves. Violent disagreements between the leaders of the army about who should rule Antioch delayed further progress in the direction of Jerusalem until the spring of 1099. In July 1099, the Holy City was captured, the original objective had been attained.

What did this army of Crusaders look like? By the standards of that time, the total force of four armies of knights must have presented an impressive sight. The exact number of combatants is not known. Mediaeval chroniclers are notoriously unreliable when they quote figures and are inclined to exaggerate a great deal. The number of participants in the first Crusade ranges from one hundred thousand to six hundred thousand in the various accounts. It is asserted in a Byzantine source that in the army of Godfrey of Bouillon alone there were ten thousand knights and seventy thousand foot-soldiers. This figure is of a purely symbolic character. The following approximate figures have been calculated on the basis of complex comparisons: some four thousand to four thousand five hundred warriors took part in the first Crusade; Godfrey of Bouillon, Robert of Normandy and Raymond of Toulouse each brought a thousand knights while Bohemund, his nephew Tancred and Count Robert of Flanders each headed contingents of about five hundred. In addition, there were about seven times this number in foot-soldiers and other personnel, i.e., about thirty thousand participants in all.

The hard core of the army consisted of the mounted warriors, who were feudal lords for the most part. They were heavily armed. The changes and improvements in fighting equipment which had taken place in the 11th century and were first depicted as a whole on the Bayeux Tapestry showing the conquest of England by the Normans in 1066 were already in general use in the first Crusade. The head of the mounted warrior was protected by a helmet of conical shape made from a single piece of metal and consequently stronger than the multi-piece helmet which had been in common use up till the 11th century. For the special protection of the nose, an iron strip extended from the edge of the forehead downwards, this being known as the nasal. This Norman-style helmet was in use for only a short time and was replaced already in the 12th century by the bell-shaped helmet and then by the heaume which was more comfortable to wear since it rested on the crown of the head. The longer side parts of the heaume also afforded better protection of the face and the nape of the neck.

The knights were dressed in a coat of chain mail which enveloped the head and extended at the sides to just above the knee. This had also been subject to change in the 11th century. Hitherto, the knights had usually worn a leather or linen jacket to which iron, copper or horn plates had been attached like scales. Iron plates for the special protection of the knees or arms, for example, appeared only in the 13th century and this is true of plate armour in general. It became the general custom in the 12th century to wear a tunic over the armour.

For personal defence, a long, triangular shield was used, mostly made of tough wood and covered with leather. The sword and the lance were used for attack.

The non-mounted part of the army was a colourful mixture. Small contingents of archers and pikemen were organized as separate military units which could be used to very good effect in defensive engagements in particular. It was not by chance that they became an increasingly important part of the active army in the following centuries. However, the majority of the foot-soldiers consisted of the direct ancillary personnel of the knights and of the pilgrims of the most diverse social origins who had followed the armies. They suffered from a shortage of military equipment. Some possessed only simple sticks and clubs and only became experienced combatants in the course of the long march to Jerusalem during which they gradually acquired a complete set of equipment from the booty taken from a defeated enemy.

It is very difficult to obtain a complete picture of those Crusaders who fought on foot. It is known that as a whole they were indispensable from the military point of view. Their major function was the protection of the camp and there are several reports of their successful defence of it against armies of mounted attackers, as at Dorylaeum and Antioch. They were also an important ancillary factor in the besieging of great fortresses both in the construction of siege engines and directly at the walls. It was also the foot-soldiers who determined the morale of the army if only from the fact that they accounted for the great majority of the combatants. However, their social status is obscure. Many received provisions from the feudal lords to whose retinue they belonged. Others were relatively independent. These included the "Tafurs" from Flanders who were given this name from the long shields which they carried and which covered the whole of the body. They had gone to Byzantium with the Peasants' Crusade and had then joined the army of knights. They went barefoot and lauded poverty. The rules that they themselves had formulated were observed with great strictness. They led a separate existence in the army and were mistrusted by many knights. However, they rendered excellent service in transportation work and in the operation of the siege-engines.

Finally, the participants in the Crusade included a relatively large group of women and clerics. Many of the feudal lords took their families with them, although Urban II, already during the preparatory stage, had warned them against taking old men, women and children to the Orient. Priests accompanied each of the four armies in the Crusade. They looked after the religious welfare of those taking part in the Crusade, provided medical help and often went into battle, bearing religious symbols.

The military power of the feudal armies was reinforced by Byzantine personnel who included not only siege specialists but also small groups of warriors. In Asia Minor, they were also accompanied for a time by armed groups from the Christian population, especially Armenians. The Byzantine Empire, which was supposed to have been given military support, was not very enthusiastic about this army. A first overall assessment contains the following report: "The emperor heard the rumour about the approach of numberless Frankish armies. He feared their arrival since he knew their irresistible enthusiasm, their changing and inconsistent character and everything which is specific to the Celtic temperament with all its consequences. He knew that they always display open admiration at the sight of wealth and that they break their treaties at the first opportunity without the slightest compunction ... Nevertheless, far from being discomforted, he took all the necessary precautions in preparation for a struggle should it prove necessary. The reality was much more serious and frightful than the rumours which had circulated since it was the whole of the Occident, all of the Barbarian nations which inhabit the land between the shore of the Adriatic Sea and the Columns of Hercules, all of them had set out in masses, in entire families, heading for Asia by marching through Europe from one end to the other ... The Celtic soldiers were accompanied by a mass of unarmed persons who carried palm branches and bore crosses on their shoulder: women and children who had left their land." Not a very flattering description—and it was not unprejudiced since Byzantium had had unpleasant experience of the South Italian Normans in particular; at the same time, however, it was realistic and exempt from any religious colouration. The idea of the Crusade made absolutely no impact on Byzantine society. Disappointment is also evident in the account quoted above. A request for mercenaries had been sent to Europe and a relatively small force had been expected. Instead of this, a great army with masses of followers had come to the city on the Bosporus. There could be no question of voluntarily accepting the military authority of the Byzantine emperor.

The actual motives of the Crusaders for taking part in this armed pilgrimage were only superficially linked with the ideology of the Crusade. Even a brief look at some of the leaders of the first Crusade is enough to explain why they took the Cross. Bohemund of Taranto, the leader of the Norman Crusaders from Southern Italy, had already attempted in 1082 to take Macedonia from Byzantium and thus acquire a feudal territory. He had failed in this ambition and was now turning his attention to the Orient.

Godfrey of Bouillon, Duke of Lower Lorraine and leader of the army from Eastern France, is seen as the ideal Crusader. His material position as a duke—the title had only been conferred on him—was so weak, however, that he hoped that he would acquire more power and influence by taking part in the Crusade. It was not without reason, for instance, that he sold his family estates before setting out on the journey. For him, piety and economics seemed to be two aspects of the same thing.

His brother Baldwin had no share at all in the family estates. He was supposed to enter the Church but the idea did not appeal to him. There was no future for him as a feudal lord in his native land and so he took the whole of his family with him at the same time.

Robert (Curthose) of Normandy, the leader of the Normans from Northern France, was the son of William the Conqueror and had inherited the duchy of Normandy. However, he had been fighting his brother for a long time, achieving little success and suffering heavy losses. Through the intermediary of the Church, he pledged his duchy to his brother and set off on the Crusade.

Count Raymond of Toulouse, who commanded the knights of Provence, had already acquired considerable combat experience against the feudal Moslem lords of Spain and consequently was originally designated by the Pope as the leader of the whole force. It is known that it was only with great bitterness that he acquiesced in the distribution of the more attractive territories in the Orient to the other princes.

The range of motives for taking the Cross was of course much broader than is indicated by those few examples. The granting of remission from penance, the desire to see the holy places of Christendom or, quite simply, the following of a general trend were all factors in the individual reasons for taking part. Some only participated in the Crusade against their better judgement. We know, for instance, that Count Eustachius III of Boulogne, a brother of Godfrey, was not an enthusiastic Crusader. Stephen of Blois, also one of the leading feudal lords, was subjected to pressure by his wife, who had the main say in all important matters, until he at last took the Cross. Then, however, and even before the capture of Antioch he wrote this to her: "You can be sure, my beloved, that at the present time I possess twice as much in gold and other riches as your love gave me for the journey."

The motives of the various feudal lords as indicated above did not assume a religious form, for instance, in the course of the march. It was rather the case that their greed for booty and feudal power became even more pronounced and the ideology of the Crusade assumed only subordinate importance. Nothing would be more unhistorical than trying to give the Crusaders a halo, attempting to set them apart from the social reality of their background and attributing to them the qualities of devout soldiers of Christ.

The closer the Crusaders came to their aim, the greater the unrest among their leaders and the sharper the contention between the different contingents. Even before the siege of Antioch, i.e., before Syria had been reached, individual groups had set off by themselves to conquer territories on their own account. It was a favourable opportunity. In the East of Asia Minor, there existed a number of small Armenian principalities with Christian subjects and a Seljuk overlord. Baldwin of Boulogne and Tancred emerged as rivals in this region. Characteristic of the mood and the aims of the knights was the way in which they came into conflict with each other. Baldwin had occupied the city of Tarsos and had refused to allow three hundred Norman knights to enter the city. The result was that the latter were attacked by the Seljuks during the night. Shortly afterwards, Tancred's knights would not allow Baldwin to enter Mamistra and stormed his camp in revenge for Tarsos. These episodes were more than just unpleasant incidents on the sidelines, even though the main armies were extremely angry about them. They are rather to be seen as only the drastic expression of a general tendency. Baldwin was intent on acquiring a feudal principality in the Orient and consistently followed this objective, even though he used somewhat strange methods to attain it. He had himself adopted by the Armenian Prince of Edessa, who originally wanted mercenaries for the struggle against the Seljuks, and in this way became co-regent. It was not long before Baldwin became the sole ruler. For him, this was consequently the end of the Crusade and he took no further part in the march on Jerusalem. However, he and his followers were not the only ones who took this view. The political events were the expression of an attitude which increasingly gained ground throughout the entire army. A number of Crusaders immediately decided not to besiege Edessa but to join Baldwin instead. While the main army continued to march towards Jerusalem, they settled down in Edessa and married Armenian heiresses.

It is quite true, of course, that this territory later became an important Crusader state but nothing of the sort was apparent in the year 1097. Adventure and the striving for feudal estates were the motivation here. This was hardly an isolated episode since two of the principal leaders of the Crusaders, Bohemund of Taranto and Raymond of Toulouse, who had the reputation of being a particularly pious Crusader, quarrelled about the mastery of Antioch even before the city had been captured. Each watched the other's actions with suspicion. It suddenly no longer mattered that the army had to wait for months on end before it could continue the march to Jerusalem only because the two could not agree. When Bohemund finally got his way, it was with bitterness that Raymond led what remained of the army on to the Holy City. After this city had been taken, there were similar arguments among the princes as to who should control Jerusalem and Raymond was again one of the losers.

These rivalries between the leaders left their mark on the army. Disagreements and brawls were the order of the day in the final phase of the expedition. This had an effect on the general atmosphere, as will be shown by examples in another connection.

All this had little in common with the sermon preached in favour of the Crusade. The motivation of those who took part in the Crusade, did not differ very much from other conquests launched with a view to expansion. Of course, a specific Crusade ideology did emerge, of which the participants were continually reminded in the course of the expedition by the efforts of individual priests and former pilgrims. The major elements of this are indeed of great interest since they reveal concrete evidence of the synthesis between feudal customs and the penetration of Christian principles.

From the numerous records which survive it is quite clear that the Crusaders felt themselves to be the instruments of divine power. For them, Christ was the supreme liege-lord. For those who took part in the Crusade, God was a "chivalrous" God and the Crusaders were the bondsmen of Christ. The sewing of the Cross to the clothing of the Crusaders was the outward sign of this, symbolizing that the knight had put himself at the disposal of God. The "eternal reward" promised when the oath to take part in the Crusade was sworn recalls the oath of allegiance which required service from the vassal and protection and reward from his lord. In the consciousness of many of the Crusaders, this general concept was understood to mean that it was a question of a quite specific liege-lord relationship. Thus, in a small group of knights who were fighting on their own, the rumour spread that the main army had been destroyed at Antioch. Their reaction was expressed in the following words: "Verily, when the message that we have received is true, all we other Christians will desert thee (this refers to God) and no longer bear thee in mind and none of us will dare to call out Thy name." This was their attitude until it was proved that the news was false. That episode vividly demonstrates that it was considered that God, as the omnipotent liege-lord, had the obligation to guarantee victory.

The princes of the Church in the expedition skilfully propagated the idea that God, the angels and the saints were fighting alongside the Crusaders and giving them direct assistance. This propaganda was generally accepted and played a part in important battles in particular. Thus the religious leader of the Crusaders, Adhémar of Puy, in the battle against the relief army of Kerbogha at Antioch, saw St George leading countless knights in white armour mounted on white horses and with white banners to the aid of the Crusaders. This vision made the knights determined to win. At Jerusalem, morale was increased when somebody reported seeing a knight waving to the Crusaders from the Mount of Olives. Even before this incident, a priest had declared that the dead Bishop Adhémar had appeared to him and commanded the Crusaders to forget all their squabbles and selfish plans, in which case they would capture Jerusalem within nine days.

The most spectacular happening in this connection was without doubt the discovery of the Holy Lance with which Christ was supposed to have been pierced in the side. It was after Antioch had been taken by storm that the Crusaders were themselves suddenly surrounded by a relief army of Kerbogha and, in a totally demoralized condition, had to withstand a siege. It was in this situation that St Andrew is said to have appeared several times to Peter Bartholomaeus, a knight from Provence, to tell him that this lance was buried in a cathedral. After several searches had been made, a rusty iron bar was indeed found. This discovery had a considerable effect in strengthening the determination of the Crusaders. They saw in it a symbol of salvation and victory and were able to defeat the forces besieging them. This was the effect of the incident although there was doubt among the Crusaders as to whether the lance was genuine or not. After all, some of them had known that such a lance had long been kept as a relic at Constantinople. The knight who had experienced the vision subsequently met with an unpleasant fate. Since more and more of the knights doubted the truth of the whole affair, Peter was obliged to demonstrate the genuineness of his divine vision by undergoing the ordeal. As a result, he was badly burnt and died from his wounds shortly afterwards. It was especially the Norman Crusaders who had insisted on the trial by fire since they wanted urgently to counter the increased prestige of the mighty knights of Provence in the army as a whole.

The belief in divine support was apparent in many other ways. Solemn religious services were held before the great battles. An impressive procession took place before the storming of Jerusalem. The entire army walked barefoot but armed to the Mount of Olives and Mount Zion and listened to impassioned sermons. During the battle, the priests prayed to God for the victory of the Christians and the defeat of the Moslems. At Antioch, the Holy Lance was carried in the foremost rank of the army.

On various occasions, the battle-cry "God wills it!" was raised when the Crusaders went into battle. After the first Crusade, this gave way to other battle cries such as "God and the Holy Sepulchre help us".

In times of need, the priests held penitential services as expiation for offending God since it was considered that the sins of the Crusaders had caused God to turn away from the army. In all, there were many different religious thoughts and actions inspired by the Crusade ideology which evolved in the crusading armies between 1096 and 1099. However, they formed part of the general process of the further feudalization of Christian ideology. They were not basically in opposition to the interests of the knights but in fact favoured them. This is why specific use was also made of them.

The preceding remarks have already indicated that even after assembling in Byzantium the Crusaders wanted to remain what they had been at the onset—four independent armies. Urban had been obliged to give up the plan of having a supreme command even before the expedition had set out. There did exist a joint council, it is true, to which the leading temporal and spiritual feudal lords belonged and which took the major decisions. This, however, did not put an end to the rivalries, as the examples demonstrate.

Apart from these deep-rooted conflicts, it was clear that discipline was often lacking even in the tactical operations of the army. In the way in which fighting was conducted, the armies were a totality of small units which operated independently at first and were only very loosely co-ordinated in a general plan. Their military experience in Europe had been dominated by engagements on a limited scale within a relatively small area. Most of the knights were unaccustomed to efficient organization in large units. Infringements of the tactics laid down, independent actions and similar goings-on were the result. However, for the most part these weaknesses were compensated by exceptional determination and valour in battle, plus the fact that the Islamic world itself was divided into small states which were in a constant state of conflict with each other.

The journey through Asia Minor and Syria was marked by hardship and heavy losses. Every city was fortified. The Crusaders had little experience of siege-engines (cf. the following chapter concerning military tactics and methods). They were unaccustomed to the climate of the country. Additional difficulties were caused by the impassible nature of much of the terrain and especially the lack of information about wells and springs. The consequence was that the armies were several times in serious difficulties as regards supplies. On the way through the Sultanate of Rum, they had neither water nor food for some of the time. A large number of horses perished so that many of the knights were obliged to continue on foot. The Crusaders ate brambles and meat obtained from the horses, donkeys and camels. Many of them contracted fever and died.

Horses and beasts of burden plunged into the gorges on the way through the Anti-Taurus Mountains. To ease their passage through the difficult terrain, some of the Crusaders sold their shields, coats of mail and helmets for a few coins while others threw their weapons away. It was only when the Christian kingdom of Lesser Armenia was reached that the situation improved. The Crusaders were hospitably received and were able to make good their losses of equipment.

During the siege of Antioch, the shortage of food became a catastrophe. Nobody in the army had anticipated a siege lasting months and consequently no supplies of food had been acquired for the winter. Realization of the need for these came too late. Throughout the winter of 1097/98, the besiegers not only sent out large groups to search the surrounding villages for food but even dispatched expeditions to Armenia for food. It is recorded that one in seven of all the Crusaders died before the walls of Antioch. Plague and other diseases were rampant. The number of knights still able to fight shrunk to seven hundred since many of their steeds had perished. The consequence was desertion on a mass scale, Cyprus and Byzantium being the places of refuge most favoured. It was not only foot-soldiers, who had suffered particular privations, that fled; many of the feudal lords also turned their backs on Antioch. Stephen of Blois, whose desertion caused much talk in Europe, got as far as Byzantium. Others, including Peter the Hermit, were caught and brought back.

The army of Crusaders was faced with similar difficulties once more during the siege of Jerusalem, when, in particular, there was an acute shortage of water since the Moslems had made sure that the Crusaders would not be able to use the wells.

As regards their greed for booty, there was no difference between the Crusaders and other feudal lords. The spoils were divided up after every victory, everybody increasing thereby his personal wealth. Valuables were taken from the dead enemies. At Antioch, those who had been buried were exhumed again for their gold and silver ornaments. The idea that when a city was captured it had to be plundered seems to have been widespread among the Crusaders right from the start. This is principally why the Crusaders were furious with the Byzantine emperor when by secret negotiation he obtained the capitulation of Nicaea since this meant that there was no opportunity for plundering. Antioch, and practically all the other cities which had been taken, made the acquaintance of the Crusaders as robbers.

The attitude towards the enemy was not clearly marked by religious fanaticism on the part of the Crusaders. In the first great battle of 1097, the knights were surprised to find that the Seljuks were brave and chivalrous warriors, worthy of proper respect. Enemy troops who surrendered were subsequently allowed time and again to withdraw without hindrance. Even at the end of the Crusade, when Jerusalem was taken, Raymond of Toulouse allowed a group of Moslem warriors, who had established themselves in the stronghold of David, to withdraw in return for a large ransom. On the other hand, there are many instances of exceptional cruelty, although it is not clear whether this resulted from religious fanaticism or simply the bitterness of the fighting. The plundering already referred to was constantly accompanied by murder and terror. The Crusaders decapitated Moslems and hurled their heads over the walls by catapults both in the fighting for Nicaea and in the siege of Antioch. Bohemund of Taranto paid a handsome reward for the head of a Moslem leader brought to him by Armenian auxiliaries during the storming of Antioch. He also had prisoners slain and roasted to make the Moslems believe that henceforth all spies and enemies would be eaten by the Crusaders.

The atrocities reached a climax at the end of the first Crusade with the frightful blood-bath after the capture of Jerusalem. This was on a scale which was practically unparalleled in mediaeval history. After a hard-fought siege, Jerusalem was taken on 15 July 1099. There followed a mass-murder of the native Moslem and Jewish population. The knights rode like madmen through the streets. Neither women nor children nor old men were spared. The hardships of three years of war, religious fanaticism and greed for booty suddenly culminated in senseless slaughter. The accounts of eye-witnesses are full of horrifying details. The principal synagogue, the place of refuge of the Jews, was set on fire and those sheltering inside perished in the flames. The Moslems who had hidden in the mosques met with a similar fate. There were mounds of corpses in the streets and on the squares. A Christian chronicler wrote the following words: "The Patriarch passed down a street and on his way murdered all the unbelievers. And so he came to the Church of the Holy Sepulchre, his bloodstained hands on the hilt of his sword. There he washed his hands and repeated the words of the psalm: 'The righteous rejoices in the Lord when he sees such vengeance which he takes. He shall bathe his hands in the blood of the godless.' He then celebrated the Holy Mass and said he had never made a sacrifice more pleasing to God." Other accounts are in similar vein.

It is not known how many people died in the massacre. The chroniclers quote figures between ten thousand and a hundred thousand. What is known, however, is that only a few Jewish and Moslem inhabitants still lived in the city of Jerusalem in the following years.

The Arab Islamic world was appalled and Europe dismayed. Immediately after the bloodbath, the Crusaders held a thanksgiving procession for their victory.

The army of Crusaders which had set out from Europe to conquer the Orient was, at the beginning, a mighty force as regards its numbers and was well-equipped. It is said that only 1,200 to 1,300 knights still took part in the besieging of Jerusalem, the total number of combatants amounting to 12,000 although this includes the Genoese auxiliaries for the siege-engines who had arrived in the meantime. Even allowing for the inaccuracy of these figures, they are nevertheless a vivid indication of the tremendous losses which had been sustained in the three years of the campaign. Many had also settled in the various areas in the course of the journey and others had returned home before reaching the Holy City.

If a balance is drawn, the description of the army confirms all that which was said about the economic, social and ideological reasons for the Crusade movement.

Many fortunate coincidences helped the Crusaders to reach Jerusalem. In a more general sense, their success was due not so much to their military superiority, as might be surmised at first sight, but rather to the fact that the Islamic world in Syria and Palestine was politically divided into numerous small spheres of power and was thus incapable of organized resistance on a comprehensive scale. Apart from this, the Orient obviously underestimated the Crusaders. Military confrontations which were already in progress were not broken off, differences were not settled. This enabled the European feudal lords to achieve a military victory. The actual task of safeguarding the dominating position thus won and seeking the real confrontation with Islamic Arab society and its material and cultural civilization was something which still had to be done.

The Crusader States

Immediately after the bloody slaughter in Jerusalem, the leaders of the Crusade turned their attention to the choice of a ruler for the City. A decision was taken in favour of Godfrey of Bouillon but it was not a whole-hearted one since Raymond of Toulouse would also have dearly loved to have been the master of the "Holy City". "Advocatus sancti Sepulchri" (Defender of the Holy Sepulchre) was Godfrey's official title. This took account of the doubt whether anyone could take the title of king in the holiest place of Christendom, but in political terms it remained an open question whether a temporal or a spiritual dignitary should be the ruler of Jerusalem. It was not until Godfrey was succeeded by his brother Baldwin in 1100 that a "King of Jerusalem" was crowned.

In all, four Crusader states were founded: the Kingdom of Jerusalem (1099), the Countship of Tripoli under Raymond of Toulouse (1103), the Principality of Antioch under Bohemund of Taranto and the Countship of Edessa under Baldwin of Boulogne. The establishment of these states does not imply, however, that well-organized realms had been formed. It was rather a question of the control of captured cities and fortresses and the domination of the countryside around them. In the following years, the conquerors used these bases to force the submission of cities and districts that were still resisting and in this way to establish coherent complexes. The expansion of the Crusader states was never planned in a systematic manner. Admittedly, the original aim of keeping Jerusalem in Christian hands and safeguarding the overland route for pilgrims always retained its relevancy, yet the size and function of the Crusader states from the very start was not determined by this but by the laws of conquest.

With the founding of the new states as the most important consequence of the first Crusade, the confrontation with the Oriental world became a matter of first importance for the European conquerors and to an extent which had not yet been apparent in 1096. It was a twofold problem. On the one hand, the establishment of feudal realms signified a direct confrontation of the Crusaders with the existing material and cultural civilization, the social structure and the customs and habits of the conquered territories. On the other, and from the very start, the Crusader states were politically, militarily and diplomatically states of the Orient. Their existence depended on the balance of political and military power in the Islamic world of the Middle East. The subsequent Crusades, which the European feudal class organized up until 1270 for the support of the Crusader states, did indeed render assistance in preserving the balance of political and military power but in no way brought about changes of a basic nature. In the course of the process of internal and external confrontation, the European knights in the Orient became the ruling class and the Crusader states developed their specific social and political character.

About three hundred knights and two thousand foot-soldiers stayed behind in the kingdom of Jerusalem after 1099. In the following period, their numbers were constantly increased by new arrivals from Europe. Although no accurate data have survived, it is assumed that there were never more than a thousand European feudal lords living in the kingdom of Jerusalem. If the clergy and adult members of their families are included, the total number of persons in the temporal and spiritual communities of the Crusader states could have amounted to some three thousand at most. Figures of about the same order have been calculated for the countships of Edessa and Tripoli and the principality of Antioch, taken together.

The structure of the ruling class of the Crusader states was not complete at the time of the conquest; on the contrary, it was only after 1099 that it began to take shape. The war was the determining factor in its development. Above all, it was the prominent leaders of the Crusade who appropriated the conquered territories by virtue of their military power and, at most, only yielded to even stronger rivals from their own ranks. A typical example of this is to be found in the person of Count Raymond of Toulouse, the leader of the knights of Provence. In general, Raymond is regarded as one of the principal personages of the first Crusade; piety and coolness of decision gave him notable personal authority. At Antioch, his followers who had occupied a part of the city were obliged to yield it in 1098 to the troops of Bohemund. After the conquest of Jerusalem, none of the tactics he employed were of any use to him and it was Godfrey who was elected Defender of the Holy Sepulchre by the leaders of the individual armies. Raymond's intention to establish a dominion in Southern Palestine was thwarted by his adversary Bohemund. When, in connection with the territorial expansion of the Crusader states, he turned his attention to the fortresses of Tripoli which were still in Arab hands, he did indeed acquire the title of Count of Tripoli. But he died in 1105 while the siege was still in progress. Thus it was only for his followers that he finally secured a territory.

The leaders took over the positions of the Moslem rulers who had fled. Their estates and dominions were given to the knights for their use, the fief of money or the tax privilege and other rights associated with money payments being the most important factor in this, to begin with. In other words, they continued all the forms of feudal exploitation which had previously been exercised by the Arab and Syrian feudal lords. These fiefs differed from European conditions in the high proportion of money payments. In the initial phase, these fiefs were not very stable and their holders frequently changed. This is explained by the fact that the knights who had remained in the country were not organized in a feudal structure; there was no feudal pyramid below the leaders, as in Europe. These knights, who had been the lowliest group of the ruling class at home, had first to fight for these positions. Prior to this, it was solely as warriors that they had acquired a reputation. Their new estates represented an indescribable stroke of good fortune for them. Even in 1120, a chronicler illustrated the material advantages in striking words: "He who was a stranger has now become a native and the new arrival an inhabitant. Every day, our families and relatives follow us and, without having desired it, leave all their possessions behind them. For he who was penniless there, God has made wealthy here, he who had little money possesses countless Byzantines (gold coins) here and he who did not even possess a village now owns an entire city here by the gift of God. Why should he return to the Occident who has found such an Orient here." This account, overflowing with tales of abundance and plenty, obviously refers to the changes which took place within the body of knights. It is a fact that many of the most important and powerful feudal families of the Crusader states can scarcely be traced in their native lands, so insignificant were their possessions there. Thus the founder of the house of Ibelin, one of the mightiest families in the kingdom of Jerusalem, was the brother of a bailiff of Chartres, a relatively lowly position in the 11th century. The founders of other equally powerful feudal families in the Crusader states are known only by their Christian names, a sure sign that their economic position in Europe had been modest in the extreme.

From about the middle of the 12th century, the inner structure of the conquerors in the Crusader states assumed an hierarchical character. A small group of mighty feudal lords emerged. The major economic and political power was concentrated in the hands of about ten families who, in particular, were the holders of the four baronies in the kingdom of Jerusalem, owned several great estates and were the rulers of entire cities. In political life, they often used the central authority to further their own interests.

This group could call on a considerable number of vassals, who came from a wide variety of backgrounds. They were former foot-soldiers of the Crusades, immigrants of a subsequent period or even knights who had not experienced the same favourable conditions at the beginning. They had to be available for military service. They possessed only small fiefs and achieved prominence mostly as responsible warriors in the garrisons of castles.

At no time was the new ruling class capable of regenerating itself. Many families existed for only three or four generations in a direct line. Above all, it was the constant warfare which reduced their numbers. Crusades and the stream of pilgrims brought the additional people needed to the Orient. The availability of relations in Europe also helped in the transferring of possessions to another branch of the family should the original one be in danger of dying out. All this could not prevent the social structure of the Crusaders from being subject to a degree of fluctuation which was high even by mediaeval standards. As a consequence, a specific institution—the knightly orders—soon became the principal element in official and military authority. This was a particular feature of the feudal nobility in the Crusader states.

In 1120, a small group of French knights under the leadership of Hugo of Payns was established to ensure the safety of pilgrims from attack in the direct vicinity of Jerusalem. From their house in a part of the royal palace on the site of the Old Temple built by Solomon, they were given the name of "militia templi" or Knights Templar. They lived according to rules as in a religious order which in general required chastity, poverty and obedience and set out their special duties for the protection of pilgrims. Their outward sign was a red cross, the symbol of the warriors of the Church, which the knights wore on a white cloak and the other members of the order on a black one.

The Order of the Knights Hospitalers of St John dates back to an institution which was in existence before the Crusades. Citizens of Amalfi had established a hospice in Jerusalem for the care of sick pilgrims. At the beginning of the 12th century, the hospice which had been set up by merchants developed into an organization of knights who were likewise of largely French origin. In addition to looking after pilgrims, this order was dedicated to the protection of public order and demanded monastic vows from its members. The fight against the heathens was also one of its principles. As an outward sign its members wore a white cross of eight points on the tunic over their armour.

The Order of the Teutonic Knights was founded at a somewhat later date.

It developed in 1198 from a hospice in Acre which had set itself the task of caring for German pilgrims in particular. Its members were mainly German knights. The rules of the Order were based on those of the Templars and the Hospitalers. It had only a brief history in the Orient since in 1241 the Knights Templar insisted on this German order of knights being withdrawn from the Crusader states. It then became the principal instrument in the policy of the German feudal lords against the West Slavs.

From modest beginnings, the orders of knights developed into the most powerful military organizations of the feudal lords in the Orient. For the Papacy and the militant priests preaching the Crusades in Europe, they represented the ideal of Christian knighthood. It was not by chance that

11 *The building of a castle. (From a contemporary manuscript in the monastery archives of Monte Cassino.)*

Bernard of Clairvaux, who passionately propagated the idea of the second Crusade, became the enthusiastic panegyrist of the Templars. Although the reconciliation of monastic rules with a militant body of knights was not always an easy matter for the Church and although the elaboration of such rules took a long time, the mutual agreement between the interests of the Church and those of the feudal lords was so complete that it even proved possible to overcome all the existing contradictions.

The knightly orders became a state within a state. There were sharp divisions between three groups: the knights, the lay brothers who served the knights and the chaplains. The orders were headed by their Grand Masters who insisted on a strict military regime. The orders soon succeeded in disentangling themselves from spiritual and temporal control within the Crusader states and in following an independent course. The legal foundation for this was provided by the numerous privileges which they had received, particularly from the Pope. Economic power provided the backbone. The orders had received gifts of great landed estates in town and country. They administered a vast amount of wealth and owned the biggest castles of the land. At a very early stage, they extended their activities to Europe, acquired landed estates there, too, and built bases in France and Italy in particular. Their possessions in the Crusader states had come initially from gifts made by the Crown and the aristocracy. The knightly orders soon adopted rapacious principles and were prepared to use any kind of brutality or treacherous trick to enrich themselves. There are countless complaints and criticisms by their contemporaries. Not only that, they competed with each other for the choicest benefices and most influential positions and carried on their squabbling in public. Despite this, they constantly grew in importance since, with the efforts they made in Europe to gain recruits to the orders, they were one of the chief sources of new knights for the Crusader states, especially when there were no Crusades or when these were unsuccessful. In the Orient, they took over the responsibility of safeguarding entire frontier regions. Thus the Hospitalers guarded the southern frontier of the kingdom of Jerusalem with Egypt, in the countship of Tripoli the dis-

tricts around the fortress of Krak des Chevaliers and frontier areas of the principality of Antioch.

Very little accurate information about the military strength of the orders is available. The Knights of St John and the Templars each had about four hundred knights in their forces, plus several times this number of foot-soldiers, archers, mercenaries, turcopoles and various auxiliaries. The Templars were estimated to have had a total of about four thousand men under arms at the end of the 12th century. It is unlikely that the Knights of St John had a lesser military potential.

In the life they led, the knightly orders soon differed markedly from the rest of the feudal lords. Fanaticism and implacability in the struggle against the Moslems were constantly renewed and developed in their ranks by the rules of the order. Any concessions to Oriental life, in the usual fashion of the temporal feudal lords, were countered by additional rules of the order condemning luxury and worldliness. They made up the group of feudal lords who were hated by the Saracens and who, on account of their cruelty, could expect no mercy from the enemy.

Governmental organization in the Crusader states developed in parallel with the social structure of the Crusaders. The great power of the kings and princes of the conquest period was gradually followed by legal provisions which conceded positions of increasing importance to the knights. At the beginning of the 13th century, they were collected, in their simple form, in the "Assises", the books of law of Jerusalem. In their principal parts, they reflect a form of state in which the powerful aristocracy dominated the scene and where the king, at most, was a peer among peers. The Crown was obliged to bring all important matters before an assembly of nobles in which the vassals of the king had the main say. From this, there developed the high feudal court which gave judgment on all offences committed by the vassals of the king. The vassals of the aristocracy possessed courts of the same kind at a lower level. The loyalty of the vassal to their liege-lord was only obligatory when the lord respected the considerable rights of the vassal. Anger, disregard of the duty to perform military service and similar things in the most diverse form frequently occurred. It was very often the case that the Crown was powerless to take any military or political action since the courts usually sided with the vassal, no matter what damage had been caused to military interests by his behaviour. The application to the Orient of the concepts of feudal law which had developed under specifically European conditions proved unworkable. In practice, this meant that the legal system was largely concentrated on the ruling class. For the most part, the native population had its own courts. The economic legislation of the Crusaders took account of the economic situation and changed but little. The constitution did not, as such, refer to society in general but rather to the conquerors.

In the political and military respects, the history of the Crusader states and thus the history of the conquerors is the story of a constant confrontation with the neighbouring Oriental realms. The situation in foreign affairs at the beginning of the 12th century was not unfavourable for the Crusaders of the Orient. The two great powers of the Middle East, the Fatimid empire of Egypt and the Seljuk empire had suffered a severe decline in their military potential. The Seljuk domination of Asia Minor and Syria had disintegrated into a number of small territories which were independent in actual fact although they were still formally subject to Seljuk rule. These small realms were constantly feuding with each other. With Damascus, Aleppo and Mosul, they lined the eastern boundary of the Crusader states. The political scene in the north and north-east was characterized by greater activity since the Armenian principalities had succeeded in freeing themselves from the rule of the Seljuks and were emerging as an independent political force. As in the past, the Fatimid empire of Egypt was still a coherent state and also laid claim to Palestine but its main attention in foreign affairs was directed at the Seljuk sultanate in Baghdad.

The Crusaders profited from this state of affairs and rapidly adapted to it. In a multiplicity of local conflicts, especially with the rulers of Mosul, Aleppo and Damascus in which they were not always successful, however, the Crusaders succeeded in extending their political position and in consolidating their rule. Aggression and temporary alliances alternated with each other in the course of this, as in 1115 when the Crusaders united with Aleppo and Damascus against the army of the Seljuk sultan of Baghdad or in 1139 when they joined with Damascus against Aleppo and Mosul. In these warlike actions, the Crusaders did not always fight as a single entity by any means. Rivalries between the Crusader states, special interests and finally open revolts, such as that of the Count of Jaffa who in 1132 ultimately hoped for Egyptian assistance against the King of Jerusalem, were just as much part of the picture presented by the Crusader states in their relations with other states. The feudal customs of the knights which they had acquired from Europe and the way in which they ruled were continued under the conditions existing in the Middle East. It was this which determined the mentality of the Crusaders and not an abstract religious ideal, for instance.

However, the signal of change in the balance of military and political power which ultimately led to the destruction of the Crusader states dates back to the first decades of the 12th century when Imad al-Din Zangi became the ruler of Mosul and Aleppo in 1127/1128. The Crusaders were now confronted with a powerful antagonist who first of all attacked Edessa (1144). The city fell and the first Crusader state was finally relegated to the past in 1146.

In the decades that followed, it was Zangi's son, Nur ad-Din (Nureddin), originally only the lord of Aleppo, who became their greatest enemy, following his subjugation of numerous Islamic principalities and especially after his capture of Damascus. There began the contest between the Crusaders and Nureddin for the domination of Egypt at a time when that country was in a state of political weakness. Nureddin's army won.

The victorious general was Saladin, the son of a Kurd. He put an end to the Fatimid dynasty in Egypt in 1171 and established the rule of the Ayyubids in the Land of the Nile. Saladin first conquered Damascus, Aleppo and Mosul and then launched a concentrated attack on the Crusader states. The army of knights suffered a crushing defeat at Hattin in 1187 and important fortresses and cities fell into Saladin's hands, including Acre, Ashkelon and, above all, Jerusalem.

Admittedly, some of these were recovered again by the third Crusade but Saladin retained possession of Jerusalem. Acre became the capital of the kingdom of Jerusalem. From this time onwards, the Crusader states were really only "rump possessions", so severe had been the losses in territory which they had suffered. The battle of Hattin and its consequences marked the beginning of the end of the Crusader states although the death of Saladin (1193) extended the presence of the Crusaders in the Orient. They endeavoured to counter the pressure of their adversaries by steering a middle course and following a policy of truces. In 1227, Emperor Frederick II succeeded once more in gaining possession of Jerusalem by treaty for the Crusader states until 1244.

The Crusades of the 13th century were directed against Egypt with the aim of striking at the Ayyubids and thus taking the pressure from the Crusader states. Lasting success was not achieved.

The advance of the Mongols in the middle of the 13th century to the frontiers of Syria brought indirect relief to the Crusader states in that the Arab Islamic world was confronted with a new adversary. In 1260, the Egyptian general and later Sultan Baybars halted the march of the Mongols on Palestine and then turned his attention to the remaining possessions of the Crusaders. Jaffa and Antioch fell in 1268, Tripoli in 1289 and, as the last bastion, Acre in 1291. Only the island of Cyprus remained in their hands as a place to which to retreat.

The military situation was the dominating factor in the specific mentality of the European feudal lords in the Orient. The extension, protection and finally, from the second half of the 12th century, the defence of their positions—this was regarded as the principal task to which everything else had to be subordinated. The result of this was that all forms of military techniques and warfare attained their highest level of development in the Crusader states and not in Europe itself. It was not by chance that the castles built by the Crusaders on a monumental scale and with every technical refinement appear almost as a symbol of the history of these states and, indeed, of the history of the Crusades in general.

The fortifications constructed in the period of almost two centuries when these conquests were made are some of the most outstanding edifices of the whole of mediaeval history. Great activity in the development of new forms and improvements is clear evidence of the specific interest of the Crusaders in castles of the most advanced type.

In the literature on the subject, there has been violent controversy in recent decades about the traditions which produced the castles of the Crusaders. Powerful fortifications had been built in the Orient since Antiquity and the experience of their architects and strategists had remained alive, despite all the changes brought by historical development, up to the eve of the Crusades in the Orient. Byzantine and Armenian influence in particular has been greatly emphasized by a series of historians and experts in the history of art. Byzantine fortifications for the protection of Asia Minor and the Oriental territories of the Eastern Roman Empire had existed for centuries and, at the same time, acted as staging points for the movements of Byzantine troops. Citadel-like structures, covering a large area, were characteristic of Asia Minor but it was also customary for cities to be enclosed within high defensive walls. Antioch, for instance, at the end of the 11th century was protected by a fortified wall in which there were about four hundred watchtowers. The general layout was such that large areas of agricultural land, gardens and orchards and a sufficient number of wells and springs were within the city walls so that the city could withstand a siege for a considerable period. The Arabs were also familiar with the construction of massive fortifications. Nevertheless, the most comprehensive knowledge and experience of castle construction was probably possessed by the Armenians of Asia Minor at the eve of the first Crusade. They were active as architects both in the Arab and Byzantine areas of the Orient.

On the other hand, it has recently been pointed out with some emphasis that when the European feudal lords came to the Orient, they brought with them not just an interest in the building of castles but also actual experience. The construction of stone castles in large numbers in the regions north of the Alps dates from about the 11th century. The Normans developed a massive stone tower which was heavily fortified and was known as a donjon. Examples of this tower were built in Northern France, in England after the conquest of

1066 and in Sicily and Southern Italy. The Norman lords and their henchmen used these towers as places to which to retire and rest after the battle. They had the reputation of being very difficult to capture since modern siege techniques were still unknown in Europe at this time. This type of construction played a not insignificant part in the design of the castles built by the Crusaders in the Orient since Normans from both Northern France and Southern Italy took part in the expansion of the Crusader states.

If the element of synthesis is a dominating feature of the castles built by the Crusaders, this just is true of the details of the military techniques employed. There is scarcely anything about them which was not already known and this applies just as much to the walls and towers as to details such as concealed entrances, battlements, pitch-spouts, moats, drawbridges, embrasures and so on.

However, it is not so much traditions as the social functions of the castles which explain their particular development in the Crusader states. It was from their fortified residences that the feudal lords dominated the countryside around them and exercised the functions of state power (supervision of taxes levied from the peasants). Castles were suitable instruments for maintaining social order while their second function was to protect the country against its enemies, against attacks by its neighbours and, if necessary in times of war, to provide shelter for the population. One is inclined to regard the second function as having been more important in the Crusader states. This, however, is only partly correct. Particularly for the initial phase, it can be shown that there were numerous fortifications which were used to dominate the local working population and to control trade-routes. In the final analysis, it was precisely the fact that these two conditions favouring the building of castles were particularly relevant in the Crusader states that led to so many castles being built. If an attempt is made to identify the phases of development in castle architecture, the following picture emerges, despite all the transitional phenomena: —

To begin with, it was mostly a question of simply taking over existing castles and town fortifications which had been built by the Byzantines or Arabs; in addition to this,

12/13   Seal of Baldwin III, King of Jerusalem (1143–1162) and of Bohemund III, Prince of Antioch (1163–1201)

48   The tomb of Bohemund of Taranto in Apulia. As the leader of the Southern Italian Normans, Bohemund took part in the first Crusade. The ulterior motives of the Crusaders are particularly clearly illustrated by his personal history. Before the Crusades, his aim was to establish his supremacy in the Balkans at the expense of Byzantium. The first Crusade gave him the principality of Antioch. In 1104, he made his nephew Tancred regent of this Crusader state and returned to Apulia to organize a war against Byzantium. In 1107, he invaded the area now known as Albania but was repulsed. He died in the year 1111.

49 Many of the people of the time, as a result of religious influence, thought that Jerusalem was practically a part of the world to come. This concept, presented according to the fantasy of the artist, appeared in many contemporary illustrations. In the centre of this miniature painting symbolizing Jerusalem, there is the Holy Lamb, with St John and an angel standing on either side (basis: Apocalypse of St John). Bibliothèque Nationale, Paris

50 The Christian concept of the world was also reflected in geographical drawings. The symbolic map dating from the 13th century places Jerusalem at the centre and arranges important cities of Europe, the Middle East and North Africa around it. Bibliothèque Sainte Geneviève, Paris

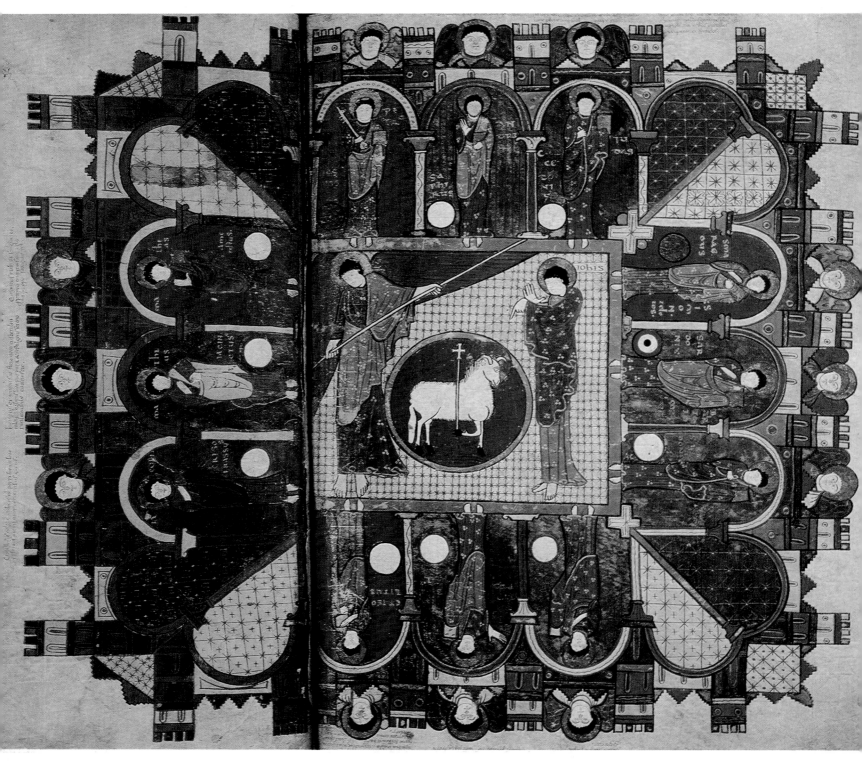

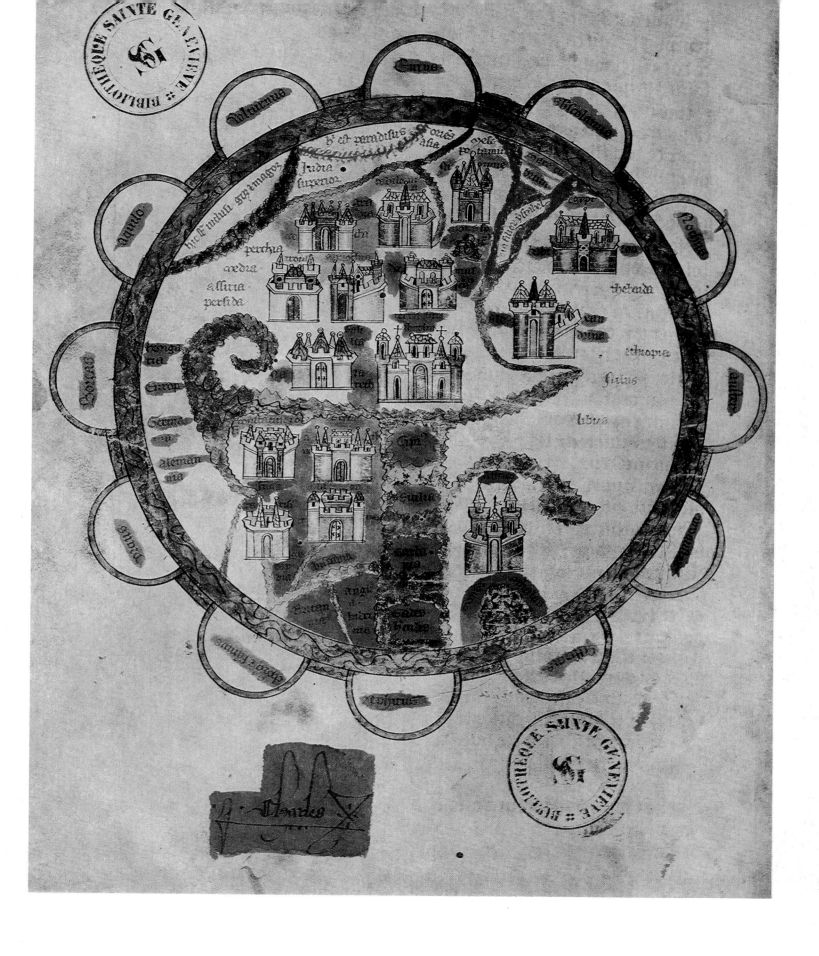

51   The Church of the Holy Sepulchre,
built in late Antiquity, was visited by all
those who made the pilgrimage to Jerusalem.

52 Interior of the Church of the Holy Sepulchre

53 Like all Oriental cities, Jerusalem was also protected against attack by a wall several metres in height. It was not only residential areas which lay within the fortifications but also gardens, springs and other facilities which, together with the provisions stored, ensured that the defenders could keep alive during a long siege and maintain their resistance.

54 Jerusalem was not just a Christian religious centre. The Wailing Wall of the Jews and the Dome of the Rock built for the Moslems were comparable in significance for these religions.

55 During the period of the Crusades, the Church of St Anne in Jerusalem and the Church of the Holy Sepulchre were regarded as the most important edifices of the city. The extensions carried out in the course of time have produced a harmonious blend of Byzantine and Romanesque features.

56   Christ as the leader of the Crusaders in battle—an illustration from a manuscript of the Late Middle Ages which symbolizes views already held during the Crusades. The Crusaders considered themselves as soldiers of Christ and the presence of Christ was the guarantee of victory in battle. British Museum, London

57   For the Crusaders, the capture of Jerusalem and its protection was one of the principal objectives of the conquest. The successes of the first Crusade in 1099 were greeted with enthusiasm while the fall of the city after the battle of Hattin in 1187 caused great dismay. Although this really decided the future of the Holy City, Emperor Frederick II succeeded by treaty in 1228 in linking Jerusalem to the Crusader states once again until 1244 when the city was finally lost. The symbolic representation in the manuscript illustration is taken from a contemporary description of Palestine. Seminary Library, Padua

58/59 These schematic drawings of scenes from the siege of a fortress clearly show the problems of military tactics. Despite the use of all the siege engines available, a sally from the fortress, when there was a sufficient number of defenders, could rapidly reverse the situation of the besiegers and the besieged. The illustration shows two pages from the Genoese Annals of events in the year 1327. Bibliothèque Nationale, Paris

60 The deeds of the Crusaders met with an enthusiastic reception in Europe and, particularly in the initial period, were celebrated and depicted by artists as meritorious achievements. This picture is in a window of the Abbey Church of St Denis and depicts the capture of Antioch during the first Crusade.

ANTIO CHIA

On the following two pages:

61 Man-to-man combat between an Islamic and a Christian knight. The ornamental armour was only worn at tournaments. British Museum, London

anni articulo mentate lin eque magna (Qd pli
Quadam die ioms q ese termata constare luebe
borib consueunt. Vigesima seda april memoz mg
dnnin Lazari gerardun glandonis feluat mour.
e mit saragimi·si pus qua re unpet· ultentingu

borib subenstedia consignaunt· n eni moram aliq
apud albigolam potestag e han faussent· nesigi
post tga nolebant aliqd dmitie indeuerun.
Thabua uo uctoria spredictis· prinua tempesta
te mans e aeris intempie e mundatomib iq·

Artuolla

querent

puid me oxano d

cam deo susceptor

62 Queen Melisande's marriage to Count Fulko of Anjou. She was crowned in 1131 and after the death of her husband (1141) reigned until 1161 for her young son or as Queen Mother. She is remembered for the encouragement she gave to the painting of illustrations in manuscripts. Bibliothèque Nationale, Paris

63 Emperor Frederick Barbarossa on the Crusade. The third Crusade was a most ambitious undertaking. Together with Richard Cœur de Lion of England and Philip II Augustus of France, the German emperor set out for the Orient with a large army. The death of Barbarossa on 10 June 1190 prematurely ended the expedition. The other armies did not achieve their objective, the recapture of Jerusalem, either. Burgerbibliothek, Berne

frederic' fortiss[im]us [I]p[er]ato[r] cu[m] inumera p[ro]ce[rum] [multi]
tudine domu[m] d[omi]ni redeu[n]t
accelerat[...]

d[...]ma frederici [im]p[er]ato[ris]

frederic[us] [im]p[er]ator i[n] flumine[...]

64 Emperor Frederick I Barbarossa
(1152–1190) was an outstanding figure
of the Middle Ages in Germany. The
illustration shows him as a Crusader.
Miniature from the Schäftlarn Monastery
1188/89. Vatican Library, Rome

small fortresses were built to secure feudal rule in the country-side and to act as local administrative centres. All the big cities which were captured belong to the first group. The second group was numerically quite important since it had not been possible to conquer the whole of the countryside by 1099. Thus Blanche Garde, Ibelin and Beth Gibelin were given the task of conquering the city and port of Ashkelon, which succeeded only in 1153, and of controlling the pilgrim road from Jaffa to Jerusalem. This type of building was usually of a simple and massive shape. In the literature on the subject it has been compared with the Romanesque style of architecture. A relative large fortified wall of square layout encloses the main tower which resembles the donjon to which reference has already been made. The fortresses of the Subeibe and Montréal type built or extended from the middle of the 12th century onwards are similar in structure and function. Subeibe, situated on Mount Hermon, controlled the road from Tyre to Damascus and threatened this latter city. The collection of taxes in the frontier districts was ensured solely by the existence of this castle. Montréal had a similar function in forcing nomadic Arab tribes to pay tribute and in controlling the trade-route from Mecca to Damascus.

At the same time, the famous "super-fortresses" were built, such as Château Pèlerin, Montfort, Margat—the biggest of all the castles in the Crusader states, Saphet and Krak des Chevaliers, which is considered to be architecturally the most beautiful of all mediaeval castles. The point has been made in the literature on the subject that the real golden age of castle architecture was in the 13th century since at this period the defence of their remaining possessions in the country was a matter of life and death for the Crusaders. The castles referred to consequently belong to this last phase. However, this is only true of the later additions to the fortifications since at least some of the castles were begun at an earlier date. All these great castles, which represented the backbone of the country's defences, belonged to the knightly orders since no single feudal lord was in a position to provide the resources necessary for the construction and maintenance of such vast complexes. Thus Château Pèlerin was in the hands of the Templars, Montfort belonged to the Teutonic Knights and Margat

(Marqat) and Krak des Chevaliers was the property of the Hospitalers. Other examples could be quoted.

From the viewpoint of military engineering, the improvement of the castles was a constant race with new developments in siege-craft, which had achieved a very advanced level in the Orient. Preference was given to a site in an inaccessible location which made it difficult to besiege the castle immediately below its walls or to storm it. Deliberate use was made of deep trenches, rocky promontories and other natural features of this kind. The layout of Say'un (Saone) is characteristic, a deep rocky fissure forming the kind of almost impassible trench considered necessary for the forward defences. There was a steady increase in the height of the curtain wall and in the number of towers incorporated in it. Whether the towers were round or of square construction was less important. What mattered was that they projected further forward from the wall than hitherto, enabling heavy flank-fire to be directed against the besiegers attacking the wall. From the 13th century, there was an increase in the number of loopholes provided since the archers in the army were becoming increasingly important. The gates were subjected to particular pressure in sieges and were consequently given extra protection by angled approaches, more pitch-spouts and a large number of loopholes in the vicinity of the entrance. The provision of several rings of defence was intended to allow the garrison to carry on the struggle after the first ring had been stormed. The size of the castles enabled the garrison to be supplied with food for even a long siege. Vast underground vaults acted as storage chambers for arms and provisions and also provided accommodation for a very large number of military personnel. Wells or springs within the fortifications ensured the reserve of water so urgently needed.

The general characteristics of such a castle can be illustrated by the most attractive of them all—Krak des Chevaliers. Set on an elevation between Tripoli and the Mediterranean coast, its function was to protect the city and countship of Tripoli and ensure military control of it. There had already existed a fortification at the same spot before the time of the Crusades and it had probably been a Kurdish military colony. This at least explains the term "Kurdish castle" still found in older literature as the designation for Krak des Chevaliers. The fortress was conquered by Tancred in 1109 and was used to dominate the countryside around it. In 1142, the castle passed into the possession of the Knights of St John, marking the beginning of the main period of building activity. It is no longer possible to accurately identify the individual phases. Yet it is certain that the final result was not a single coherent complex planned from the very start but a combination of architecturally very successful additions and extensions. The total area covered by the buildings is about 2.5 hectares and the diameter in the north-south direction is 220 metres and from east to west 135 metres. Closely-hewn limestone was mostly used as building material. A double perimeter wall is a dominating feature of the fortress. The outer wall encloses the zwinger and is strengthened by thirteen towers, most of which have a semi-circular ground-plan and are provided with loopholes. Within the shelter of this outer wall and partly underground there are the stables, the rooms for the garrison and the storage chambers, beneath which there is a vault of 60×90 metres. The inner wall encloses the upper castle which is situated on a rocky plateau and is likewise reinforced by massive towers. Inside the courtyard and again partly underground, there are the numerous living quarters and halls. The heart of the fortress is the citadel on the south-west side which is the keep, in fact. All the military refinements of the age were utilized for the protection of the main entrance. The actual gate, protected by a drawbridge in front of it, gives access to a covered way leading upwards and arranged at right-angles to the gate, this covered way being protected by at least one portcullis and four more gates. Loopholes and pitch-spouts in the covered way helped the garrison of the castle to repel any enemy troops which had forced their way past the gate.

For the time at which they were built, fortresses of the type of Krak des Chevaliers represented nothing less than miracles of military engineering and were considered to be impregnable when manned by a sufficient number of defenders. The real problem was to find the numbers necessary for this. Even the Kurdish castle at the beginning of the 13th century had a garrison of two thousand men but in 1268 not even ten per cent of this figure was available. Castles were almost always undermanned. The chronic shortage of soldiers for the defence of castles was not so much a problem of transport or communications. It was really the case that the maintenance of fortifications was too heavy a burden for the society of the time, especially when account is taken not only of the size but of the density of the castle-network. Even when full use was made of all reserves, the economy of the Crusader states was not in a position to maintain this system. The sophisticated network of castles, some areas of which were so dense that communication over long distances by light-signals was possible, was a last vain attempt to delay the collapse of the Crusader states by a few more decades.

Special siege-techniques for the capture of such fortresses had been developed, particularly in Byzantium and the Orient. The following weapons and equipment were some of the more important elements of these techniques.

The simplest pieces of equipment were the scaling ladders, made from wood or rope. They were usually employed in massed attacks on the wall and generally only in combination with other weapons.

Siege-towers were more important. These were wooden frames which had to be higher than the parapet of the castle under siege and were mostly up to 20 metres in height. They were mounted on wheels or rollers and, when completed, were pushed up to the walls. Many of them were also equipped with a kind of drawbridge so that the soldiers in the siege-tower could not only direct their fire against the wall-walk but had also easier access to the battlements of the fortress. The construction of such towers took much time and they could only be used in long drawn-out sieges. Sometimes weeks of work were necessary and it was also necessary to level the ground along which the tower had to be moved up to the wall. During the siege of Jerusalem, three days were needed for simply filling up the trench in front of the city wall. For protection against missiles and fire, siege-towers were covered with mats and the wet skins of animals.

Catapults of the most diverse types were in widespread use and stones or giant arrows (iron bolts) could be hurled at the walls or the enemy.

Battering rams consisted basically of a stout tree-trunk, sheathed in iron and suspended horizontally in a covered frame. This was rhythmically swung against the wall of the castle until a breech was made in it and the attackers could penetrate the interior.

Mining was also carried out on a relatively large scale. Underground passages were dug out underneath the walls of the fortress and filled with wood which was set on fire. The resultant heat could cause the wall to collapse.

A weapon of quite a specific nature which the Crusaders had to face was "Greek fire", known for centuries in Byzantium and used in military actions. Its exact composition was kept a secret by the Byzantines for hundreds of years but its essential constituents were saltpeter and a mixture of tar and resin. The Byzantines probably obtained the mineral oil products used in its manufacture from their possessions in the Sea of Azov. It was ignited in copper tubes and could be hurled at the enemy from some distance away, the charge exploding with great noise and accompanied by hissing and dense smoke. The Byzantines used this weapon chiefly in naval warfare. In imitation of Greek fire, the Arabs developed something similar on a naphtha basis, being likewise designated as "Greek fire" in contemporary literature, although it was not of the same quality as the original. It proved to be an effective weapon for combating attacks by siege-towers and was soon used by the Crusaders as well.

The whole range of complicated siege equipment was unknown to the Crusaders in its totality. They learned how to use it from experts of mainly Byzantine, Venetian, Genoese and subsequently Arab origin in particular. The march from Constantinople to Jerusalem is clear evidence of how rapidly the army of knights learned to use the new techniques of war and include them in a systematic manner in their sieges. They built stone-catapults and battering rams at Nicaea but did not achieve any notable success with them. An attempt to cause the walls to collapse by mining also failed since the Seljuks repaired the damage overnight. In the struggle for Antioch, building materials and specialists were requested from Constantinople to build counter-fortifications before the principal gates of the city as protection against sorties from inside. This practice subsequently became widespread in the Crusader states when reducing powerful fortresses.

A vivid description of the use of siege-towers is contained in a chronicle on the siege of the city of Marra in 1098: "When our noble lords perceived that nothing could be achieved and that their efforts were in vain, Raymond (of Toulouse) had a stout and high wooden castle constructed; this castle was set up and constructed on four wheels. On the upper floor several knights took up their position . . . , among them were knights in armour to push the castle up to the wall by a tower. When the heathens saw this, they immediately built a machine which hurled great stones at the castle so that almost all our knights were slain. They threw Greek fire on the castle in the hope of setting it alight and destroying it. But Almighty God did not wish the castle to burn this time since it stood higher than the walls of the city. Our knights who were on the upper floor . . . hurled huge stones at the defenders on the walls. They struck mightily at their shields . . . Others held lances with curved tips and endeavoured with the aid of their lances and iron hooks to pull the enemy towards them." In the siege of Jerusalem, where three siege-towers were brought up to the walls, the struggle followed a similar pattern. Stone-catapults or trebuchets were also used by both sides.

From the end of the 12th century, all kinds of siege equipment were in use. Of the siege of Acre by the army of the third Crusade, the following account has survived: "The miners of the King of France dug so deep that they found the foundations of the walls. They supported them with props and laid a fire so that a great part of the wall collapsed." At least ten stone-catapults were in action on the side of the Crusaders, in addition to siege-towers. The Moslems in the city used stone-catapults and Greek fire for their defence. "When the right moment had come, he (a pyrotechnist) hurled a pot which was completely in flames. In an instant, the fire spread everywhere and the tower was consumed by it. The fire appeared so rapidly that the Christians did not have time to get down; men, weapons, everything was consumed by the flames . . . The two other towers were destroyed by fire in the same way. This time, the Christians were able to flee."

Contemporary descriptions contain accounts of the major forms of military confrontation in the history of the Crusader states as far as sieges were concerned but not a comparison of attack and defence as understood in modern military history. Right from the start, the besiegers were confronted with the same problems as the besieged, for instance, the question of supplies for the army. Many sieges had to be abandoned because the countryside was incapable of supplying the food required over a long period, because there was not a sufficient supply of water or because the springs had been rendered useless. There are only a few examples of a besieged city being forced to surrender by lack of food since, as a rule, hostilities were broken off during the winter season. On the other hand, the garrisons of castles seldom remained inactive. Sorties and attacks on the enemy camp were an established part of tactics on both sides. Only when castle garrisons were numerically too weak was a siege a one-sided affair in respect of military actions and in this case capitulation was inevitable. In all other cirumstances, siege tactics were supplemented by battles in the open.

Despite the fact that there was the same social structure and although armies of feudal lords and their followers confronted each other on either side, there were considerable variations in tactics and strategy. The Crusaders were forced to recognize this fact already on the first Crusade. A contemporary description of the first great battle with the Seljuks under the leadership of Kilij Arslan at Dorylaeum illustrates the problem: "At the first attack (on the Crusaders' camp), the Turks fired such great numbers of arrows at us that neither rain nor hail could have made it darker, so that many of us were pierced by them. And when the first had emptied their quivers and shot their arrows, there came behind them a second line, in which there were even more horsemen, who began to shoot even more arrows than before, in such a manner that cannot be conceived. This manner of fighting was totally unknown to our soldiers. They were unable to stand this with equanimity, the less so when they saw their horses fall at every moment. They (the Crusaders) endeavoured to drive back their enemies by storming forward and attacking them with sword and lance. But these, for their part

incapable of withstanding this kind of attack, immediately disengaged themselves to avoid the first thrust and since our warriors, deceived in their expectations, no longer found anyone before them, they were forced to retire without achieving success with their sudden advance while the Turks rapidly reformed and began to shoot their arrows once more..." Only when the Crusaders attacked the Seljuk camp in the closed ranks of a phalanx, were they able to exploit their military superiority and put Arslan and his troops to flight.

The different tactical concepts followed from the different kinds of weapons. The armies of the Islamic princes which confronted the Crusaders in the following centuries were largely organized along the lines pioneered by the Seljuks as regards the overall military concept. These warriors were decidedly more mobile and quicker in battle than the European knights. This is explained on the one hand by the superior quality of their mounts and secondly by their lighter weapons. Instead of heavy armour, they mainly wore leather reinforced with iron fittings. Their principal weapons of attack were the bow and arrow, though lances, swords and clubs were also used when fighting at close quarters. On the average, it seems that their weapons were lighter than those of the European knights. For protection, they used only a small round shield, while the Crusaders had a heavier one in the shape of an extended triangle. This is an indication of the different ways in which they fought. Whereas the Crusaders sought a man-to-man contest, in the manner to which they were accustomed in Europe, and were then able to take full advantage of their superiority, the Seljuks preferred to fight at a distance, as illustrated in the account quoted above. One of their special tactics was to feign retreat to encourage the enemy to break ranks while another stratagem was the skirmish on the flanks, particularly when the enemy was on the march, and a third variation was the use of archers from a safe distance to open up the ranks of the foe. The armies of the Crusaders endeavoured to counter these tactics by maintaining a close order. Random actions by individual groups of knights, which had led to heavy losses at first, were soon discontinued. Better observation of the enemy by reconnaissance parties helped to prevent the Crusaders from being

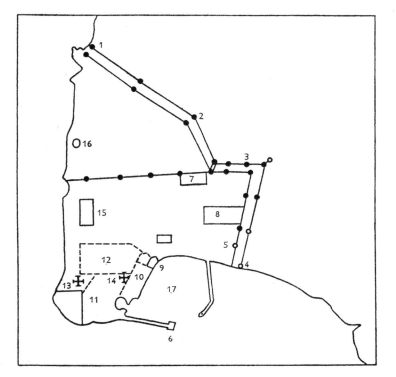

14   Acre in the year 1291

1	Fortification of the Knights Templar	9	Arsenal
2	Fortification of the Hospitalers	10	Venetian quarter
		11	Pisan quarter
3	English Tower	12	Genoese quarter
4	Tower of the Patriarchs	13	St Andrew's Church
5	German Tower	14	St Sabas
6	Tower of the Flies	15	Hospital
7	Castle	16	Hospice of the Hospitalers
8	Knights of the Teutonic Order	17	Harbour

taken by surprise. In addition, the military structure of the army soon changed under the new conditions. The more lightly armed mounted archer appeared at the side of the heavily armed knight. These troops were largely recruited from the local population. As "turcopoles", these units played a not inconsiderable role in the army of the Crusaders from the end of the 12th century in particular.

It is exceptionally difficult to estimate the number of troops in the armies of the Crusader states since no exact figures are available. It has been estimated from incomplete data that 675 knights from fiefs of the Crown were at the disposal of the kingdom of Jerusalem in about 1180, i.e., shortly before the battle of Hattin. Then there were the members of the knightly orders. The cities and the clergy had to pay the cost of equipping the foot-soldiers or serjeants, as they were called, a total of some five thousand men. Turcopoles, mercenaries, pilgrims and suchlike completed the army. The aim of the Crusaders was always to localize the conflict right from the start and if possible to avoid battles of a crucial nature. The relatively high proportion of foot-soldiers on both sides did not change the feudal character of the armies in any respect. The decisive actions in the campaigns were fought by the mounted feudal lords. The foot-soldiers were responsible for the protection of the military camps or fortresses. This was extremely important, particularly when these were without the protection of the knights. A number of battles were won because the troops guarding the camp were able to repel attacks. The duties of the foot-soldiers also included the protection of the flanks, logistics, tasks of a technical nature in connection with siege works and, not least, the manning of fortifications. Only in emergencies did they take part in pitched battles.

The field camps were of exceptional importance with respect to tactics. They were the real centres of the army; not simply because all military operations were directed from them but even more because it was here that the whole of military life was concentrated. The heavily armed knight could only spend a very limited time fighting on horseback, after which he needed rest in the protection of the camp. It was the custom in the Oriental armies in particular—the Crusaders often had castles at their disposal to which to withdraw—to have everything in their camps to which they were accustomed. All the comforts of civil life accompanied them on their campaigns. Kilij Arslan even had the whole of his treasure of gold and jewels constantly in his vicinity. Libraries were likewise a part of the camp facilities of Oriental princes as was also a large retinue of personnel to cater for the needs of the feudal lords. It is related that Saladin's camp at Acre included a bazar with several thousand shops; numerous bathrooms, swimming pools of clay and so on allowed a life to be led hardly different to that in the cities. Reference has already been made to the layout of the Crusaders' castles.

The picture of the enemy contained in contemporary reports is not at all clear. The Crusader ideology during the first Crusade and also afterwards was characterized by a religious fanaticism which was expressed, militarily, in merciless slaughter. This attitude continued to be held by the knights of the following centuries as well, not only because it was propagated time and again by Rome and the preachers of the Crusades. There was no lack of defamatory utterances about people of other creeds and how to deal with the vanquished. The Islamic rulers reacted in a similar fashion. Before the capture of Jerusalem, Saladin is said to have remarked: "I will deal with you (the Crusaders in Jerusalem) as the Christians dealt with the Moslems when they took the Holy City, that is to say, I will slay the men and make slaves of the rest, I will repay evil by evil." Incidentally, Saladin did not act as he said he would. On the contrary, he generously allowed the defeated knights to withdraw but the Arab chronicler was certainly accurate enough in his account as regards the mood in Saladin's army. Although the religious differences continued to be stressed, there are unmistakable signs in practice that they were regarded as less and less contentious. In political and diplomatic terms, this meant: truce agreements, peace treaties, diplomatic actions and missions, a policy of alliances including the agreement of special peace terms and so on. Was this betrayal? The fanatical Crusade ideologists of Europe certainly thought so. There was no lack of sharp attacks from the Papal Court but little was achieved by these moral pronouncements. Once the European knights had become estab-

lished in the Orient, they had to follow the laws of feudal foreign policy. The various religions were by no means the principal factor in this. For the small feudal states, the matters which took first priority were the characteristic feuds including a policy of alliance and the tactical variations in diplomatic affairs. The Oriental states were guided by the same basic considerations. This general situation in political matters largely determined the relations between the Christian and Moslem knights. The principles of a chivalrous code gradually developed. Respectful treatment of the vanquished became increasingly more common, the same applying to the release of captives in return for ransom money which did not exclude slaughter, however, if the conditions agreed were not observed. This is reflected in a series of episodes which, although not characteristic, are nevertheless worth noting. It is reported that Saladin at the siege of Tyre was so impressed by the courage of a Crusader that he offered to take him into his service. At Acre, the fighting stopped for some time and friendly conversations were held: "It is the custom for gifts to be exchanged among us kings, even in times of war." Since they had to live in close contact with each other, patterns of behaviour developed which had little in common with religious fanaticism, even though it made an appearance time and again. These patterns were determined by the basic principles of the struggle between two ruling classes of the same kind. This practice developed more or less in parallel with a new attitude in the chivalrous epic poems of Western Europe where, as will be illustrated later, the non-Christian feudal lord is given signs of respect and knightly appreciation and the concept of the "noble heathen" emerges. However, the warlike character of the Crusader states conveys only an incomplete picture of the nature and prospects of these states. A superficial examination seems to indicate that it was the fortune of war and the balance of military power which determined the fate of the conquests. The building of castles, modern military tactics, constant warfare and diplomatic negotiations cannot conceal the fact that the Europeans in the Orient were only a small upper class. They made use of the economic and political positions acquired by conquest to enrich and extend their possessions but they were essentially

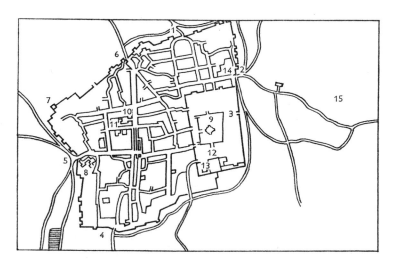

15 Jerusalem at the time of the Crusades

1	Herod's Tower	10	Church of the Holy
2	Stephan's Gate		Sepulchre
3	Golden Gate	11	House of the Knights
4	Zion Gate		of St John
5	Jaffa Gate	12	Royal Palace of Jeru-
6	Damascus Gate		salem (Al Aqsa Mosque)
7	Tancred's Tower	13	House of the Templars
8	David's Tower	14	Church of St Anne
9	Temple	15	Mount of Olives

an isolated group. The economic structure of the Crusader states remained Oriental and it developed in accordance with the laws of the Orient. The Europeans did not give a major stimulus to developments in the economic or cultural spheres.

The great majority of the inhabitants of the Crusader states were Orientals, though there were significant ethnic and religious differences between them. The hard core consisted of Syrian Christians, who were divided into Orthodox Christians, monothelitic Maronites and monophysitic Jacobites. The latter two churches date from Late Antiquity. The monophysitic Jacobites rejected the concept of the two natures of Christ and insisted on the divine aspect. Thus they did not accept the decisions of the Council of Chalcedon (451). The doctrine of the Monothelites developed in a similar manner in the 7th century from the dispute whether Christ had one or two wills. The Monothelites took the first view. These theological disputes were linked with the struggle of the Syrian (Antioch) and Egyptian (Alexandria) Christians against the ascendancy of Constantinople. The fact that many of these sects were able to exist for such a long time is due not least to the Arab conquests which prevented persecution by Byzantium. In addition, large groups of Armenians and Greeks, members of the Armenian and Orthodox churches respectively, lived in the principality of Antioch and the cities of the other Crusader states and in the countship of Edessa. The massacre of the first Crusade had drastically reduced the numbers of the Jewish and Moslem population. A large number of Jews who had survived subsequently left the region, only an insignificant group remaining. It is said that in the second half of the 12th century there were four hundred Jewish families in Tyre and about two hundred each in Jerusalem and Acre. They still lived in fear of pogroms. The account which relates that at the end of the 12th century there were more Jews living in the city of Damascus than in all the other Crusader states together is probably indicative of the atmosphere as a whole. Large numbers of the Moslem population of the most diverse ethnic origin likewise tried to find refuge from the Crusaders. Thus the unhindered withdrawal of the Moslems formed part of the conditions of surrender of the cities of Arsuf, Gibelet, Tyre and Acre. Nevertheless, there were numerous villages which were populated exclusively by Moslems, as can be shown for Northern Galilee, the valley of the Orontes and other districts, too. Nomadic Bedouin tribes frequented the south of the kingdom of Jerusalem in particular and came within the jurisdiction of the Crusaders, although they did not care much for the state frontiers which had been established.

All the elements of this indigenous population considered themselves to be first and foremost Oriental and an integral part of this society and civilization. Consequently, the frontiers of the Crusader states were not natural frontiers for these people since there were the same social and religious groups on the other side as well, in the neighbouring Moslem states or in Lesser Armenia. The Christians among them did not feel threatened in any way by their Moslem rulers since, from their own experience, they knew of their tolerance in religious affairs. In social and cultural respects, contacts between Christians and Arabs had become so close that Old Syrian, for instance, was eclipsed as a language by Arabic to such an extent that it died out in the 13th century, evidence of the influence of Arab culture even at the time of the Crusaders. On the other hand, there was very little which united the native Christians with the European feudal lords and nothing in the social and cultural sense. The Christian religion to which they both subscribed was not capable of bridging the great gap between them, especially as the differences between the practices of the Catholic Church and the Eastern Churches had become so marked that they were more likely to be the cause of dissent than a common bond. Even the action taken by the Crusaders to make up for the decline in the numbers of the working population by encouraging immigration had little effect on the basic composition. It was principally the Syrians and Armenians living in the neighbouring Islamic realms who were urged to settle as peasants and artisans in the Crusader states. In religion, they were Christians but if the intention had been to strengthen the Christian element these systematic measures did not help at all to shape the population in the religious respect. The Catholic hierarchy in particular regarded the increasse in the congregations of the Eastern Churches and sects with suspicion and only permitted this immigration with great reluctance. In 1168, for example, the clergy were able to prevent a large number of Armenians from taking up residence, something which had already been agreed with the authorities, by demanding that these peasants and artisans should pay additional taxes. Apart from the religious factor, a characteristic of all these immigrations was that they reinforced the Oriental element in production and consequently, in the final analysis, in society as a whole.

Of course, not all the people who came to the Crusader states from Europe were of aristocratic origin. Peasants, artisans and merchants were also represented. The success of the first Crusade had resulted in more than just a wave of enthusiasm in France, Italy, England, the German Reich and other territories.

The subsequent Crusades and even more the very numerous pilgrim expeditions brought a continual stream of people with the most diverse interests and ideas to the Orient. The misery of life in their native lands caused many peasants to seek their fortunes in the Crusader states. There is evidence in various regions of peasant settlements granted on a free hereditary basis, roughly comparable with the conditions for peasants clearing new land in 12th and 13th century Europe. We know of a village in the vicinity of Ashkelon which was inhabited around 1168 by peasant immigrants, a total of thirty-two families, from the Auvergne, Gascony, Lombardy, Poitou, Catalonia, Burgundy, Flanders and Carcassonne. Settlements such as this existed in other districts, too, but were not of major importance in the peasant population of the Crusader states as a whole. In comparison, there was a larger proportion of roving knights and adventurers who wanted to rapidly win fame and fortune in the new land, i.e., in the cities, for the most part. There must have been a relatively large number of shady characters among those pilgrims who had the intention of remaining in the Orient. A chronicler characterizes this in the following sharp words: "Since he who committed evil, the murderer, the robber, the thief, the adulterer, crosses the sea to the East, ostensibly to do penance but in actual fact he does not dare to remain at home for fear of the punishment that threatens him. Thus they stream there from all directions but they only change the clime in which they live, not their way of thinking. For after they have spent with all haste the resources they brought with them, they must acquire some more and then commit worse things than before."

In contrast, the body of merchants streaming in from the European cities of the Mediterranean was relatively coherent and exercised an influence on the structure of the cities, at least. Pisa, Genoa, Venice, Amalfi and Marseilles had established settlements in all the important cities of the Crusader states soon after the first Crusade. It was from here that they carried on commerce with distant countries. However, these merchants were never part of the population of the Crusader states in a real sense. They were primarily traders who had an interest in Oriental merchandise as a whole. As a rule, they stayed only for a few years in the cities of the Crusader states and lived according to the laws of their own states under an administration of their own. As merchants, they had an interest in the fate of the Crusader states. Even though the assistance they rendered in the shape of naval support during hostilities was considerable, the fortunes of the European merchants did not depend on the existence of the Crusader states, a fact confirmed by the centuries which followed.

It is true that the constant stream of temporal feudal lords, priests, pilgrims of the most diverse social backgrounds, merchants and to a certain extent peasants as well helped in the course of the history of the Crusader states to ensure that there was a certain minimum number of inhabitants from European territories in the "Holy Land". Yet they never exercised a major influence on economic and social affairs. The Europeans remained a thin stratum of conquerors.

In comparison with other Oriental regions, the territories of the Crusader states were not outstanding centres of economic prosperity. To the Crusaders, however, it seemed that they were in Paradise, not so much from the feeling that they were in the land of Jesus Christ but mainly because of the substantial difference in the standard of production as compared with Western Europe and the fact that many commodities of agricultural and craft origin were unknown to them. It is likely that many shared the opinion of Burkhard de Monte Sion: "One should know that the Holy Land is to-

day the best and, in truth, always was the best of all countries. Only people who have not observed it closely can assert the contrary. For the land is very fertile for the cultivation of grain which grows and flourishes almost without effort. All kinds of wild herbs grow in the soil. Fennel, sage, rue and roses are found everywhere in the fields. Cotton grows in bushes and the sugar cane likewise flourishes there. Many fruits are found there on the trees throughout the year and the people gather them the whole year through. At one and the same time, blossoms, half-grown and ripe fruit are to be seen on the same tree. The most important fruits are apples, limes and Adam's apples (tomatoes) from which the inhabitants living there make a sauce which is eaten with fowl, fish and other dishes. There is also a kind of apple which is called lemon from which an excellent sorbet (lemonade) is made in Acre ... The wine of the Holy Land is very good and of a noble quality... There are also figs, pomegranates, honey, oil and the most diverse kinds of vegetables such as melons and cucumbers. Many other fruits likewise flourish there in plenty." This profusion of agricultural produce must have seemed like another world to the people who came from countries where famine of the worst kind was the order of the day. This was only one side of the coin, however. On the one hand, there were the fertile regions especially along the coast and in the river valleys around the great cities, whose yields were increased still further by artificial irrigation which was largely unknown to the Crusaders, while on the other there were the vast and barren steppes and deserts. Natural catastrophes were no rarity either. For the first half of the 12th century alone, the records mention earthquakes (1114), great plagues of locusts (1114, 1117, 1120) and destruction of the harvest by mice (1120, 1127). It was in years such as these, in particular, that the Crusader states lived on large food imports, especially grain, arranged and organized by the merchants of Northern Italy. The variety of horticultural and field crops quoted was only partly the result of an ancient tradition of agriculture maintained at a high level. Of equal significance at least was the integration in the Arab Islamic world. Thus, sugar cane had been introduced from India via Persia at the time of the Arabs in Syria. It was already an important agricultural crop in the regions around Tripoli, Beirut, Sidon, Acre and other cities in the 10th century. There were centres for the processing of the crop from the crushing of the cane to the boiling of the sugar in Tripoli and Tyre. The Arabs had shown similar initiative in the propagation of other agricultural crops in Syria, such as cotton, even though these had been less successful.

The tilling of the soil, market gardening and the breeding of livestock were almost entirely in the hands of the indigenous population. Nowhere was this structure changed to a significant extent by the conquerors. The villages varied in size. Some were small settlements the size of hamlets with only a few farms, others contained forty families or more while others in a central location specialized in the exchange of goods from a certain area. An impression of such a village is conveyed in the following report:

"Dunayar (in Northern Syria) lies on a vast plain, surrounded by sweet-smelling plants and irrigated vegetable-gardens. It is of rural appearance and has no wall; crowds are attracted to it by its well-visited and richly stocked markets... It possesses wide fields and produces numerous foods ... The market is held on Thursdays, Fridays, Saturdays and Sundays. The people from the neighbouring communities congregate there, for a succession of villages and lodgings line the left and right of the road. This market, to which the people come from different directions, is called a bazar."

The majority of the native peasants lived in a state of feudal dependency. The tax they had to pay was in proportion to the yield of the crops they harvested, varying between one quarter and one half of the total harvest. There was scarcely any socage in the cultivation of the land since most of the conquerors did not possess land, in the European sense, which their vassals had to till. However, it can be shown that compulsory labour and the provision of draft animals was frequently demanded for the building of castles in particular. There was also a poll tax. In addition, the Moslems had to contribute a tithe tax which was paid to the local Catholic Church via the state. It is significant that the Catholic clergy constantly fought for the extension of this tax to the Christians and members of the Eastern Churches.

The European peasants were given land—in one case there is evidence of 62 hectares (about 150 acres) per family—from which they had to make payments in kind, this depending on the yields. In addition to this, they were sometimes required to perform military service.

In contrast to European feudal society, it was the existence of powerful and flourishing cities which largely determined the economy of the Crusader states. Ashkelon, Jaffa, Haifa, Acre, Tyre, Sidon, Gibelet, Tripoli, Laodicea and Antioch, to mention only some of these cities, and not least Jerusalem united large numbers of the total population within their walls. Their traditions dated back to Antiquity. But at the time of the Crusades they were largely Oriental Islamic in character since this area had fallen under Islamic control, following the conquests in the 7th century and later. Byzantine influence was also present in varying degrees, this being most apparent, perhaps, in Antioch which had belonged to Eastern Rome until the 11th century. The cities had become integrated within the Oriental economic system. As seaports, they were the gateway on the Mediterranean to Byzantium and Europe for Arab merchants and warriors and were regarded as important terminals for the caravan routes from the interior of the region, from Central Asia and the Far East. With their numerous craftsmen, they were part of the not inconsiderable manufacturing potential of Syria within the Oriental world, although the main centres were at Damascus, Aleppo, Mosul and other cities in the interior.

The size and structure of these cities must have been impressive for the European Crusaders. At the beginning of the 11th century, Tripoli had 80,000 inhabitants and its fortifications enclosed an area of about 12,000 hectares. Not only did it possess a series of palaces, its five- and six-storey buildings were also an impressive sight. It was a similar picture in the other cities. The bustling crowds and the busy atmosphere of the bazars where numerous craftsmen and merchants sold a wide range of wares excited the astonishment and admiration of the conquerors. In the cities, there were centralized water-supply systems, some dating from Antiquity, these being either in the form of cisterns with pipes leading to the houses of the wealthy citizens at least or, in individual cases, consisting of an integrated mains-supply system for the entire city. Street lighting had been common in city centres since the 10th century, vegetable oil being used as fuel in Syria, for example, for this purpose. Public baths, with strict male and female segregation and sometimes of considerable artistic merit, were just as familiar a part of the urban scene as the great hospitals, libraries and schools. It was a new and alien world with advanced economic and cultural standards which confronted the Crusaders. Manufacture and trade on an unprecedented scale for European concepts of the time were the material foundation of this world.

The merchandise produced by Syrian craftsmen for export to the great Oriental Islamic market came mainly from the following trades: glass making and associated products, pottery and ceramics, cloth manufacture of various kinds and metalworking.

The glass makers of Syria had maintained exceptionally high standards ever since Antiquity and, at the time of the Crusades, Syria and Egypt produced not only coloured glass objects of a high artistic standard but also a wide range of glassware for everyday use. It is said that bottles and glasses were the usual form of packaging for food as early as the 10th century. In Tyre, Tripoli, Jaffa and other cities, glassmakers and grinders turned out work of the finest quality. None of this was changed by the conquests of the Crusaders. It is rather the case that this branch of the economy continued to develop in the 12th and 13th centuries as well, this being parallelled by the growth of glass production in such cities as Aleppo and Damascus, i.e., Syrian cities which were not on the territory of the Crusader states. It is not possible to distinguish any particular specialization and the term "Syrian glass" applied to the whole of the country. The same is true of decorative pottery, a trade which was found in Jaffa, Beirut, Tyre and other cities. Raqquah, on the edge of Syria's frontier with Mesopotamia, was the leader in decorative design up to 1259, the year in which it was destroyed. Figurative design, arabesques and lettering as ornamentation on turquoise ground were the special features of this artistic direction. Large silk-weaving establishments existed in Tyre, Antioch, Tripoli and other cities, four thousand weavers be-

ing engaged in this craft in Tripoli alone. Silk cloth was a popular export product and was regarded as equalling Chinese in quality. However, the actual centre of silk weaving was in Damascus.

In addition to these branches of trade which characterized the economy, each of the great cities naturally disposed of all the crafts necessary for the requirements of the population.

These craftsmen were native to the region. For them the Oriental standards of material culture remained the criteria for the quality and quantity of their products. European artisans, who had settled in the cities of the Crusader states, were unable to exercise any lasting influence worth mentioning.

The structure of commerce was similar. In times of peace, the Crusader states were directly linked with the main centres of Arab intermediate trade. Trading caravans to Damascus, Aleppo and other cities of the Arab states were a part of everyday commercial life. The significance of commerce has been much discussed in scientific literature. The advance of the Mongols to Central Asia had blocked the overland route to China and trade with India was in the hands of the Egyptian cities, Alexandria in particular. The conclusion was drawn from this that Alexandria was the really important factor in trade between Europe and the Orient. In actual fact, the seaports of the Crusader states had access to the whole of the Syrian, Persian and Mesopotamian economic area. In addition, at least to a limited extent, Indian spices were brought from Mecca to Syria via the pilgrimage route. The advantages of this economic situation had immediately been recognized by the merchants of Italy and Southern France at the end of the first Crusade. Genoa, Pisa, Amalfi, Venice and also Marseilles, Montpellier and other cities had won the privileges of sea-trade between Europe and the Crusader states. They established settlements in all the seaports and other cities: Genoa in Antioch, Laodicea, Caesarea, Acre, Jaffa, Jerusalem, Beirut; Pisa in Jaffa, Laodicea, Tyre, Jerusalem, Acre; Venice in Sidon, Tyre, Tripoli, Jerusalem; Marseilles in Acre and other cities. The main settlement of the Venetians was in Tyre and that of Genoa and Pisa in Acre. These settlements were usually complexes of buildings in a particularly favourable location where the merchants lived according to the law of their native land and carried on their commercial activities. The Genoese quarter in Antioch, for instance, consisted of at least thirty houses, a church and a set of buildings used as warehouses and stores.

The European merchants were principally interested in sea-trade. Overland trade remained in the hands of the Syrians, Arabs and Jews. They organized the transportation of merchandise from Damascus, Mosul, Aleppo and other cities of the Islamic empires to the coast. It was only later, at about the end of the 12th century, that the merchants of Northern Italy in particular tried to acquire a greater share of this trade for themselves.

The range of merchandise which the Northern Italian merchants obtained via Acre and Tyre and sent to Europe was exceptionally wide. From the wares produced in the Crusader states, it included silks and velvets, glassware, pottery, wine and other agricultural produce in particular. Apart from this, commodities were constantly imported from the Islamic states, too. Medicinal products included ginger, aloe, camphor, bitter-wort and also incense; there were spices such as pepper, cinnamon, muscat and cloves; silk, damask and muslin; textile dyes such as indigo and Brazil-wood while other articles included Damascus steel, perfume, jewelry and porcelain. Acre and Tyre especially became seaports to which European goods were exported for the whole of the Islamic world. Textiles from France, Flanders and England, copper, lead, iron, wood and pitch, all materials needed for shipbuilding, largely arrived in Egypt by way of the Crusader states.

And not least, Acre was also a staging point in the flourishing slave trade which had developed between the Golden Horde and Egypt, a sphere in which the merchants of Northern Italy likewise acted as intermediaries in many cases. The provision of supplies for the Crusaders themselves was also an important aspect of these trading activities, of course. Cereals, weapons for the knights and building materials for the fortresses were supplied by the Italian cities. It was precisely in this connection that they were indispensable for the Crusader states. In addition to this, the Northern Italian cities also organized regular ship services for passengers to the

Orient. In this way, pilgrims, relatives of the Crusaders, adventurers, immigrants and others were able to visit the Holy Land and avoid the onerous overland route with all its dangers. The sea voyage took four to five weeks and, where possible, followed the coastline for greater safety. Thus a relatively good and direct link with Europe was established which proved to be exceptionally important for the survival of the Crusader states.

The economic union of the Crusader states and the Oriental world was not seriously disturbed since the European conquerors were not in a position to replace it by any other. Having assumed positions of feudal power, they contented themselves with the appropriation of the surplus product from agriculture, craft production and trade. Apart from the contributions made by the dependent peasants to their lords, the most revenue was obtained from taxes, rights of coinage and customs duties. The latter revenues initially flowed to the central state authority, this source of profit being exploited by the kings of Jerusalem in particular. They were paid tribute and poll-tax by the indigenous artisans, possessed monopoly rights for a series of trades, such as sugar production, for instance, which they contracted out for an appropriate sum, charged anchorage dues for the ships using the ports of the kingdom, collected market fees and even demanded a property tax from the pilgrims who came from Europe. These revenues were used for paying the Crusaders employed by the state administration as administrators, judges and so on and for financing the military equipment of a number of castles. Special economic manipulations were not associated with this taxation and revenue system.

The minting of coins throws a vivid light on the nature of the economic policy of the Crusader states. Gold and copper coinage in the Byzantine or Islamic tradition was struck in all the mints. Greek or Arab inscriptions predominated. Sayings from the Koran and portraits of Caliphs were not at all rare. Tancred was depicted in a turban on a coin of the principality of Antioch and was described as the "great emir Tancred". It is possible that at the beginning much of this was due to the private initiative of the mints which were left in their original structure. However, it is just as likely that in the following decades no change was made in this practice once it had been adopted because there was no wish to disturb the confidence of the native merchants or those of the neighbouring territories in the familiar currency. It was only at the beginning of the 13th century when Pope Innocent IV, who knew about this practice, made an energetic protest, that a change was made to Biblical quotations for the inscriptions on the coins, though the Arabic alphabet was retained. Coins with Christian symbols were slow to appear, preference being given to heraldic signs, especially those of cities.

The history of the coins issued in the Crusader states is admittedly only a detail of their economic policy. Nevertheless they are a vivid reflection of the contrast between the economic structure of the country and the isolation of the conqueror class which, it is true, concentrated on military affairs but was neither in a position nor wanting to reshape the economy. This touches on the central question of the long-term prospects of conquests during the Middle Ages. Assimilation or downfall were really the two alternatives

which confronted every feudal conqueror class, when it was not supported by large numbers of peasant settlers. This problem already follows from the circumstance that social renewal requires a constant influx from the people and it only becomes directly relevant in the shaping of habits and customs, ideology and language, in short, the whole sphere of intellectual culture. Since the Crusaders were socially renewed by the steady stream from Europe, the cultural question acquired special significance since at the beginning there was the Crusader ideology and a consciously displayed sense of mission.

About twenty years after the foundation of the Crusader states, Fulcher of Chartres described how the Franks had adapted to the situation in these words: "We who were Occidentals have become Orientals; they who were Romans or Frenchmen have become Galileans or inhabitants of Palestine; those who came from Reims or Chartres are now from Tyre or Antioch. We have forgotten our native cities and several of us no longer know them or have long since not

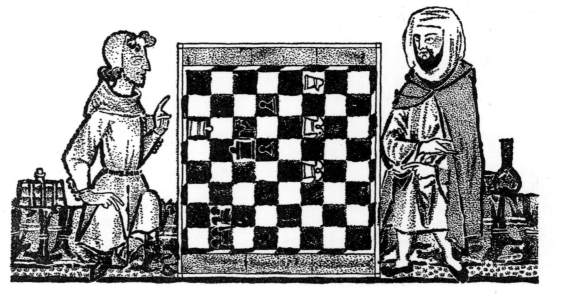

16 One form of contact between the European knights and the Moslem feudal lords which was certainly not the most common but not the least interesting either was the game of chess. (*From a contemporary manuscript, El Escorial Library, Madrid.*)

heard them named. Many of us possess houses and servants in this country, as if inherited from their fathers, others have married not a countrywoman but a Syrian or Armenian, sometimes even a baptized Saracen..." Although this description would appear to be unequivocal, it does not indicate anything more than that the conquerors liked it there and were determined to stay. In other respects, some corrections are appropriate. The feudal lords did not consider themselves "Orientals" in the sense indicated by Fulcher. Not many of them married natives of the country. It was only at the beginning of the reign of the Crusaders that some of them married Armenian princesses. This was primarily motivated by political considerations since they wanted to be sure of Armenian support in their military campaigns. This tendency soon disappeared afterwards. The Crusaders arranged for wives to come from Europe. We know, for instance, of only four cases where kings of Jerusalem married Armenian or Byzantine princesses. Relations with local women took the form of concubinage, as proved by many old records, and little distinction was drawn here between a Christian or a Moslem woman. The clergy also participated enthusiastically in this form of contact. Heraclius, Patriarch of Jerusalem and the highest-ranking priest of the Catholic Christians in the Crusader states, openly kept a married woman as his mistress, the lady then being sarcastically addressed as "Madame Patriarch". However, this is more a question of the moral state of the Crusaders rather than their genealogical development. In this connection, it is more significant that only few families were able to maintain a direct line of descent for several generations. A high mortality rate as the result of war and disease weakened the basic substance. Child marriages were no rarity in the Crusader states either but could not prevent continual changes in ownership of property or save families from dying out. From this aspect, the growing importance of the knightly orders, which obtained their members from Europe in a different manner, is understandable.

It was a different story as regards the family relations of the European population who were not members of the nobility, the foot-soldiers, peasants, artisans, merchants (with the exception of those from Northern Italy and Southern France) and other city-dwellers with the local populations. Marriages to Oriental Christian women and even converted Moslems were so frequent that a specific social group, the Pullani, had already emerged by about 1150 and took part as infantry in the wars of the time. It is reported that in the mid-12th century there were about five thousand of these Pullani in the army of the Crusaders. Even if this figure is exaggerated or included members of the native population as well, it does provide a clear illustration of the basic problem. And when it was demanded at a church conference as early as 1120 that relations with Moslem women should be punished by castration and the cutting off of the nose, this drastic measure indicates that the Church wanted to take action against a problem which really existed. The practical solution was very simple: baptism of the Moslem women.

In contrast to this, the process of assimilation made rapid headway among the common population. It adopted Oriental civilization not just because of family relations but mainly on account of the general economic life with which the ordinary people were confronted. They were not only able to speak Arabic, they also used it in their ordinary dealings to a greater or lesser extent. These people assumed all the customs and habits of the Orient. There are many historians who consider that this group of the population had already lost a large part of their intrinsic character by the 13th century and, to use the words of Fulcher, had become "Oriental".

This was not so with the Crusaders. As a necessity of war and conquest, they endeavoured to lead an independent existence. Among themselves, French remained their customary speech and this to such an extent that a German Crusader who visited the country at the end of the 12th century was astonished at his inability to find a German-speaking group. They knew Arabic, of course, but it remained an alien language for them.

It is rather the case that another process was characteristic of their situation. This may be defined in general as a passive acceptance of the civilization of the Orient. This process developed in parallel with a decline in the ideology of the Crusades. This is evident from the account of an Arab chronicler who, when praying in the Al Aqsa mosque, was jostled on this account by a Frank "who was not known to him". The friends of this Frank, Crusaders who were resident in the land, apologized to him with the words "He is a stranger who has just arrived from the country of the Franks. He has never seen anyone pray who did not turn to the East." Even if this was only an episode, it is nevertheless representative of the astonishment or anger felt by the new arrivals in regard to the intellectual and material view of life which had emerged among the Crusaders. These changes in their attitudes and habits were due, on the one hand, to the harsh necessity of accepting the conditions with which they were confronted and, on the other and to an even greater extent, to the fact that life in the Orient was more attractive than in their homelands.

Like the original Oriental rulers, the Crusaders became accustomed to living in the cities. It was only to a limited extent that the castles were used as residences in peacetime, too. City maps clearly show the quarters of the knightly orders but the other feudal lords also had their residences here. The palace of the lords of Ibelin in Beirut, built by Byzantine, Syrian and Armenian craftsmen, is described in the chronicle as a truly splendid building. Marble was used for the floors, ceilings and walls and was employed to such advantage that the floors, for instance, conveyed the impression of water rippled by the wind. Mosaics on the walls provided additional decoration. An object of particular magnificence was the fountain with its marble ornamentation in the centre of the house. The purpose of this was to provide a kind of air-conditioning for the rooms. Large windows looked over the sea and on to gardens which surrounded the entire palace. Even if not all of the Crusaders possessed such establishments as this, much less was still enough to convince travellers from Europe of the difference between this and their own material life-style. Carpets, curtains, exquisite furniture, vessels of porcelain and glass, gold and silver utensils and other objects could be found in the dwelling of every Crusader. Only the richest princes of Europe were accustomed to luxury of this order. The Crusaders rapidly adjusted to the customs and comforts of life in the Orient. Their palaces had a constant supply of piped water. The "Franks" used the public baths if they did not possess one of their own.

Meals were prepared according to native traditions and were composed of local foods with the appropriate spices. It did not take long for the Crusaders to make a complete change to the Oriental cuisine. They despised the meagre and plain meals of their own countries. Many Crusaders refused to eat pork and there is no lack of remarks to this effect.

All of their very numerous servants were recruited from the Oriental population. Not a few of them were slaves and they continued as such. Only when they embraced Christianity did the law require from their master that a change be made in their legal status, though this did not affect their actual position to any great extent. These servants considerably influenced the general atmosphere in the Crusaders' houses, i.e., they were directly responsible for the introduction of the Oriental way of life. Many of the old literary sources indicate that there was a certain pride on the part of the European feudal lords in possessing only Egyptian cooks, in being attended only by Oriental physicians and so on.

Pilgrims were shocked to notice, in particular, the adoption of Oriental clothing. Silk burnous and turban were the normal attire for the Crusaders, made of exquisite Oriental cloths, of course, and richly embroidered, as was the custom of the country. Trimmings of gold and silver thread were normal, as was the decoration of bridle, saddle and weapons. In keeping with the custom of the country, the knights wore a linen cloak over their armour as protection against the heat of the sun when they went to war.

The Crusaders started growing beards as early as the 12th century. In contrast to Europe, it was regarded as a disgrace in the Orient to have one's beard cut off. Baldwin of Edessa exploited this attitude in an enterprising manner by pledging his beard to his creditors and thus compelling his scandalized Armenian father-in-law to pay his debts.

Even more striking were the long and clinging garments, made from exquisite materials and embroidered with gold thread and jewels, of the wives of the Crusaders. The veil was a normal article of clothing and naturally they were quick to learn the art of Oriental cosmetics.

The acceptance by the Crusaders of the customs and habits of the Orient was so striking for visitors to the Cru-

136

sader states that numerous chroniclers considered it worth recording. Extreme luxury and the decline of moral standards, as reflected in the existence of brothels and so on, were the main points of criticism. However, it must be added, with some caution, that much of this derived from a comparison with European life. It is clear that the reason for such sharp criticism of many Oriental customs was that they were totally unknown. This is very apparent from the astonishment which many pilgrims felt when they saw how jealously the wives of the Crusaders were guarded by their husbands, this being some sort of reflection of Oriental harem attitudes. On the other hand, they were shocked that the same ladies were wont to use the public baths two or three times a week, likewise in accordance with local custom. Speculation about loose morals may have been based on this, although there was no real foundation for it.

Oriental influence on everyday life strengthened the inclination already present to accept Islamic feudal lords as members of the same class and to develop relations which had little in common with the ideology of the Crusades. The exchange of legations, accompanied by the presentation of gifts of friendship, was no rarity but an important means of establishing and maintaining diplomatic relations and of concluding military alliances of at least a temporary nature. Private visits, receptions, hunting parties and similar occasions consolidated these contacts.

Through the haphazard nature of the accounts which have survived, it is not possible today to measure the extent of personal contacts. It can be regarded as a fact that friendly relations were common and, which is perhaps even more significant, that the Crusaders who were resident in the country considered such links as completely natural. Only Europe and the knightly orders rejected this attitude in a more or less drastic manner. Of course, the closer contact between the Crusaders and the Oriental lords did not bridge the difference in their intellectual standards. The Oriental world with princes who took an interest in science, literature and art, recruited scholars to their courts, were poets themselves, possessed great libraries which they also used and even wrote books themselves, all this was alien to the European feudal lords. The men-

tality of the Orient is apparent from an episode in which an Arab ruler, whose ship had been wrecked and plundered on the coast of the Crusader states, complained that "The well-being of my children, the children of my brother and of our wives allowed me to accept the loss of my wealth with ease. What distressed me was the loss of my books. These were four thousand volumes, all precious works. Their loss was the cause of life-long sorrow for me." The unfortunate man was well-respected as a warrior. Reactions such as this were beyond the understanding of the Crusaders. The adoption of the outward forms, however, as already mentioned in connection with the everyday life of the Crusaders, was an easier matter. Reference must also be made to the imitation of special practices, such as the display of coats of arms on shields and the use of flags and standards and so on. Since these elements were adopted not only in the Crusader states but also spread rapidly in Europe, more attention will be paid to them in connection with the effects of the Crusades on Europe.

Science and literature in the Crusader states followed a similar pattern to that in the economy and material civilization. A question which has been raised many times is whether the Crusaders were responsible for cultural achievements of their own in the conquered territories. Even when all the evidence available was conscientiously examined, the answer has always been in the negative. Traces in this direction naturally exist and are most obvious in the buildings erected by the Crusaders. Apart from the castles with artistically significant details which they built, they were also responsible for a series of ecclesiastical structures. The best-known of these are the Church of St Anne in Jerusalem, the Cathedral of Tortosa and also the new surround to the entrance of the Church of the Holy Sepulchre in Jerusalem. Apart from the fact, however, that the number of buildings was relatively small, their activities had little of an original nature about them and the adoption of European or Oriental forms predominated. The Church of St Anne was built about 1140 in Romanesque style while the dome is imitated from Aquitainian churches of the same period. The Cathedral of Tortosa, constructed in the middle of the 13th century after an earthquake, reflects the transition from the Romanesque to the Gothic style. Worth

67   Krak des Chevaliers (Kurdish castle), west and south sides with the two perimeter walls. Even the surroundings of the fortress made it extremely difficult for it to be taken by storm. When Baybars captured the castle from the Knights of St John in 1271, his troops had to storm it tower by tower under heavy fire. Despite their courage they only succeeded because the fortress was undermanned. The water supply for the castle was a weak point. Within the walls, there were only cisterns which were filled by rainwater. Water was also brought from the hill close by (right foreground).

On the preceding two pages:

66   Krak des Chevaliers, architecturally the most beautiful of the castles built by the Crusaders, was rebuilt time and again in the course of the centuries. Many models, such as this one from Paris, give a clear idea of its constructional details. Musée de Monuments Français

68   Underground rooms and gigantic halls, such as the 120-metres long hall of Krak des Chevaliers shown here and located beneath the inner perimeter wall, not only enabled vast quantities of provisions to be stored but also provided accommodation for horses and beasts of burden.

69   The sharp angles in the approach to the fortress of Krak des Chevaliers made it easier to hold back any of the enemy who had forced their way into the castle.

70–72 The interior of Notre Dame in Tortosa. The 13th century capitals are evidently the work of European craftsmen, probably of French origin. This church is one of the edifices built by the Crusaders.

On the following pages:

73 Margat, a fortress of the Order of St John situated near Tortosa, also had to be abandoned during the last days of the Crusader states. It is said that it had room enough for 2000 families and 1000 horses.

74 Kir Moab was built in 1142 to maintain control of the caravan route from Damascus to Arabia but it was captured by Saladin in 1183. It is said that a marriage took place in the fortress while the siege was in progress. The mistress of the castle permitted Saladin to bring part of the wedding feast and reminded him that he had carried her in his arms when she was a child. Saladin accordingly gave instructions not to bombard the tower in which the newly wedded pair had their rooms.

75 Covering an area of five hectares (more than 12 acres), the fortress of Say'un was one of the largest castles built by the Crusaders. It stood on land which had long traditions in this respect since a Byzantine fortification had been built here in the 10th century. Say'un was captured by Saladin in 1188.

76 The impregnability of a castle was one of the principal objectives of those who built it. Say'un, which dominated the port of Laodacia, was situated on a plateau. A trench, 28 metres deep, 20 metres wide and 130 metres long, protected it in this direction and probably dates back to the time before the Crusades.

noting as regards an original tendency is the fortresslike character of the church with its massive walls and arrow-slits, unmistakable evidence of the political and military situation in the land. In contrast to this, the palaces of the Crusaders in the cities were based on Oriental architecture, supplemented by Byzantine influence.

A similar mixture of European Romanesque and Gothic elements and Syrian and Arab influences can be found in sculpture and in the mosaics which were produced.

There are remarkably few signs of the emergence of an independent literature. There is scarcely any trace in the Crusader states of a poetic presentation of the ideology of the Crusades, with the exception of the Chansons de Chetif, recalling in poetic form the events of the campaign of 1101 between the first and second Crusades. They were written in the middle of the 12th century at the court of Antioch. There are also a few lesser poems but it is not clear whether the author was a pilgrim on his way home or a permanent resident of the land. The few works composed in the Crusader states can in no way be compared with the poems celebrating the Crusade which flourished in Europe during the same period. Otherwise, it was chroniclers who recorded political and military events, mixed with descriptions of their milieu. The "History of the Holy War" by William of Tyre who, as Archbishop of the kingdom of Jerusalem, was well informed about the military situation of the country, provides valuable testimony and a detailed description of this time. Other clerics, too, such as Jacques de Vitry, who was Bishop of Acre for a time, wrote chronicles of no mean importance.

The art of illuminating manuscripts, centred around the Patriarchate of Jerusalem, was of general importance for mediaeval book decoration in the history of art. Magnificent work was carried out here in the decoration of liturgical books in particular, this being specifically at the behest of the royal family. The artists were obviously Greeks who followed the Byzantine models but English and Italian influence can also be identified to a limited extent. This tradition continued until the middle of the 13th century.

As a whole, this was very little when compared with the overall cultural scene in the Crusader states. Even after the conquest, it was the native scholars and artists who determined the tenor of intellectual and cultural development. The ancient cultural centres of Syria at Tripoli, Antioch and other cities continued to exist. Philosophy, medicine, literature and other disciplines continued to be taught in the existing schools. Gregory Bar-Hebraeus (1226–1285), the important philosopher, historian and ecclesiastical historian, lived in Tripoli. His works reflect some of the characteristics of the Syrian philosophers who concerned themselves with the heritage of Antiquity, with Aristotle, but did not disdain the influence of Arab philosophy. It is typical of all the academic disciplines cultivated in the Crusader states that they developed under the influence of other Oriental centres. By tradition, the links with Damascus, Aleppo, Cairo, Baghdad and so on must have been relatively close even in the time from the 11th to the 13th centuries. At this time, too, the libraries of Tripoli, Antioch, Tyre and other cities were constantly receiving new books from the Arab centres of learning. However, the barbaric behaviour of the Crusaders during the first Crusade in particular had been a serious blow for the schools and libraries as well. Thus the great library of Tripoli was totally destroyed and the equally valuable and very large Jewish library at Jerusalem was scattered in every direction. Despite these setbacks, the losses were soon made good again through hard work and good contacts with the scientific centres of the Orient outside the territory of the Crusader states.

For large numbers of physicians, pharmacologists, biologists and other scientists, the schools of the Syrian cities were part of the Oriental world as a whole, even during the time of the Crusaders, and they felt just as much at home in Antioch or Tripoli as in Cairo, Damascus or Baghdad.

In view of this cultural situation, the Crusaders were left with no choice but to enjoy the benefits of this world. A great many Arab and Greek works of learning were translated into Latin, principally by the priests resident in the Crusader states. Philosophical writings of the Ancient Greeks and medical treatises were especially popular. Schools of translators started to emerge and the best-known translators were Stephen of Antioch and Philip of Tripoli. Nevertheless, the reception of the Oriental world of science proceeded at an exceptionally slow pace. The difference in standards was simply too great, as is demonstrated very clearly by the example of medicine. For the whole of the Crusader period, the European feudal lord in the Orient showed a preference for native physicians and counsellors. Numerous contemporary reports tell time and again of the primitive methods of European physicians even in the Crusader states, even though the Oriental medical schools were in the direct vicinity. It is possible that these reports were wildly exaggerated but the basic situation was clearly stated and consequently often quoted in literature. An Arab physician recorded his experience of the art of healing as practised by the Franks: "They brought me a horseman on whose leg an ulcer had formed and a woman suffering from a hectic fever. I applied a blistering plaster to the horseman. The ulcer opened and took a benign course. I prescribed a diet for the woman and improved her physical condition by prescribing vegetable food." The account states that a physician of the Crusaders who appeared on the scene insisted that treatment should be carried out according to his own diagnosis. He had the leg of the horseman amputated, at which the patient died.

The woman had her head shaved and the scalp removed since the Devil had entered her head. She, too, did not survive this therapy. In another case, a wound which refused to heal was washed with strong vinegar but this time with success, as the astonished Arab physician records. It is not difficult to understand why the Crusaders had such confidence in the native physicians. Many of them kept personal physicians in their houses. They readily accepted the precepts of Oriental medicine, the only condition being that the physician should be a Christian or a converted Moslem, if possible.

When the Crusader states were militarily defeated, this only affected the surface of society. The essential nature of the hopelessness of their position resulted from the economic and cultural situation. The Crusaders had remained a small and isolated ruling class without roots in the common people and were alien to their economy and culture, despite all the relations which had developed. Such a state, even under mediaeval conditions, could be maintained by its military potential for a long time but a permanent solution could not result from such a situation.

The Concept of the Crusades in the 12th and 13th Centuries

The feudal society of Europe did not remain unaffected by the events in the Orient and this was true for the entire history of the Crusader states. Although the concept of the Crusade changed in the course of time and new motives gave it a different accent, the European feudal lords, inspired by the Catholic Church, continued to react to the military happenings in the Holy Land. Defeats and loss of territory in particular were regarded as reason enough for military expeditions in the shape of new Crusades.

At first, it was the success of the first Crusade which mobilized the feudal lords of Europe. Around 1100, armies of knights from Northern Italy under the leadership of Archbishop Anselm of Milan, from Southern France under the command of Duke William IX of Aquitaine and groups of knights from Northern and Eastern France, Flanders, Bavaria and Austria, each led by bishops and great temporal princes, set out separately for the Orient. All these armies were overwhelmed by the Seljuks in Asia Minor so that only small, scattered groups reached the Crusader states. When Edessa fell into the hands of Zangi, this loss gave a new stimulus to the propaganda for the Crusades in Europe and led to the second Crusade with contingents under the command of Louis VII, King of France, and Conrad III of Germany (1147/1149). They reached Jerusalem after hard-fought battles and achieved only modest military success. The decision to attack Damascus proved to be politically premature. The aim of preventing the union of Aleppo and Damascus was not achieved; the attack was a failure.

The third Crusade (1189–1192) was a reaction to the overwhelming victory of Saladin at Hattin (1187) and the capture of Jerusalem in the same year. The forces of the third Crusade were the greatest ever sent. Three armies under the command of Frederick I Barbarossa of Germany, Richard Cœur de Lion of England and Philip II Augustus of France set out for the Orient, the leaders of European feudal society and their retinues. The English and French knights took the sea-route and achieved some military success, capturing Acre, one of the major seaports of the Crusader states, and inflicting a series of defeats on Saladin. Richard Cœur de Lion was an outstanding figure here but Jerusalem could not be taken.

The army of German knights received a setback on the march through Asia Minor at the death of Barbarossa, who was probably drowned when bathing in the River Saleph on 10 June 1190. The reaction to this was devastating. Disillusioned, many of the feudal lords returned home again, doubting the support of God for the undertaking. Those who were left fought in small groups in the ranks of the English and French knights. It was intended that the mortal remains of the Emperor should be buried in Jerusalem but in fact it was in Tyre that they found their last resting-place.

At the beginning of the 13th century, the situation of the Crusader states was as complicated and militarily hopeless as it had been in the past. This led to several Crusades in rapid succession. In the course of these, the main emphasis was increasingly directed against Egypt, the most powerful opponent of the Crusader states in the Orient.

French and Flemish knights led by Margrave Boniface of Montferrat and Count Baldwin of Flanders had planned the fourth Crusade against Egypt (1202/1204). The sea-passage was in the hands of the Venetians, yet the destination was not Egypt but Byzantium. Inspired by the Venetians, the Crusaders stormed Constantinople. This event has gone down in history as an example of the subordination of the idea of the Crusades to mercantile ambitions. This Crusade is also clear evidence of the interest in expansion on the parts of the European knights.

The fifth Crusade, fanned by the passionate propaganda of Pope Innocent III, lasted from 1217 to 1229 and was marked by a whole series of military campaigns. In 1217, Andrew II of Hungary attempted to move forward from Acre but he was unsuccessful. Other armies from various parts of Europe under the direct command of the Church in the person of Cardinal Pelagius laid siege to Damietta, took it in 1219 but were forced to abandon it again in 1221. In 1228/1229, Emperor Frederick II set out for Acre with a relatively small force and, through skilful diplomatic negotiations with the Egyptian Sultan Al-Kamil, persuaded him to cede Jerusalem and the surrounding territory to the Crusader states. This success, too, was only temporary. In 1244 Jerusalem finally passed into the hands of the Egyptians.

The sixth Crusade (1248–1254) was the exclusive affair of Louis IX (the Saint), King of France. Damietta was captured for a short time but military defeat brought Louis into captivity, from which he was freed only after the payment of a large ransom. His last Crusade (1270) was directed against Tunis but was of no military or political significance whatsoever for other Crusader states.

Even the bare facts confirm what has been stated in connection with the history of the Crusader states. With the change in the political and military balance of power in the Orient through the union of the forces led by Saladin and his successors, the fate of the Crusader states was sealed. They had never possessed any long-term prospects of survival even before this, either. The events which followed the fourth Crusade appear to confirm this from the viewpoint of the internal dynamics of the undertaking.

In the course of the two centuries which spanned the age of the Crusades, significant changes and developments occurred in the Crusade ideology, in the attitude of the knights and in military practices in Europe.

Without doubt, Urban II could scarcely have foreseen at the Council that the Crusade idea would remain a major element of Papal propaganda and of the thinking of the European feudal lords for such a long time. Up to the beginning of the 13th century, Rome was therefore constantly occupied, among other things, with the re-definition of the idea of the Crusade and with adapting it to the new conditions of European feudal society which was developing at an unprecedented rate precisely during this period. Two high-points stand out in this: the preparation of the second Crusade and the time of the Pontificate of Innocent III at the beginning of the 13th century.

In the preparations for the second Crusade, all the elements of practical experience which had been acquired, sometimes by chance, in the preceding years were given a systematic basis summarized as a directive which applied to all participants. The proclamation by Eugene III of 1146 expressly granted the Crusade indulgence to all those who took part in it, extended the protection of the Church from the start to all the dependents and property of the Crusaders and clarified their financial problems by stating that no interest was to be charged for loans made to Crusaders. In the arguments put forward for taking the Cross, two lines of approach were evident. On the one hand, there was the appeal to the feeling of tradition. In the sermons preached in favour of the Crusade in particular, no effort was spared in lauding the meritorious deeds of the fathers and in stressing the duty of the sons to emulate them. There is no doubt that this had a very strong impact on many sons and grandsons. The second approach put a new accent in the motivation for the Crusade. It was asserted that Edessa had been lost by the great sinfulness of the Christian world. Atonement could be made to God by a Crusade and remission of sins would be obtained. This concept had its roots in the mysticism of the 12th century and was derived from it. Humility and penitence were the principal elements of piety which opened the way to God who would forgive the meek their sins. It was no accident that the Cistercian Abbot St Bernard of Clairvaux, the leading representative of this mysticism, gladly accepted the command to preach the Crusade. A powerful speaker, these were the arguments that he used: "The Earth is on the move because the Lord in Heaven has begun to lose his land... Has the hand of the Lord been cut off or become weak that he appeals to pitiful little worms to protect his part of the Earth and to return it to him?... I say unto you, God is testing you... What is it then but a matter of salvation, chosen and invented by God alone, when the Almighty privately reminds murderers, adulterers, perjurers and those arrested for other misdeeds, together with those who acted righteously, of His service... He wishes to be the debtor so that he can pay the wages of those who fight for him, forgiveness of sins and eternal glory." This change in emphasis was retained in the following centuries, too and, since it was so significant, was taken up by the critics of the Crusade movement and the message reversed.

There was no change in the essential nature of the Crusade movement but it did take on a more military character. In 1096, it was still the simultaneous timing of the expansions which caused Urban II to bar the way to Jerusalem for the Catalans whereas Bernard of Clairvaux framed the call in such broad terms that the expansion of the Saxon feudal lords in the East could be accommodated without difficulty. Since the Saxon nobility refused to set out for the Orient on the grounds that there were peoples practising paganism, St Bernard is reported by Otto of Freising to have granted them the privileges of the Crusade for a campaign against the Slavs. "Baptism or death!" was the infamous slogan which accompanied the Crusade against the Obodrites in 1147. With this, the idea of the Crusade was given an accent tailored for the specific situation. In its social implications, the battle-cry "Baptism or death!" really meant "Feudalization or death!". Conversion by force was the specific form in which the rule of the Saxon nobility was extended. Even though the Crusade against the Wends met with failure, this was nevertheless a momentous event. The idea of a religious war against the heathens caught on and became the theoretical basis for the "missions" to the Slav peoples. These "missions" reached a sad climax in the 13th century when the Teutonic Knights established themselves in the land of the Pruzzi and carried on their cruel "conversion of the heathens".

For other feudal lords, too, the proclamation of 1146 was only an excuse for participating in feudal expansion under the banner of Christ and with the blessing of the Church. English and Flemish nobles took part in the Reconquista and, among other cities, captured Lisbon, everything taking place under the sign of the Cross and with the attributes of a Crusade.

The unexpected outcome of the fourth Crusade prompted Pope Innocent III once again to devote all his zeal to the promotion of the Crusade movement. A sharp tone was the keynote on this occasion and there was practically no change in the arguments employed. The call was addressed to everybody although in actual fact it was the knights for whom the Pope's words were intended. Central offices were established in many dioceses to win over the knights for this undertaking. The preachers of the Crusade were provided with specially selected literature, the "books of letters", as they were called, containing all the arguments in favour of the Crusade and in connection with organizational questions. A hectic atmosphere was organized. In France, the legate Robert de Courson distributed crosses to children, old men, women,

blind persons and lepers. There were similar tendencies in other regions.

The ecstasy fanned by the Papal legates reached a macabre climax in the Children's Crusade of 1212. Contemporary accounts report that the following events took place. In the region around Cologne and Southern Lorraine, children and teenagers up to about 18 years of age came together and followed a boy by the name of Nicholas on a journey to the Holy Land. They are said to have numbered twenty thousand but the sources are very unreliable and doubtlessly exaggerate a great deal. Nicholas wanted to lead them there by the overland route. They crossed the Alps on their way to the South. It is said that a fairly large group reached Genoa and others Pisa. Individual children got as far as Brindisi. There is evidence that some young people begged Pope Innocent III to release them from their vow but it was only in few cases that he granted their request.

At the same time as this undertaking, it is reported that young people assembled in France with the same idea in mind. Led by a boy by the name of Stephen, who asserted he was sent by God, they walked to Marseilles to find ships to take them across the sea on their way to Jerusalem. It is not known what happened to them after this.

The accounts of the Children's Crusade are not very precise at all and, since they understandably aroused the emotions of the people, they included tendencious elements. Opinions were divided from the beginning. Some of the advocates of the Crusade among the clergy were not displeased to see children marching forth since this stimulated people's feelings about the matter. Innocent III and his advisors welcomed this development as a means of shaming the grown-ups. On the other hand, it also met with opposition. The official acting on behalf of the King of France was able to disperse several groups and the populations of several cities stopped the children from continuing their march. Despite all this information, it cannot be assumed that only children took part in this expedition. It is likely that they only formed a part of it and were used as an ideological front, guaranteeing the success of the venture by virtue of their innocence. It seems to have resembled the Peasants' Crusade in its basic structure, though a great deal of activity and energy was not apparent. The column from the Rhineland disintegrated when it had only got as far as Italy. Many of the children found a home in the Italian cities. Of those who reached Marseilles, many were sold as slaves, five ships full of them arriving in ports of North Africa and Egypt. For these, the slave markets were the end of the road. Viewed as a whole, the Children's Crusade is one of the many examples of the horrifying consequences of religious fanaticism.

Let us return, however, to the question of the organization of the propaganda for the Crusade. To make sure that the Crusade was adequately prepared, Innocent III established a system of various measures which had a profound effect on the Crusade movement and its ideology in the period that followed.

The Curia needed money for financing the undertaking. Many of those taking part in the Crusade were not able to pay for their equipment themselves. The vigorous development of a money economy in Europe had created new conditions of which the Papacy endeavoured to take account. For material provisions, a Crusade tax was raised on all the estates owned by the Church and placed at the disposal of the Papacy. An innovation of even greater importance was the principle that the equipping of a substitute was equivalent to taking the Cross and carried the same rights. This meant that the vow to take part in the Crusade could be fulfilled by the payment of money instead. There seem to have been many cases where substitutes accepted the money but never went to the Orient since it was not long before they were required to bring back confirmation from the knightly orders that they had completed their task. This was no longer compatible with the ideal of the Crusader preached hitherto. To Innocent III, the solution seemed very obvious. In the Papal Bull of the Crusade, it is said "For we hope with certainty that there will be no lack of men when there is no lack of money."

This marked the end of the original Crusade movement and its ideology from this aspect, too. Adapted to the new conditions, the distorted organization of the Crusade opened the way to every kind of political ambition. The tax originally intended to help poor Crusaders soon became a permanent institution and filled the coffers of the Papacy. The Papal fiscal system prospered and the Order of Knights Templar became the unscrupulous treasurer of the Curia. Already under Innocent III and even more in the time of his successors, these funds were used to promote the concept of Papal universalism, as in the struggle with Frederick II, in the crushing of the uprising of the Stedinger peasants or the Crusade against the Albigensians in Southern France.

The temporal lords were no better in this respect. By taking the vow to participate in the Crusade, they obtained possession of the tax and used it to strengthen their financial basis, only deciding to go on the Crusade very much later, if at all. Henry III of England (1216–1272) had the tax placed at his disposal several times but a Crusade was never organized. King Haakon of Norway (1240–1263) did exactly the same three times, too.

From the early days under Urban II up to the 13th century, numerous revisions were made to the Crusade propaganda organized by the Papacy but it always remained the instrument of economic and political interests. The influence of Innocent III caused the Crusade idea to become a specific ideology of feudal expansion. The conquest of Byzantium, a Christian state, under the sign of the Cross was followed by deliberate propaganda for a Crusade in the Southern French county of Toulouse. The murderous campaign which has gone down in history as the Albigensian Crusades (1209–1229) was initially directed against the followers of the Cathari heresy who were extremely numerous in this region. Since the Crusaders, mostly nobles from the North of France, were neither in a position nor prepared to make detailed investigations, brutality was rife. It is said that the Papal legate urged on hesitant Crusaders with the words "Kill them all, the Lord will recognize his own." Thus, at the beginning of the campaign, seven thousand inhabitants of Béziers were slaughtered, their town plundered and set on fire. The result of the Crusade was that a culturally prospering Southern French district lay in ruins in the hands of its conquerors with the political advantage passing to the kingdom of France since, as a result of the confiscations which took place, it had a firm footing on the Mediterranean for the first time. However, there was no direct connection between the result and the events which had initially led to the campaign.

In Germany (the Holy Roman Empire), the risings of the Stedinger peasants against the feudal repression of the Archbishop of Bremen were crushed by a Crusade organized with the permission of the Curia. In this case, too, the nobles recruited from North-West Germany, Flanders and Holland laid waste the countryside under the sign of the Cross.

The adaptation of the Crusade idea and its practical organization to the interests of the Curia at that time did not fail to leave a mark on the concepts of the Crusade which were held by the nobility. There was no evidence of a firmly established ideology along these lines in the knightly armies of the first Crusade. The 12th and 13th centuries brought about a complete change. This was the heyday of courtly culture and chivalry in Europe which was based on the development of the economic and political power of the knightly class and had an influence on the whole of society. Above all, the "ideal of chivalry" was formulated in numerous lays, sayings and epics. Standards, customs and habits were evolved and propagated and knights were expected to conform to them. Troubadours spread these ideas throughout the land and all aspects of knightly life were influenced by them. There were many factors which contributed to the evolution of the "perfect knight", some of these originated in the Orient.

A firm part of courtly poetry was the confrontation with the Crusade idea. Very many poets of the age of chivalry expressed their opinions on this subject. Pilgrimage and Crusade songs were written, the subject appeared in epic poems and even the great names of the literature of the time devoted much of their work to the Crusades. Walther von der Vogelweide composed several sayings and songs about the Crusades and Wolfram von Eschenbach set out his views in his epic poem "Willehalm". The general view was that Crusades were a part of chivalry. Walther von der Vogelweide urged the knight to take part in the Crusade since he possessed suitable weapons for it: ". . . dar an gedenket, ritter: ez ist iuwer dinc. ir tragent die lichten helme und manegen herten rinc, dar zuo die vesten schilte und diu gewihten swert." (Don't forget, Knights, that it is your task. It is you who have

the bright helmets and many a strong armour, the solid shields and the consecrated swords.) The subject was explained in every possible variation. Christian humility was important as an essential condition, as was the simple behest to free the Holy Sepulchre. "If the Holy Cross freed you, then free the Holy Cross with the sword" was the demand made in a Crusade song in Latin dating from the second half of the 12th century. Anyone who broke his vow to take part in the Crusade is the subject of moral scorn. "Accursed be he and all who do not say 'Fie!' . . . Now ye will lead a life in shame for ye did not wish to die freely for God. Ye will now be counted among the cowards"—this is how a French song of the same period reviles a knight who broke his promise. The general opinion was clear; at least until the beginning of the 13th century. The idea of the pilgrimage under arms was propagated. The knights accepted it and regarded it as a part of their life. The Christian virtues were joined by an element of tradition. It had become customary to take the Cross. In this, the knight did not see himself as a fierce soldier of God, aflame with religious zeal; it was rather considered as something which everybody did.

Although there was agreement with Papal propaganda for the Crusades in the basic orientation, an intimate identification of the spirit of chivalry with Christendom, there were definite discrepancies in other respects. This was especially apparent in relation to the Islamic warrior: "Slay him for his different faith" plays almost no part at all in chivalrous poetry. The fierce but honourable combat took priority. The antagonist was a knight who was assumed to have all the virtues that a knight should have. Much space is devoted to this theme in Wolfram von Eschenbach's "Willehalm", for example, where, before the combat of the Christian knight with the "heathen" Matribleiz, both are considered equals as regards the courtly idea of the "perfect knight". Willehalm's superiority is due to the Christian faith alone. In the poem "The Crusade of Ludwig the Pious of Thuringia", the author stresses that Moslem and Christian knights are separated only "durch den gelouben, durch niht mêr" (only by their faith, by nothing more). And once victory is won, he mourns the many courageous Saracens who have been slain.

This appreciation of the adversary reflects the actual military events. Not only in the actual Crusader states but also in the battles which took place in the course of the Crusades at the end of the 12th and the beginning of the 13th centuries, a form of warfare predominated in which the adversary was respected as a human being.

To begin with, the newcomers in the Crusader states were still shocked at the mutual tolerance displayed by Christians and Saracens. They accused the Crusaders of the Holy Land of attaching more importance to the defence of the rich coastal regions than to the protection of Jerusalem. They were angry about the truces and treaties with Moslem princes and they asserted that in the Crusader states self-interest took priority over the affairs of Christ. In short, they wanted a "Holy War". The background to this attitude was the greed for booty which could only be acquired through war.

However, a change soon took place in this attitude. Moslems were treated as chivalrous foes, as amply demonstrated by the confrontations with Saladin during the third Crusade. It was known in Europe that Saladin had acted in a very humane manner towards the Crusaders at the capture of Jerusalem and had agreed to allow the Christians to withdraw in return for ransom money. Chivalrous gestures of this kind were recorded only in the accounts of the meetings between Richard Cœur de Lion and Saladin. During the siege of Acre, Saladin had fruit and confectionery sent to the English king, who had fallen ill. The latter responded to this by returning a prisoner. Saladin, in turn, allowed an elderly Crusader, who had been taken captive, to go free. Saladin's brother had two fresh horses sent to Richard during the battle. Even before this, during the siege of Acre by Saladin, the two enemies had had a friendly talk during a pause in the fighting. It is even said that Richard Cœur de Lion played with the idea of marrying his sister, Joan, to the brother of Saladin. Regardless of whether these accounts derive from fact or legend, they were widespread and helped in the development of an ideology.

Emperor Frederick II and Sultan Al-Kamil of Egypt exchanged gifts on several occasions during the fifth Crusade, these being brought by official envoys. In order to bring the negotiations on the return of Jerusalem to a conclusion, Frederick sent a letter to Al-Kamil in which he addressed him as his dear friend and explained that he needed Jerusalem if he were not to lose his authority in the eyes of the European princes. Neither the Pope nor the population of the Crusader states forgave him for being on such cordial terms with the enemy. When Frederick departed, he was bombarded with animal intestines by the butchers of Acre who had expected great military victories of him.

From the beginning of the 13th century, instances are reported where Saracens and Moslems dubbed each other as knights. Although this is to be considered as no more than an isolated gesture, it is nevertheless an indication of the widespread respect which the adversaries had for each other.

The hostilities were characterized by hard and sometimes brutal combats. Losses were often very severe and a series of atrocities are reported to have been committed by both sides. Richard Cœur de Lion is known to have had thousands of Moslem captives executed while Saladin personally decapitated some of his prisoners. At the capture of Damietta in 1219, the captives and inhabitants were massacred by the Crusaders. More examples of such actions could be quoted. Both sides tell repeatedly of prisoners being subjected to frightful mutilation. Some of the Crusaders were enslaved. Interestingly enough, it is only in rare cases that such brutalities are given a religious justification. They seem to have resulted from certain traditions rather than from the difference in creed. However, everything stated here as an illustration of the chivalrous Crusade ideology can only be understood in its correct relationship when the actual background is considered at the same time. Political motives dominated all the Crusades and were the decisive factor. Their leaders, in particular, never allowed themselves to be influenced by religious hysteria and always subordinated their Crusade to the overall political interests.

King Louis VII of France had already planned his Crusade of 1147 before Pope Eugene III issued his proclamation and was not at all inclined to take orders from Rome.

All three monarchs allowed themselves a great deal of time for the preparation of the third Crusade. Frederick Barbarossa needed several years to settle all the internal political problems. The English Crown was expected to equip an army for the Crusade already in the 1160's but hostilities with France delayed the undertaking until a settlement had been reached. There was no longer any trace of the spontaneity which characterized the first Crusade.

For political reasons, Emperor Frederick II waited several years before keeping his promise. He took the Cross in 1215 but did not set out for the Orient until 1228.

Louis the Saint likewise needed several years of preparation. Other rulers did not fulfil their vow at all in the 13th century.

None of them displayed any religious fervour at all and at most were only complying with a traditional duty and a desire to help the hard-pressed Crusaders in the Orient, whose families were still living in Europe for the most part.

In the final analysis, the majority of the knights followed their liege-lord—assuming that they had no direct interest in the Crusader states by virtue of their relatives there or did not want to join the knightly orders—in a military undertaking like any other.

The inclusion of the Crusade movement in the ideology of chivalry had to lead, sooner or later, to a critical confrontation. In actual fact, rejection of it was always apparent, as demonstrated by the refusal to take the vow to participate in a Crusade, by the failure to keep the promise given or by the premature abandoning of armed pilgrimages. From the beginning of the 13th century, there was an increase in the verbal and written dissent within the ruling class to such an extent that it took the form of an intellectual movement.

Primarily, there were two main reasons for this: the failures of the Crusades and the development of the organization of the Crusades by Innocent III. Time and again, their contemporaries asked themselves why God had not looked favourably on the Christian knights in the Orient. Where the blame was to be sought had already been indicated by Bernard of Clairvaux—in the sins of the Christians. In contrast to the 12th century, however, the fire of criticism was not directed against temporal lords but against the Papacy itself. The decisions taken by Innocent III met with the sharpest opposi-

tion and the financial manipulations especially caused great dissatisfaction. Greed and deceit were the words used for Rome. It was said that the Papacy was to blame for the lack of success, Greek Orthodox and Catholic Christians had been kept apart and the Saracens spared. For Walther von der Vogelweide, the introduction of the Crusade tax was incompatible with his ideal of the Crusade: "Sagt an, hêr Stoc hat iuch der babst her gesendet, daz ir in rîchet und uns Tiutschen ermet unde pfendet" (Say, this box (i.e., for the Crusade tax contributions) has been sent to you by the Pope so that we Germans pledge ourselves again) was his reaction. In the "Money Evangelium", a parody written about 1200, the author puts these words in the Pope's mouth: "Love silver and gold with all thy heart and soul and the rich as thee thyself."

The use of Crusade money for military expenditure in Europe angered the people of the time. French troubadours criticized the Pope for using indulgence money for a Crusade against the Albigensians in Southern France. The words of the priest Mathieu of Paris were sober enough: "The faithful were astonished that the same complete indulgence of all sins was granted for the spilling of both Christian and infidel blood."

The situation became even more serious when the massive criticism of the Pope's Crusade policy became linked with the quarrel between the Papacy and Frederick II, the Holy Roman Emperor. The ruling class was now split into two commanding factions.

In addition to the anti-clerical criticism, it was also doubted that there was divine support for armed pilgrimages. Walther von der Vogelweide asks the archangels: "Was habet ir der heiden noch zerstoeret? sit iuch nieman siht noch niemen hoerst, sagens, waz hant ir noch dar zuo getan?" (What injury have you caused the heathens since nobody sees or hears you, say, what have you done?) Impressed by the constant failures, a Knight Templar wrote the following in the middle of the 13th century: "Verily, when God doth approve all that which should displease Him, then indeed we must be content with our lot. He who goes to war against the Turks is therefore a complete fool since God allows them everything." The mood of the time expressed the total lack of confidence in the omnipotence of God propagated by the Church. It was openly questioned whether Islam might not be the better religion after all and whether the Crusade was worthwhile in any respect. The individual complaints were very specific but the general opinion of many knights was probably expressed by a poem of Southern Italian origin composed about 1220: "The Cross is the salvation of humanity but it sends me astray." The Crusader ideology was starting to disintegrate by the beginning of the 13th century. The ruling class no longer needed feudal expansion in the sense of the 11th century, either. With the economic prosperity of the 12th and 13th centuries and the necessary development of political power associated with this, the knights began to concentrate on these tasks to an increasing extent.

The critical confrontation with the Crusade movement and, in particular, with the Church which had now become wealthy was not restricted to discussions within the ruling class. There was a remarkable increase in the opposition of ordinary people, of the peasants and artisans, to the wealthy and immoral clergy, particularly in the economically advanced districts of Northern Italy, France, Flanders and the Rhineland in the course of the 12th and 13th centuries. Movements extolling poverty became widespread and their adherents consciously dissociated themselves from the wealthy Church and regarded apostolic poverty as their ideal. Heretic doctrines and their advocates found a ready reception among the common people. Many subscribed to the heresy of the Cathari while the sect of the Waldenses emerged as a rapidly spreading mass-movement. A series of popular movements and numerous contemporary dissidents adopted the arguments of the critics of the Crusade ideology, this being most apparent in connection with the uprising of the Pastoureaux (shepherds) in 1251. This was essentially a peasants' revolt with its centre in North-Eastern France. A preacher by the name of Jacques appeared on the scene here and announced that the Virgin Mary had commanded the people, through him, to free the Holy Sepulchre. He said that the knights were too proud and arrogant for God to favour them. This was a clear reference to the Crusade of Louis IX who was taken captive in Egypt in 1250. God would give his protection only to the people. It

was his, Jacques', mission to carry out the divine command. The movement spread rapidly and the Pastoureaux moved southwards from Amiens, Rouen, Paris, Orléans, Bourges, Limoges and Bordeaux in the direction of Marseilles. More and more new followers joined them. The numbers quoted range from twenty thousand to a hundred thousand participants and, though exaggerated, convey an idea of the mass-character of the movement.

The Pastoureaux owed their popularity and the support they received to the anti-clerical leaders of their movement. In their sermons, they called the priests by such names as loafers and hypocrites and accused them of being covetous, avaricious and slaves of lust. They were not content with simply preaching this but in various cities and monasteries they also made direct attacks on priests and persecuted them.

For the Pastoureaux, the Church was no longer necessary. They blessed the people, granted absolution and gave the Cross to their followers. The Pastoureaux were crushed by armies of knights which had rapidly been assembled for the purpose.

This movement was essentially a peasants' uprising, directed against the increased degree of exploitation under the conditions of the expansion in commodity-money relations. Many peasants were impoverished and had lost much of their land. Emerging for objective reasons from the consequences of pauperization, the criticism of the Crusade movement and the clergy met with such a popular echo that it became the main substance of the ideology of the Pastoureaux movement.

Holy Wars and the conversion of the heathens by force could not really be equated with the character of Christianity so that the solution which the knights found with their recognition of the Moslem feudal lords as worthy and equal adversaries was not the only form of rejection.

Even in the first phase of expansion, religious tolerance had never been totally abandoned in the military and political actions. It is only necessary to recall the life led in the Crusader states themselves and even in Europe there was never a total absence of criticism. Thus in a minstrel's epic of the 12th century the defeated "heathen" says, "an dinen got geloube ich niht wie halt mir darumbe geschiht" (whatever happens

17 *Development of shield designs*
The early Middle Ages were dominated by the round shield but from the 11th century the almond-shaped long shield, designed to protect the left side of the rider from head to knee, came into increasing use. It was probably the better protection of the head (heaume) that led to the shield becoming smaller and triangular in shape at the end of the 12th century

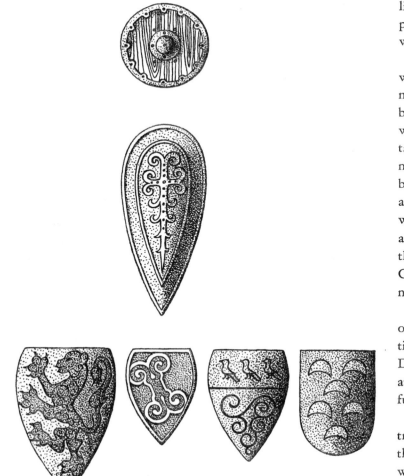

to me, I do not believe in your god). The Christian knight then endeavours to demonstrate the superiority of God but does not kill his prisoner, even when the latter remains stubborn. This element appears time and again in the courtly epics of the time, despite the fact that the Papacy insisted on intolerance.

A change in the ecclesiastical attitude occurred at the beginning of the 13th century when the call for peaceful conversion became an intellectual movement. St Francis of Assisi (1182–1226) played an influential part in this. As the founder of the Franciscan Order (1210) which had emerged from the poverty movement, St Francis was already a legendary figure in his own lifetime. Powerful religious persuasion emenated from him and his practice of apostolic poverty and evangelism met with an enthusiastic response from the ordinary people at a time when criticism of the wealth of the Church was at its most virulent.

It was the desire of St Francis of Assisi to fight for God with peaceful means. The lack of success of the Crusade movement made a great impact on him and he sought the solution by renouncing the use of force. In 1219, he set out for Egypt where an army of the fifth Crusade was laying siege to Damietta. It was his aim to convert the Sultan to Christianity but, naturally enough, he was unsuccessful in this. The meeting between the two is wrapt in legend. It is said that he met with a friendly reception from the Sultan who offered him gifts which he declined. He was permitted to preach to the Sultan and his retinue. St Francis asked to be allowed to pass through the ordeal of fire in order to demonstrate the omnipotence of God but the Sultan rejected his request with the remark that no Islamic priest would go through fire for his faith.

This encounter was important since henceforth the idea of the peaceful mission became an integral part of the activities of the Franciscan Order and, not long afterwards, of the Dominicans, too. At about the same time, the Franciscans attempted to convert Moslems in Tunis but were not successful, either. Five monks suffered a martyr's fate in Morocco.

Soon afterwards, the two Orders set up missionary centres in Palestine. Only a little later monks began to concern themselves with the languages and civilizations of peoples who were to be converted to Christianity.

The Popes of the 13th century were shrewd enough to incorporate the missionary fervour of the poor monks in their Crusade policy. Monks were sent on behalf of the Papacy to individual sultans with messages urging them to adopt Christianity.

Missionary activity and the furtherance of the Crusade policy were combined in the efforts to win the Mongols as allies against the Egyptian sultans and, at the same time, to convert them to Christianity.

The Mongol Empire, which had emerged in the first half of the 13th century after a mighty campaign of conquest under the leadership of Genghis Khan, had brought about a basic change in the political map of Asia. China, Central Asia, Southern Siberia, Persia, Mesopotamia, Transcaucasia, the region along the lower reaches of the Volga and parts of the Rus of Kiev had been subjugated by the nomadic Mongol tribes in only two decades. Syria was part of the area in which they had a military interest. It was only in 1260 that their ambitions were ended by a crushing defeat at the hands of the Egyptians. The Papacy speculated on an alliance with the Mongols since it was known that they had a tolerant attitude towards religion and that numerous Nestorian Christians held offices of high rank in their administration and possessed influence.

In 1245, Innocent IV sent Franciscans headed by Joannes de Plano Carpini to the Mongols. Louis IX of France tried to develop a system of alliances in 1253 and he despatched the monk William of Rubruk with offers to this effect. Further delegations followed.

All these efforts failed and the Mongols rejected both the offers of alliance and the attempts of the monks to convert them. The accounts of the monks are interesting for the insight they convey of the way in which negotiations were carried out between peoples of very different backgrounds in the 13th century and of the arguments used to persuade them to become Christians.

William has the following to say about the reception given to him by Batu, the Khan of the Golden Horde: "We were taken to the middle of the tent ... He studied us attentively and we did the same ... At last, he commanded me to speak. Our escort then told me to kneel and speak. I knelt on one knee as before a human being but he indicated to me that I should kneel on both knees, which I did so as not to quarrel. Then he told me to speak ... I began with a prayer and said 'Merciful lord, we beg God who created you and gave you these worldly goods that He may afterwards give you heavenly wealth for without that these are vain.' He listened to me carefully and I continued: 'But know for certain that you will not enjoy the wealth of heaven if you are not a Christian. It is namely said by God: He who believes in Me and is baptized shall be saved and he who does not believe will be damned!' At these words he began to smile and the others began to applaud so as to mock us ..." When calm was restored again, the monk handed over the letters from Louis but the Mongols did not accept the offers they contained. The Franciscans also soon noticed that Moslem envoys and merchants were received with more interest than they had been.

Nevertheless, the journeys by the monks were important and they opened the way to Asia, to a world hitherto unknown to Western Europe. Within a short time, the merchants of Northern Italy followed in the footsteps of the Franciscans.

As with the concept of the Crusade, there was a significant change in the structure of the armies of the Crusaders after the first campaign.

Due to the unreliability of the mediaeval chroniclers to which reference has already been made, we have no accurate knowledge about the numerical strength of the individual armies. It is reported that 70,000 men each were led by Louis VII and Conrad III on the march to the Orient. The old chronicles state that the army of Barbarossa on the third Crusade, doubtlessly one of the most powerful of them all, numbered 100,000 men. This evidence may be greatly exaggerated but the transportation by ship, which was organized by the cities of Northern Italy, presents a more detailed picture. The French army of the third Crusade crossed the sea in ships provided by the Genoese. The contract specified the conveyance of 650 knights and 1,300 squires, plus the same number of horses. The army of Richard Cœur de Lion, which was carried by the English fleet, needed one hundred merchant ships and twenty warships. It is estimated that it consisted of about 1,200 knights and many times that number of foot-soldiers. For the fourth Crusade, a contract was concluded with Venice for the transportation of 4,500 knights, 9,000 squires and 20,000 foot-soldiers. In actual fact, however, only 1,000 knights, 4,000 squires and 8,000 foot-soldiers appeared. The figures for the fifth Crusade are again very vague, especially as numerous individual actions took place during the long time from 1218 to 1228. Louis IX is said to have undertaken his first Crusade to Damietta with 25,000 Frenchmen.

Despite all their inaccuracy, the figures clearly show that the entire body of knights of Western Europe was involved in the Crusade movement for generations. There could scarcely have been a single family that did not take part in it, particularly when it is considered that in the periods between the principal Crusades numerous smaller expeditions were organized, such as the campaigns of 1101, the Crusade of Henry the Lion in 1172, the only military expedition which did not fight in the Crusader states since their relations with other states were relatively good at that time, or the Crusade led by Emperor Henry VI in 1197. The awareness of tradition of the knights of Western Europe derived from a well-developed military practice.

The expeditions to the Orient were organized as military operations covering a long period of time. The baggage trains were of considerable size. Equipment, tents, provisions, war material, personal belongings and so on were carried in waggons hauled by oxen and sometimes by horses. The knights were accustomed to having at least two mounts at their disposal. Some of the provisions and equipment was purchased locally by the Crusaders on the way or simply stolen. As in the past, plunder was part of the recognized spoils of war. Byzantium was compelled to make payments to the crusading armies on a number of occasions.

It is difficult to imagine how colourful these baggage trains must have been. Apart from the actual military contingent plus the servants and maids for the personal attendance of the knights, each army was accompanied by a substantial number of pilgrims, adventurers, prostitutes, criminals and so on. The leaders of the Crusades were repeatedly obliged to issue orders restraining this element which was a hindrance for the actual military objectives. Calls were issued time and again to the Crusaders not to take women and old men with them and to reduce the number of non-combatants. This appears to have been best achieved on the third Crusade when the command of the expedition was firmly in the hands of the kings. When the army embarked in Venice for the fourth Crusade, the non-combatants were simply left behind.

From the end of the 12th century, the crusading armies displayed an increasing preference for the sea-route to the Orient. The fleets of the Italian cities, Sicily and the French cities of the Mediterranean were capable of carrying out this task. This method of transportation was unavoidable when Egypt was viewed as the military objective. The journey to the Orient was not rendered any safer by this. Although they largely kept to coastal waters, ships repeatedly foundered in storms or were attacked by pirates for whom the fighting knights were no match on board ship.

From the end of the 12th century, the custom began of paying the Crusaders, the practical and moral effects of which have already been discussed. Even in the first Crusades, it had been customary for the princes not only to meet the needs of their direct retinue from time to time but also to give financial and material support to the poorer knights and this was to become official practice in later Crusades. In 1097, Emperor Henry VI equipped an army of 1,500 knights and the same number of squires. He paid each knight 30 ounces of gold and each squire 10, plus allowance of grain. This was in return for one year of service for the Crusade. Henry took care that the Byzantine emperor more than made up for these expenses by the gifts which he forced from him. When in 1204 the Crusaders were unable to pay the cost of the passage to Egypt, they practically became mercenaries of Venice and captured Zara in return for the costs of transportation. In the 13th century, it became customary for the Crusaders to be paid from the Crusade tax which was also used to cover the cost of equipment and other military expenditure. According to legend, Louis IX of France is said to have taken forty beasts of burden loaded with gold on the sixth Crusade for the payment of his troops. At first sight, the practice of paying for military service seems understandable. It is known that not only the foot-soldiers but also many of the feudal lords were not in any position to pay for their equipment from their own pocket. The emergence of the Crusade as a traditional warlike expedition in the service of the feudal lord thus becomes clear. For many of the knights in the armies of Frederick Barbarossa, Philip II Augustus, Richard Cœur de Lion or Emperor Frederick II, for instance, the march to the Orient was practically no more than a change in the theatre of war. As before, numerous Crusaders remained in the Orient of course, and in particular reinforced the knightly Orders established there.

Military equipment, strategy and tactics and the composition of the military potential developed in approximately the same direction as in the Crusader states themselves. The knights resident in the Orient participated in the military actions and in this way the experience acquired in specific battles was passed on. Two elements of military tactics in particular appear to be characteristic: the deliberate inclusion of the infantry in all phases of fighting and the systematic direction of major operations, including the adoption of tactics developed by the Moslems, such as the preparation of ambushes, the simulation of flight and so on. The principal innovation was the combined use of knights and foot-soldiers.

The following examples of tactics convey some idea of the form of warfare which was used. In September 1191, a pitched battle took place between the troops of Saladin and the army of Richard Cœur de Lion at Arsuf. The objective of the Crusaders was to push forward from Acre along the coast, which still offered the best protection, in a southerly direction to create an operational basis for an attack on Jerusalem. Saladin sought to prevent this by forcing Richard Cœur de Lion to do battle. This occurred at Arsuf. The tactics of the Crusaders in marching order proved to be of decisive importance for the outcome of the battle. The army of knights was placed in deeply staggered formation in the centre of the columns. Foot-soldiers armed with crossbows protected the flanks and were also responsible for the baggage train. Despite heavy losses, the infantry could repulse Saladin's mounted archers to such an extent that they were only

able to strike at individual parts of the army of knights. A Moslem eye-witness noted that the coats of mail and thick felt jackets of the foot-soldiers afforded very good protection against arrows. The knights, on the other hand, were harder hit since their mounts were shot away from underneath them by the archers. When the knights launched an attack and Saladin responded by directing his reserves against the baggage train, it was again the foot-soldiers who provided the principal defence until the knights came to their aid. Saladin's army was defeated primarily as the result of the part played by the infantry.

Similar tactics can be observed in other battles, too, but the army of knights and the foot-soldiers were always used in combination with each other. When the material situation of the crusading army deteriorated at Acre in 1190, the foot-soldiers launched an independent attack on Saladin's camp with the intention of plundering it but were thrown back with crushing losses.

The increased importance of the foot-soldiers is clearly apparent from the sieges, the principal form of confrontation between the Crusaders and the Moslem armies. This may be illustrated by examples taken from the struggle for Damietta, a major seaport with a variety of defences. Situated in the Nile delta with a triple wall around it, it proved difficult to cut it off from the outside world completely since the arms of the Nile constituted a natural obstacle over considerable distances. A watch-tower was located outside the city walls on an island and an iron chain spanned between this tower and the city wall denied access to the harbour. Foot-soldiers, mainly from Cologne, Friesland and Flanders, constructed two siege-towers which were ferried across on ships and facilitated the storming of the defences. This coup de main made such a mighty impact that when the Frisian, Flemish and Cologne troops announced that they had done enough and now wanted to return home, they were permitted to do so. This is also evidence of the greater independence of the foot-soldiers within the army.

When Louis IX laid siege to Damietta in 1250, his reserves of manpower were so great that he toyed with the idea of draining a part of the arm of the Nile. For this purpose alone, he had two wooden towers, eighteen ballistae and other defensive works built for the protection of the men working there. The Egyptians replied with sixteen ballistae and catapults and they also hurled missiles wich were filled with Greek fire which most effectively thwarted the work of the besiegers.

These examples are representative of many other actions and demonstrate how the Crusaders adapted to the specific problems of warfare in the Orient.

A particular characteristic of the Crusader armies were the constant rivalries between the individual military units and also the differences with the knights of the Crusader states. There were many reasons for this. From the military viewpoint, the reluctance to submit to a superior command played a part in this. The feudal armies in Europe were accustomed to fighting independently in fairly small groups and it was difficult to break with this tradition. There was often opposition between the political and military concepts of the Crusader states and those of the Crusader armies—reason enough

for irritation to develop into serious hostility, as occurred during the second Crusade, for instance when the knights of the Crusader states sabotaged the siege of Damascus. A major element in the differences and friction between the two groups was the fight for the lion's share of the plunder which influenced the course of military operations in a series of cases and was even the cause of quarrels after victory had been achieved. After the capture of Damietta in 1219, for example, the individual armies spent weeks in search of plunder. Many a knight returned home with hard feelings because he considered he had not received his fair share.

The few remarks made by the chroniclers about the nature of the crusading armies confirm what has already been said about the development of the Crusade ideology. The principal interest was a military one. The great majority of the knights never even got near Jerusalem. The original objectives in the sense of expansion deteriorated into warlike undertakings which resulted in heavy losses and no apparent prospect of success.

The Commercial Expansion of Northern Italian Cities

While it was becoming increasingly apparent to those directly concerned in it and to their contemporaries that the feudal Crusade movement could never achieve its aims and that the end was evidently not far off, the outlook for the Italian and Southern French merchants was becoming brighter and brighter in the very shadow of the military events. Even before the Crusades, the Northern Italian cities in particular had shown a growing interest in the expansion of trade with Byzantium and the Orient and this interest had not ceased in 1096 but had become associated with the expansion of the feudal lords. The principal markets which interested them, Syria, Palestine, Egypt and Byzantium, were directly involved in the happenings of the Crusades in one way or another. The struggle for them emerged as a part of the Crusade movement and was not in opposition to European expansion, even if individual events convey this impression.

The trade with the Orient increased during the 12th century, this being mainly the result of relations with the Crusader states. There was a continuous chain of common interests, beginning with the support of the first Crusade by fleets from Genoa and Pisa, and including the granting of privileges to merchants in the major trade centres of the Crusader states and the constant supply of food and military equipment to the Crusaders. The development of communications by sea, the establishment of regular trade-routes and other achievements followed from this. The extent and quality of the merchandise imported and exported during the 12th century were largely determined by the trade carried on in the Crusader states. The expansion of the naval and mercantile fleets was directly related to the requirements of commerce and communications in these states. The fact that at the end of the 12th century the fleets of the Italian cities were capable of carrying the crusading armies to the Orient is evidence of the upswing in shipbuilding and Oriental trade. The Crusades and the conquests which resulted from them were an important stage in the development of Levantine trade for the merchants of Italy and France. Despite this evident interrelation, merchants were never prepared to subordinate their commercial interests to the feudal concept of the Crusades. Of course, citizens from the cities in question also took

the Cross, took part in the campaigns and, as participants in the Crusades, tried to establish themselves in Jerusalem, Acre and other cities but as a whole this was only of secondary importance. The principal form of commercial expansion was the obtaining of privileges by just these Italian and French cities.

The second sphere of interest in Oriental trade, Egypt, proved to be much more difficult to develop. For the European merchants, Egypt was a particularly worthwhile trade-partner not only on account of its indigenous products but even more because the trade routes from Africa, India and China ended here, bringing an indescribable galaxy of commodities of all kinds. Even in the 10th century, the Arab scholar Al-Kindi lists perfumes, spices, jewels and tools from China, Ceylon, Aden, Mecca and Medina and silk, brocade, coral, saffron, furs, iron, copper, silver, lead, tin and timber from Syria, Constantinople, Cyprus, Rhodes and Western Europe, all of which could be bought in Egypt. There had been no decline in the variety of merchandise offered by the time of the 12th century. The Egyptians, too, were interested in trading with the European merchants. Timber for ships, pitch, weapons, various metals and tools were imports for which there was a vigorous demand. Thus there was no relaxation in the efforts to stimulate commerce during the whole of the 12th century, either. Egypt was nonetheless the principal adversary of the Crusader states. For the Italian cities, this necessitated the development of two alternative policies. On the one hand, they supported the thrusts forward of the kings of Jerusalem into Egypt in return for the promise of trading stations in the ports on the Nile. On the other, they established direct contacts with the rulers of Egypt, the Fatimids and, after 1171, with the Ayyubids as well.

At the end of the 12th and the beginning of the 13th century, merchants from Pisa, Genoa, Venice, Amalfi and other cities were frequent visitors to Alexandria, Damietta and Cairo. Pisa and Venice, for instance, maintained permanent trading stations in Alexandria. The treaty of 1173 between Egypt and Pisa granted the Italians the right to set up a "fondaco" (Oriental trading post and warehouse) there and Venice and other cities soon did the same.

78 Emperor Frederick II of Hohenstaufen was one of the outstanding monarchs of mediaeval Europe although he played a rather fateful role in German history since it was during his reign that the princes of the Holy Roman Empire north of the Alps were granted decisive privileges at the expense of central state authority. His personal territory was in Sicily and Southern Italy. It was here that he shaped a modern state in which, despite harsh class rule, there was a place in society for Moslems, Jews and Orthodox and Catholic Christians alike. His participation in the Crusade did not stem from the influence of the Crusade ideology but primarily from the position of his empire in the critical area of the Mediterranean between Europe and the Islamic Orient. Gold coin, diameter 15.5 mm; formerly in the Geldmuseum der Deutschen Reichsbank.

79 Emperor Frederick II set out in 1228/29 from Sicily in the direction of the Orient with a small but well-chosen force (knights and various units of foot-soldiers). The expedition, which was the subject of controversy at the time since Frederick had been excommunicated by the Pope, was a success since negotiations led to the return of Jerusalem to the Crusader states. Despite this, it did not win the approval of the Papacy since Frederick, as a political adversary of Rome, was never prepared to defend the interests of the Curia. Burgerbibliothek, Berne

80   Castel del Monte was one of Frederick II's most famous hunting lodges. It was said by his Papal opponents that orgies took place here and that the Emperor maintained a harem.

81   The castle of Lucera in Apulia was built around 1233. It was near this fortress that Frederick II established settlements of Islamic peasants from Sicily. Although this was, strictly speaking, an internal affair, it did have another aspect, too, since the settlement was in the direct vicinity of the Papal State.

82 The tomb of Emperor Frederick II was not erected in the German Empire north of the Alps but there where he had grown up and where his policies had left clear marks—in Sicily, in Palermo Cathedral. His unusual policies and his continued attacks on the Papal Party resulted in the person of Frederick II being associated with the expected end of the world, an idea which had prevailed throughout the 13th century. Even during his lifetime and after his death as well, he was held to be the Anti-Christ whose activities or return would herald the Last Judgment. This belief which was propagated by Joachimite monks in particular, reached a climax in 1260, the year which had been predicted as the year of the Anti-Christ. This belief also spread to Germany but underwent a change in the following decades, being applied to Frederick Barbarossa as the last Holy Roman Emperor, whose return would mark the beginning of an era of peace, help for the poor and the emergence of a powerful empire.

83 In its interior decorations, fountains and Arabian mosaics, this palace, which was built in Sicily at the time of Frederick II, clearly bears the hall-mark of Islamic craftsmen.

84–103 From the very beginning, all the Crusader states were very active in the minting of coins. This was in accordance with tradition and was a result of the high standard of commodity production. As in other states, too, there was no standard currency of gold or silver. Gold and, to a certain extent still, silver coins were used for trading with the Islamic states whereas small coins (bronze) were used only for domestic trade. State Museums, Berlin, Numismatic Cabinet

Countship of Edessa,
Baldwin II (1100–1118);
bronze, 7.354 g

Countship of Edessa,
Baldwin II; bronze, 2.395 g

Principality of Antioch,
Tancred (1104–1112); bronze,
3.67 g

Principality of Antioch,
Bohemund IV (1201–1232);
silver, 0.961 g

Kingdom of Jerusalem
(Acre 1175), based on Arab
model; gold, 2.836 g

12th century coin of the
Crusader states. Imitation of
an Arab dinar; gold, 3.452 g

Kingdom of Jerusalem,
John of Brinne (1210–1237);
silver, 2.678 g

Countship of Tripoli,
Raymond III (1187–1200);
silver, 0.98 g

Principality of Antioch,
Bohemund IV and V;
silver, 4.25 g

Principality of Antioch,
Bohemund VII (1274–1282);
silver, 4.157 g

104 Mosaic ceiling of the Palazzo Reale in Palermo with the Hohenstaufen eagle between two griffins as a motif.

105 Byzantine influence also continued to be present in the buildings which have survived from the Norman period in Southern Italy. This is particularly apparent in the cupola mosaic of the Capella Palatina (Palermo).

These fondachi were complexes of buildings, the central one of which was not unlike a castle. They served as a warehouse and, at the same time, as a residence for the merchants who were usually not permitted to reside outside. The complex also included a large open area as a stockyard, gardens, a bath-house and sometimes a private church and other outbuildings. During the night and the principal Islamic hours of prayer, the fondaco was sealed off by Egyptian guards. The complex was administered by a consul who was responsible to the Egyptians for the behaviour of the merchants.

The permission granted to the merchants to establish living-quarters for their staff was linked to specific demands on the part of the Egyptians. In the treaty referred to, the merchants of Pisa were required to supply strategic materials such as iron, timber for shipbuilding, weapons and pitch. In times of peace, trading proceeded relatively smoothly on account of the mutual advantage derived from it. When the mother-countries of the merchants became involved in the Crusades, the merchants were imprisoned and their merchandise confiscated. After the struggle for Damietta from 1218 to 1221, the Genoese, Venetians and Pisans were expelled from Alexandria for the time being.

The Catholic Church was not strong enough to prevent these trading relations. It did indeed mobilize the provincial synods of Southern France and Italy and passed resolutions penalizing trade with Egypt and describing it as an outrage. Innocent III forbade the selling of strategic materials but none of this had any real effect. Pisa openly supplied Saladin with timber and weapons and Venice, with some justification, feared reprisals against its own merchants in Alexandria in 1202. This was one of the reasons why the fourth Crusade, which was originally directed against Egypt, was finally diverted against Byzantium.

The commercial policy of the Italian cities appears to have been at variance with the expansion in the Orient. Nevertheless, if it is compared with the military practices of the feudal lords, such as peace negotiations, the presentation of gifts, alliances and so on, the actions of the merchants were not so very different at all. In general, they follow the characteristic pattern of trading relations in the Middle Ages.

Wars could not prevent trade and only interrupted it at most, otherwise no trade at all would have been possible. If the princes maintained friendly relations with each other in times of peace, there was no reason why trade should not be carried on as well.

It will be appreciated that there were still disputes and even attacks which had a religious motivation. Phases of mistrust occurred again and again, especially when the crusading armies laid siege to Damietta at the beginning of the 13th century but in the history of this area of trade as a whole these were only shadows.

However, the decisive phase of the commercial expansion in the Eastern Mediterranean was initiated not by the struggle to obtain privileges in Egypt but by the conquest of the Byzantine market. This is linked with the events of the fourth Crusade between 1202 and 1204 which led to the storming of Constantinople and the establishment of the Holy Roman Empire on Byzantine territory.

Viewed from the basic configuration of power, the hostility towards Byzantium had been present for a long time, although the actual Crusade came as a surprise. Byzantium could not accept the fact that from the time of the first Crusade the military initiative in Syria and Palestine had been retained by the knights of Western Europe. All the attempts to build up mercenary armies had failed already by 1096, discord and mistrust being the consequence. This was noticed by Conrad III during the second Crusade. The anti-Byzantine feeling in the French army was so widespread that the possibility of attcking Constantinople was considered when it was learned that the Byzantine emperor had concluded a truce with the Seljuks of Iconium. On their way through the Byzantine Empire, Barbarossa's troops first of all met with a reserved reception but in the district of Philippopolis (Plovdiv) hostilities practically broke out, in the course of which the Crusaders devastated the area around the city. An attack on Constantinople was planned and the Italian seaports were asked to appear with a fleet before the walls of the capital.

However, the real initiative in deciding the marching route of the fourth Crusade came not from the crusading armies but from Venice. The Lagoon City had enjoyed important privileges in the Byzantine Empire and had been largely exempt from customs duties. These advantages had appeared in danger since the second half of the 12th century. The Venetian merchants had been repeatedly expelled from Byzantium and the Byzantine emperor had allowed Genoa and Pisa to open trading posts in various cities of the empire. This meant undesirable competition for Venice and by 1200 it looked as if it could only recover its former privileged position against the will of Byzantium.

The fourth Crusade itself conveys the impression of a grotesque succession of coincidences but essentially reflects a skilfully organized subordination to the aims of Venice which that city was not yet able to achieve by relying on its own resources. It was planned that Venice should take the Crusaders across the sea and should provide fifty warships to give support. The Crusaders, who had arrived in Venice, were unable to pay the price agreed. As an alternate form of payment, the Venetians suggested that the feudal lords capture of Zara on the coast of Dalmatia which, shortly before this, had

18/19   Increasing use was made of the sailing ship by the Venetians for the transportation of freight in the 13th century. Sketch from a miniature of the late Middle Ages; right: a reconstruction

freed itself from the rule of the Venetians. Thus a Crusader army moved against a Christian city, a city which belonged to the King of Hungary who was likewise preparing to take part in the Crusade. Zara was besieged, laid waste and plundered. This monstrous action—only some of the smaller groups in the army had refused to take part in it— aroused the displeasure of the Pope, it is true, but he soon cancelled the sentence of excommunication which he had pronounced. Alexios, the son of the deposed Byzantine Emperor Isaac, appeared in the camp and requested the Crusaders, on their journey to the Orient, to stop off in Constantinople and assist him to regain the throne. The armed pilgrims were promised riches as a reward.

Admittedly, voices of dissent were heard but in the end almost the entire army marched off in the direction of Constantinople. It was known as a rich city and the hope of booty outweighed all the misgivings. It seemed that Venice would achieve its most cherished wish and the Doge, Enrico Dandolo, emerged as the leading personality of the Crusade.

He spun the diplomatic threads and set the conditions which the army of knights, split up into several independent groups, had to accept. After a fairly prolonged period of disorder, the city was stormed for the second and last time in 1204, the programme for the crushing of the Byzantine state having already been prepared. The Crusaders had been able to inspect the city even before its final capture. They were impressed by the size of the metropolis, its gigantic fortified walls protecting it from attack on both the sea and the land sides, its numerous religious houses, its palaces, the city gates and the collections of gold and silver which were to be found everywhere. The plundering of the city lasted three days. Some idea of their barbaric behaviour is conveyed by the following account of an eye-witness to the scene: "In the morning they forced their way into the Church of St Sophia and, after the sun had risen, destroyed the choir which was ornamented with silver and twelve silver columns. They smashed four altar panels on the wall which were decorated with icons, the holy table and twelve crosses on the altar . . . The walls of the altar within the columns were of beaten silver. They also stole an admirable table set with precious stones and a great gem, without knowing what damage they were causing. They then took forty chalices which stood on the altar, together with silver candelabras whose number was so great that I could not count them, likewise silver vessels which the Greeks used for their most solemn celebrations. They took the Gospel Book which was used for celebrating the Mysteries and the holy cross with the images of Christ and the altar cloth and forty incense vessels of pure gold and everything of gold and silver which they could find . . ." This dramatic picture of the plundering of a church was no exception. All buildings containing objects of value such as churches, monasteries or palaces, were plundered. Reliquaries and gold and silver vessels were especially popular. This plundering was not a regrettable side-effect of conquest but was carried out in the shape of sytematic actions with the leaders of the Crusade taking the lion's share. A not insignificant part of the treasures of mediaeval Byzantine art to be found today in the museums and collections of Europe were originally acquired in the course of the plundering of 1204. Thus the nucleus of the Halberstadt Cathedral treasure,

for instance, was brought home from the fourth Crusade by Bishop Konrad of Krosigk in 1205. It included reliquaries, all with precious settings, such as a finger of St Nicholas, a thorn from the Crown of Thorns and a hair of the Blessed Virgin, a communion spatula and other precious vessels of gold and silver, reliquary boxes, likewise with costly ornamentation, and lengths of exquisite cloths. Other participants in the Crusade naturally took their share as well. The reliquaries alone "collected" by a French abbot included a trace of the Lord's blood, a piece of the true Cross of Christ, a part of the body of St John, an arm of St Jacob, a foot of St Cosmas, a tooth of St Lawrence, reliquaries from another twenty-eight male and eight female saints and pieces of stone from sixteen sanctuaries. It seemed to the Byzantines, the unwilling witnesses of this ferocious spectacle, that the European knights were the enemies of Christ. "Most of these fellows were still intoxicated from the wine which they had drunk from the communion chalices; and they ate mackerel from the platens used for Mass. They rode on donkeys draped with priests' robes and controlled the animals with reins made from surplices . . . Then came mules, loaded down with candles, candelabras, censers, incense vessels and holy water sprinklers."

In addition to the stolen objets d'art contributed by private persons, the collection of Byzantine art in St Mark's received donations from the city of Venice. To commemorate the victory, the famous quadriga, dating from the 6th century, was brought from Byzantium to Venice and placed in front of St Mark's Cathedral.

Constantinople, this wealthy city, never really recovered from the plundering of 1204, in the course of which a great number of precious books and documents were also destroyed. This meant that the evidence of a long historical development was lost to a large extent. Exquisite manuscripts disappeared from libraries. To those contemporaries who could assess the plundering in its true perspective it seemed that these events were disgraceful and unparallelled in the previous course of history.

Once Constantinople had been conquered, the next item on the agenda was the division of the empire. Once again, it was Venice in the person of the Doge, Enrico Dandolo, which had the main say in this matter and it made full use of this opportunity. The Latin Empire was established (up to 1261) and Count Baldwin of Flanders was elected as its first ruler. Its territory consisted of large parts of Byzantium, Thracia, the north-western part of Asia Minor and some of the islands of the Aegean. Boniface of Montferrat, the real military leader of the Crusade, established for himself and his followers a kingdom in the region of Macedonia and Thessalonica. The Venetians, who exercised considerable influence on the new states, secured a system of trading posts which gave them a decisive advantage in their trade with all parts of the former Byzantine Empire. The treaty on the division of the country ceded three-eighths of it to them but they were not able to retain all of this. As a result, they concentrated their attention on their corresponding share of Constantinople, which included the Hagia Sophia, coastal

strips along the Adriatic, the seaports of the Peloponnesos, a large number of the Greek islands centred around Naxos, the major ports of the Hellespont and the Sea of Marmora and the island of Crete, which proved to be of great significance in the later development of trade. Thus Venice had not only occupied positions of prime importance in Greek trade but also possessed a sea-route, flanked by strategic bases, from the Lagoon City to Constantinople. With the conquests of 1204 and despite all the subsequent changes, it laid the foundations for intercontinental trade which endured till the end of the Middle Ages and also created the operational basis for further conquests.

For the brief period of its existence, the Latin Empire was always an instable state. The conquerors were unable to create a firm basis for their relations with Greek society and civilization. The Byzantine population regarded the Latins as

20   The maritime traffic of the Mediterranean was dominated throughout the Middle Ages by galleys which also carried sails. 15th century woodcut.

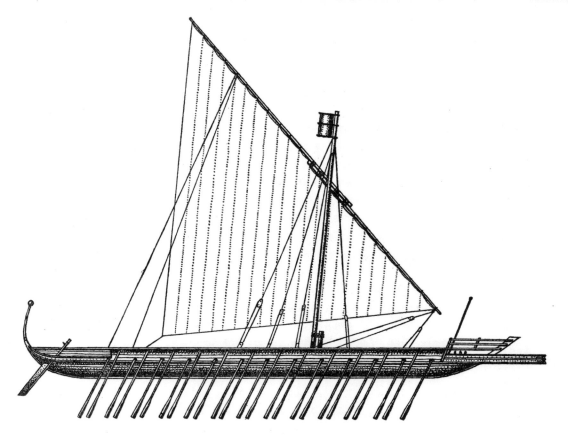

21   Reconstruction model

foes who had to be despised. It was only a question of time until the newly established state of 1204 could be dismantled again by the Byzantine states which had emerged from the ruins of the empire. By 1225, the whole of the area of the Latin Empire in Asia Minor had already been conquered by the kingdom of Nicaea. A short time later, the kingdom of Thessalonica fell into the hands of the Greek ruler of Epiros and in 1261 the victory of the emperor of Nicaea marked the end of the Latin Empire. Only the Peloponnesian principality of Achaia continued until 1482 as a small Frankish state. Venice survived the change in the balance of power but had to accept the competition of Genoa which had given military support to the Greeks.

As a whole, the balance-sheet of the fourth Crusade was a favourable one for the merchants of Northern Italy. Venice was the dominant power, it is true, but Pisa and Genoa were also able to maintain and develop their positions in the former Byzantine Empire, even if they had to pay due respect to the Lagoon City. The merchandise of the Greek world and of Asia Minor was popular and easily sold in Europe. The Greek islands around Naxos produced grain, citrus fruits, olive oil, honey, wine, cotton, wool and silk. Cretan wine, which was exported in considerable quantities, was famous and popular not only in Europe but also in Egypt. The cities, headed by Constantinople, were famous for the products of their craftsmen. From the bases acquired in 1204, the Northern Italian merchants moved as far afield as Asia Minor. The trade links with the Seljuk sultanate of Iconium were expanded nor did trade with the empire of Nicaea and Trebizond ever cease. Italian merchants were to be found on the northern coast of the Black Sea as early as the first half of the 13th century. It is recorded that several Italian merchants visited Kiev around 1247. However, they had not yet displayed any interest during this time in the link with the silk route from China since they were more concerned with the agricultural produce of the region. The trading stations in the Crimea and along the Sea of Azov had already been established by the Byzantines before 1202 and merchants from Syria were also familiar with the trade route to Rus and to the nomadic peoples in the area to the north-east of the Black Sea. The principal commodities in which they traded were animal skins and slaves. From the 13th century, Northern Italian merchants also appeared on the scene here. The political changes following the advance of the Mongols and the establishment of the rule of the Golden Horde in Southern Russia did not interfere with these trading links. On the contrary, they were developed even further.

The merchants followed in the footsteps of Franciscan missionaries and envoys. The establishment of contacts and relations was associated with the journeys of the Polos, a family of merchants from Venice. Active in Byzantine trade, Nicolo and Maffeo Polo visited the Khanate of the Golden Horde about 1255 and then reached the court of Kublai Khan in China. They returned in 1269 and repeated the expedition in 1271 when they were accompanied by the seventeen-year old Marco Polo. They did not arrive back in Venice until 1295, having passed through practically all the regions of Central Asia, China and India. Marco Polo's records have provided us with informative descriptions of economic, cultural and social life in the Mongol empires. Although the newly acquired knowledge of Asia was only very gradually converted into active trade, the expeditions of the Polos were unmistakable evidence of the increasing importance of merchants. Marco Polo's account of his travels caught the public imagination to such an extent that centuries later even Columbus was inspired by them to seek the sea passage to these peoples.

The protection and development of the trade with the Orient shaped the picture of the Northern Italian and Southern French seaports. Just as the merchants did not venture to the Orient as individuals but with the authority of their city behind them and with the privileges that that city had secured, it was the city in its totality, i.e., the patricians and the city administration, that determined the entire development and all the prospects of trade and navigation on its own territory, too.

There was a rapid upswing in the extent and importance of shipbuilding since the 11th century. Numerous new shipyards were built and existing ones extended. The quality of their work was subject to strict supervision by the municipal authorities since not only did the weal and woe of seafarers and passengers depend upon it but also the existence of trade in general. The biggest shipyard of Venice, the Arsenal, was actually owned by the city, which employed several thousand workers there. The construction of a trading ship must have cost a great deal of money and, as a rule, was financed by several merchants in each case. It is known that in Venice up to twenty-four merchants had shares in a single ship.

Very little is known about the types of ships built at that time. More detailed information is only available for the ships of the 12th century and later and then only for a few types. Dromonds were the most common type of warship. There is also evidence that they were used in a combined form for both naval and mercantile purposes. Based essentially on Byzantine models, the dromond was about 35 to 40 metres long and had a beam of five to six metres. It had two or three banks of twenty to twenty-five oars on each side and was also fitted with two small sails, making it very swift and manoeuvrable.

The most widely used types of merchantmen could carry up to two hundred tons of cargo. There are even records of individual ships with capacities of up to five hundred tons. They were relatively roomy and could also convey a large number of passengers and horses. It seems that it was with a craft of this class that Jacques de Vitry voyaged to the Orient as the Bishop of Acre in 1216. He had five cabins for himself and his luggage. According to an account from the middle of the 13th century, this type of ship was 26 metres long, 6.45 metres in the beam and 6.60 metres deep. Its superstructure included two pilot bridges, several cabins and two masts. It was slow and relatively clumsy which is probably the reason why it was not found everywhere. Dromonds, as a dual-purpose type of vessel, predominated.

In the same way that they controlled shipbuilding, the city authorities also supervised everything that was related to maritime operations, such as the loading of cargo, the recruitment of ships' crews and so on. From the 13th century onwards, detailed regulations were drawn up, specifying the burden, armament, rigging, principles for the contracts applying to the conveyance of passengers and so on. Since this time, it became usual to keep a logbook on the larger ships.

As in the past, it was usual to voyage along the major routes in convoys and, in this case, too, it was the city which was in charge. In Venice, it was the city council which organized convoys to Constantinople, Syria and Alexandria. It specified the number of armed galleys which had to accompany the merchant ships and named the captain of the escort who was in overall command of all the other crews.

Despite this, journeys by sea remained dangerous and hazardous. Captains avoided the open sea and preferred to voyage along the coast. In addition, the principal shipping routes passed via a series of islands which functioned as a system of bases. Commercial practices developed in parallel with navigation. Up to the 13th century, the usual type of commercial contract was the "colleganza" or "commenda". Two merchants would form a partnership for a particular transaction, one of these being a sleeping partner. Profits and losses were shared. Merchants endeavoured to reduce the great risk factor involved in trade by never committing their capital to a single venture. It was usual to conclude several colleganzas to run at the same time.

The consequences of the upswing in trade of the Italian seaports in the 13th century affected not only shipbuilding and navigation but also every sphere of social life. The great majority of the urban population was engaged in trade or in activities associated with it. The merchants rapidly became wealthy and, as a result of the commercial prosperity, gold coins were again minted as currency. The first gold guilders appeared in Genoa and Florence in 1252 and gold ducats in Venice in 1284. This meant that equality with the Byzantine and Oriental gold currency had been achieved. However, the use of the new money was restricted to the markets for which it was intended and silver money continued to be used for ordinary requirements. From the 13th century onwards, the Italian seaports as a whole experienced a cultural development of a high order and this also exercised an influence on the regions around them. This is examined in more detail in the final chapter.

Although the Crusade movement and concept declined in importance during the 13th century, this was not true of the trade with the Orient. The expansions of the 12th and the beginning of the 13th century had created many opportunities and had given the Italian merchants considerable economic and political power. They were no longer dependent on the wanted or unwanted assistance of the knights. The cities of Northern Italy had made such progress towards the status of mediaeval city-states that they could call on a significant political and military potential which, through money, could be expanded still further at any time. Thus, in the course of the 13th century, the links between the Crusade movement and the interests of the Northern Italian cities became looser and looser and the importance of the latter increased with every decade. The period of the Crusades was followed in the late Middle Ages by the ascendancy of the Italian merchants in the Mediterranean.

The Norman Empire and the Reconquista

Up till now, we have been mainly concerned with the expansion of the European feudal lords in the Orient. The developments in the Norman empire in Southern Italy and in Spain were not considered although these conquests followed from the same motives and a similar configuration of power and, from the initial situation at the end of the 11th century, represented similar points of concentration in the advance of European feudal lords into the Islamic Arab world of the Mediterranean.

On the eve of the Crusades, the Norman empire in Southern Italy and Sicily presented the picture of a mixed society of Catholic and Orthodox Christians, Moslems and Jews, each group retaining its own material civilization and culture. In the early stages of the Norman conquest, this relative independence was still marked by an element of chance, due to the fact that the Normans had not yet consolidated their ruling position. In the following centuries, however, an economically and culturally flourishing feudal society emerged from this and all the ethnic elements had a share in it. This development began under the Norman King Roger II (1101 to 1154) and reached an absolute climax during the reign of Emperor Frederick II (1212–1250).

From its geographical position and political situation, no state could have been better suited to emerge as a pioneer of the Crusade idea than the Norman empire. Some Crusades started out via Southern Italy and many pilgrims preferred to set out on the sea-voyage from here. The Normans themselves took part in several Crusades. The most important trading city of their empire, Amalfi, maintained bases in a number of cities in the Crusader states. Nevertheless, it was precisely in this territory that the Crusade idea never became dominant. All the expeditions to the Orient were subordinated to political interests, these being primarily the consolidation and development of Norman rule. The Norman counts and kings never allowed themselves to be bound by a Crusade policy and considered Islamic and European princes, the Byzantine Empire and the Papacy alike as enemies or allies, depending on the needs of the particular situation.

Roger II fought against the German Emperor Lothair to extend his possessions in Southern Italy, invaded Byzantine territory in Greece at the time of the second Crusade, in which he originally intended to take part, was the enemy of the Pope and sent expeditions to North Africa where he occupied Tunis and Tripoli for a time.

This foreign policy was not the result of chance. It corresponded to his internal concept of building an efficient, centralized state to maintain the high material and cultural standards which already existed. For this, he used all his resources available to suppress resistance, whether this came from the cities, the Norman barons or the Islamic population. All those classes and groups which supported his policy of centralization enjoyed his confidence, no matter what their religious belief. Moslems, Jews and Greeks occupied posts in the economy and state. The entire machinery of the local administration of Sicily was in the hands of Moslems. Jews, Greeks and Moslems alike were entrusted with important functions in the central state apparatus. Arab units commanded by Islamic officers were some of Roger's best and most courageous troops.

The cities were a major factor in the economic and cultural progress achieved by the Norman empire. However, in their political and social position within the state, they were closer to Arab models than to Western European ones. Communal freedom and the resultant social and political privileges, which divided the towns and the countryside in law, were very largely unknown. The Norman state was characterized by the integration of the towns in the centralized structure of the state. This had no effect on their economic prosperity during the period with which we are concerned. Artisan and agricultural production flourished just as it had done before the Norman conquest. The Arab craftsmen made scarcely any change in their traditional designs. The subsequent coronation coat of the German kings and emperors, which was made during Roger's reign, is the most famous but by far not the only example of this. Numerous other objets d'art which are now to be found in European museums demonstrate this. Byzantine influence was particularly marked in Southern Italy. On the other hand, numerous churches were built by Roger in which largely Western European traditions are apparent.

Palermo, the capital of the empire, experienced its real heyday during this period. Contemporaries describe the babble of different tongues in its cities and streets, and note the existence, side by side, of churches, mosques and synagogues. The royal court itself combined all the Oriental and Byzantine comforts and luxuries of the ruling class. Chroniclers list numerous palaces and pleasure seats, hunting expeditions, collections of Oriental and African animals and various technical masterpieces, such as water-clocks. Oriental and Christian elements mingled at the royal court. In addition to Norman barons, the immediate entourage of Roger included Jews and Greeks. It is said that Roger himself wore Moslem clothes. One of his most trusted advisers was the illustrious Arab geographer Al-Idrisi, who had come to the Norman court from Spain and lived and worked there for a long time. He aroused Roger's interest in geography and it is said that the Norman king gave Idrisi substantial assistance in the writing of his principal work, entitled "The book of Roger, a geographical description of the world". Not only Oriental but also Greek authors were active at Roger's court. Despite all this, however, the different cultures and their peoples retained their separate identity. In Islamic poetry, this is shown by the fact that although Roger's positive features were lauded, it is not forgotten that it is an "infidel" who is being praised. Love lyrics deal with the theme of unhappy love between young people of different creeds. Roger himself probably viewed the various confessions from a certain distance, not in the sense of an atheist but rather in the Byzantine tradition, as is more clearly evident with Frederick II. The following anecdote seems to be characteristic of him: After a victory of his fleet off the coast of North Africa, Roger asked an Islamic courtier about the help of Mohammed and whether he had forgotten this country and its inhabitants. He received the answer that Mohammed had been far away at Edessa which had just been recaptured from the Crusaders. Roger was satisfied with this answer. It seems that he saw little purpose in religious quarrels.

This was the atmosphere which marked the childhood of the later Emperor Frederick II, who was born in Southern Italy in 1194. His mother, Constance, was a daughter of Roger II and his father was the Emperor Henry VI. The Norman kingdom thus became part of the Holy Roman Empire.

No change took place in the internal political structure of Southern Italy, although Innocent III devoted a great deal of effort to stimulating the Crusade movement in this time.

Frederick II regarded the South as the focal point of his empire. It was here that he had grown up. He spent only eight years of his life on the northern side of the Alps. Under Frederick, the Norman part of his heritage continued its economic and cultural upswing. The emperor promoted a system of political and economic measures which shaped this trend. It is noteworthy, from the viewpoint of the present work, that the different religions continued to enjoy equal rights. Moslems and Jews were excluded only from the highest offices of the state.

His residence at Foggia in Northern Apulia was a complex of palaces, hunting lodges and pleasure seats which featured all the luxuries of the Orient. His enemies even said that he kept a harem there. It was natural that the knightly epic should have been held in high esteem at his court. Minstrels from France and Italy and also from the Islamic area sang their songs of heroism and love there.

It was not decadence which marked the essential spirit of this court-life but a liberal attitude which was unique by mediaeval standards and had arisen from the specific situation of Southern Italy and Sicily. Legend states that Frederick himself spoke a number of different tongues—Sicilian, Latin, Arabic, Greek, Hebrew, French and German. He maintained contacts with Arab rulers and scholars, European princes and the emperor of Byzantium. Scholars and artists from all parts of the world gathered at his court. The illustrious mathematician Fibonacci of Pisa worked here. The Scottish philosopher Michael Scotus stayed at the imperial court just like many Islamic scholars. Frederick himself took an interest in many branches of knowledge. Mathematics, philosophy and alchemy were only some of the subjects in which he had scholars inform him of the latest findings. The chroniclers state that Frederick held long and detailed conversations with the men of learning. He himself wrote a treatise on falconry for his son in which experience and the observation of Nature were regarded as the primary sources of knowledge. In Naples, Frederick founded a university, the first "state university", i.e., it was not subject to the authority of the Catholic Church. Salerno, the most famous medical school of Europe in the 12th and 13th centuries, attracted students from Northern Italy and France. Seafarers from the Northern Italian cities served as commanders in the Sicilian fleet. Although these are only external factors, they do represent an alternative to the policy of the Crusades which, despite the fact that it could only be practised within a small territorial area, did offer a long-term prospect of survival.

It would be historically incorrect to assert that there was no social discord. The reign of Frederick in Southern Italy was a period of harsh rule by a single class. Vast sums of money were extorted from the peasants and artisans. Saracen women worked as slaves in the weaving establishments which were famed for their exquisite silks. Unrest among the peasants and revolts in the cities occurred repeatedly. In 1223, Frederick had 15,000 Moslem peasants from Sicily resettled in Northern Apulia so that they could be more effectively kept under control. This was unmistakably intended as a reminder to the Papacy since the settlement area around the town of Lucerca was in the direct vicinity of the territory of the Church. Conflict and exploitation did not have a religious colouring, however, and affected the ordinary people without distinction, whatever their creed.

Frederick II had aroused the active hostility of the Popes and their followers, though not on account of his internal policies but by reason of his actions in foreign affairs. Rome was not prepared to be enclosed between a German empire to the north and south. This was how the curious situation arose in which not only German and Norman knights but also Saracen archers fought in the Imperial army against Rome and its allies during Frederick's campaigns in Italy. It is difficult to imagine the "Holy War" taking a more grotesque course.

Frederick also provided an alternative in the relationship between the State and the Church or between the State and religion. He wanted the Churches to be subject to the authority of the State. His enemies, the supporters of Papal univer-salism, spread deliberate rumours, suggesting that Frederick was more inclined to the doctrine of Mohammed than to the teachings of Jesus Christ. They asserted that he displayed more friendship towards Saracens than to the Christians and he was accused of saying that "three swindlers deceived their contemporaries in such a cunning manner that they were able to dominate the world: Moses, Jesus and Mohammed". Whether this was slander or otherwise, these accounts nevertheless express Frederick's outlook which favoured something like an absolute monarchy. It is said that at the end of his life he envied the emperor of Byzantium since the Church there was subordinate to the monarch. He considered that he occupied his own position in a similar way by Divine right. It is thus understandable that although he had been excommunicated by the Pope he set out on his Crusade to the Orient in 1228/1229 not as a repentant sinner and pious soldier of God but in full consciousness of his independence and imperial rank. He carried out skilful diplomatic negotiations with the Islamic rulers, resulting in the return of Jerusalem to the Crusader states. This is when he is said to have remarked that he would be glad to hear the call of a muezzin again. On the other hand, despite being excommunicated, he had himself crowned in Jerusalem.

For his contemporaries, Frederick II was a very controversial figure. For those who took the side of the Pope he was an Anti-Christ whereas he was honoured and admired by his followers. He became a legend immediately after his death and even centuries later his return as the last emperor was awaited. What he actually did and his view of the world can be explained not so much by his strong personality, however, but by the specific mixed forms of material civilization and culture which prevailed in the South of his empire. The unique cultural revival in Southern Italy and Sicily rapidly declined after his death which coincided with the end of the Crusades and the economic, political and cultural configuration in the Mediterranean area which was associated with them. It was not long either before the saga of the return of the emperor was also modified. After several intermediate stages, it was transferred to the person of Frederick Barbarossa (Kyffhäuser Saga). It was he whose return was awaited by the ordinary people to re-establish a centralized authority in the land and to save the poor from poverty and oppression.

It was a similar story in Spain but it is only possible here to present a brief review of developments there. The Reconquista was launched initially from the Christian states of Northern Spain—Castile, Léon, Navarre and Aragon—which also received the principal benefit from it since every new district conquered helped to increase these realms. As already described, at the beginning of the Crusades European knights took part in the expansion to the South, just as they did in the conquests in the Orient but this parallel rhythm disappeared after the second Crusade. The kingdoms of Northern Spain received military support from the constant arrival of French knights in particular and were reinforced by the peasants that settled in the new areas. The Crusade idea was soon forgotten and the climaxes of the Reconquista were linked by the local authorities with the idea of the "Holy War". Three orders of Spanish knights were founded on the model of the knightly orders of the Crusader states. The Knights Templar also tried their luck in Spain but in general all these factors were subordinated to the expansion of the Christian kingdoms. The first phase of the Reconquista ended in the middle of the 13th century with the capture of Cordova (1236), Valencia (1238) and Seville (1248). The Moslems were forced to withdraw to minor possessions in Southern Spain, centred around Granada. The reasons for the success of the Reconquista are to be found in the Moors themselves. Their rule was marked time and again by disintegration into numerous small states which waged feuds with each other and thus made it impossible for effective resistance to be organized.

In their material and cultural standards, the conquered territories still followed the traditions of the Omayyad Caliphate of Cordova. As in the past, Islamic civilization continued to be maintained by the Moslem, Jewish and Christian communities who differed only in their faiths since they had adopted the language and culture of the Arabs. The Jews were respected and wealthy merchants; from their ranks came outstanding scholars.

The crafts were in the hands of Islamic artisans and Moslems were also responsible for the cultivation of special crops. The Christian kings of the 12th and 13th centuries and their retinues relied on these groups and for a long time their rule was characterized by religious tolerance.

The Influence of the Crusades on Europe

In 1808, the "Institut de France" issued a call for historical investigations on the subject of "The influence of the Crusades on the civil liberties of the European nations, on their civilization and education, on trade and industry". The result was a flood of works which, to a greater or lesser extent, related the entire material and cultural developments of the main and later periods of the Middle Ages to the Crusades. There was a rapid reaction to this, too. The relationship between external influences and an independent development was examined in detailed studies and a precise distinction drawn between the Crusades, the commercial expansion of the Northern Italian merchants, the Norman empire and the Reconquista. It was clearly shown that the Crusades had only a minimal share in the Byzantine and Arab Islamic culture which had left a mark on Europe.

We considered the whole of the expansion of European feudal society in the Mediterranean area after the 11th century as a relative unit. The Crusade movement, the Reconquista and the conquest of Southern Italy and Sicily had emanated from the same feudal forces and the same causes could be identified. The same patterns were also evident in the confrontation with the civilizations of the subjugated peoples, as may be observed in all the expansions of the main feudal period.

Only by taking the features which they have in common is it possible to identify their specific aspects. The principal differences resulted from the degree of stability of the conquered territories. From the beginning, the Crusader states were politically and militarily extremely vulnerable. In the first half of the 12th century, it was a question of consolidating their positions while after the rise of Saladin they were primarily concerned with the defence of that area of their territory which they still held. In these circumstances, questions of the confrontation with Arab Islamic culture, which assumed an ethnic and social rapprochement of the classes, did not play an important part. In addition to this, the Crusade ideology was unsuited to encourage interest in Arab culture. On the contrary, wherever Crusaders acted in its spirit, they became isolated and the differences between Europe and Islam were emphasized to such a degree that any interest in Arab Islamic culture was suffocated. Only the amenities of Oriental life were accepted and used. Wherever contacts were established in the Crusader states, this took place in opposition to the Crusade ideology. In their content and form, the Crusader states had little chance of enduring. Byzantium, which was supposed to be the recipient of "military aid", suffered such heavy losses at the hands of the Crusaders that it never really recovered from them even after 1261.

In contrast to this, the Normans of Southern Italy and the Christian states in Spain succeeded in developing stable feudal class-structures. This laid the foundations for the inclusion of Arabs, Greeks and Jews in society, the basic condition for a flourishing material civilization and culture which survived the period of the Crusades. Despite suppression from time to time, religious tolerance was regarded as self-evident. It was not by chance that it was primarily through these states that more was learned in Europe about Arab Islamic culture.

It sometimes happens that the feudal expansion and the commercial expansion in the Orient are compared with each other, the former being presented as a warlike development, the other a peaceful one. This proposition appears to be of doubtful validity since although the merchants used different means they were nevertheless a direct part of the expansion as a whole. They were the immediate beneficiaries of the feudal conquests and helped to direct them. Despite all the differences which emerged, as in connection with Egypt, for example, the specific course of the commercial expansion was only made possible by the military campaigns. The fourth Crusade is not the only example of this. The development of Levantine trade in the 12th century did not take place in addition to the feudal expansion and certainly not in spite of the Crusades but grew with it. The development of shipping, trading posts, trade-routes, the accumulation of commercial capital and so on took place in parallel with the Crusades. After the decline of the Crusade movement, the cities had achieved such economic and political power that they were able to finance and organize the necessary military support themselves. The influence of Arab Islamic culture, which had come to Europe via the trade routes in the Crusade period, must be considered in connection with the developments of the time.

An indication of the degree to which a specific society is influenced by another can be found in the extent to which its language is enriched by borrowed words. Even a short list is sufficient to show the variety of these words and the objects they describe. It should be noted, however, that this process was not restricted to the period of the Crusades. Words borrowed by English from the Arabic or from Persian and Greek by way of Arabic include lime, lemon, apricot, citrus, sugar, orange and other names denoting fruits hitherto unknown in Europe, the names for spices such as nutmeg, cinnamon, caraway, tarragon and saffron and terms for craft products such as damask (Damascus), muslin (Mosul), atlas, mohair, chiffon, taffeta, satin, carafe, baldachin (Baghdad), pantofle, mattress, divan or sofa. Lilac and azure are likewise names for colours which come from Arabic. Words of Arabic origin are very numerous in the scientific sphere. Almost all the names of constellations and the basic terms of astronomy come from Arabic. Algebra and algorism are distortions of Arab names or book titles. Camphor, benzene, alcohol, alkali, soda, borax and so on also come from the same source. Similar examples could be quoted from other sciences. In the maritime sphere there are the words admiral and corvette and mention can also be made of a series of special terms such as tariff, sequin, arsenal, alcove, bazar, amulet, talisman, elixir and others.

However, this philological evidence does not indicate the extent of the content and forms of the confrontation with Arabic Islamic cultural achievements. These loan-words can roughly be divided into three main groups: agriculture, trades and crafts, science. In addition, there were the highly diverse influences on European society, particularly on the life led by the feudal lords.

As a result of European expansion in the Orient, Europeans were introduced to a large number of crops and fruits hitherto unknown to them: lemons, oranges, apricots, peaches, plums, cucumbers, melons, maize, rice, saffron, artichokes, sesame, carob, dates, sugar cane and others. Many descriptions of the milieu in the Crusader states are full of praise for the extensive gardens and their tasty fruits. Europe heard about this and many Crusaders and pilgrims brought seeds back with them on their return. However, this had little effect on the spread of these plants since the feudal lords knew little about their cultivation or propagation. From contemporary accounts, it seems that their attempts were regarded more as curious experiments than as serious efforts to bring about changes in European agriculture. The route by which these plants actually came to Europe was via Spain, Sicily and Southern Italy. The Moslem peasants had the necessary knowledge and skills for the cultivation of these crops and it is known that a rapid change took place in the character of agriculture in these areas after the Islamic conquest. In Sicily, for instance, date palms were planted immediately afterwards in a totally systematic manner. They then gradually spread from here to Italy and Southern France in particular. This was a matter of major importance for the producers and not for the feudal lords—which was likewise the case in Spain and Italy, too. However, it was during the time of the Crusades that this change was initiated and it continued during the centuries that followed. A second route, which was especially significant for Eastern Europe, was from Byzantium via the Balkans so that it seems likely that many of these crops, such as melons, maize and cucumbers, became known in Central Europe by way of the Balkans.

From the 12th century onwards, the trade with the Orient and Byzantium led to a substantial increase in the consumption of spices, dyes and perfumes and a wide variety of artisan products. Pepper, cloves, nutmeg, amber, incense, saffron, alum, indigo, red sandalwood, lacquer, damask, muslin, silk, velvet, atlas and other products were constantly offered for sale at the great markets of Europe, in addition to splendid apparel and blankets. Oriental carpets were in great demand and high prices were paid for jewellery of pearls and precious stones, enamel work, fine glassware and ceramic articles, ivory carvings and other objets d'art. The same applied to gold and silver work and ornamental weapons of Damascus steel.

To some extent, these and other products were imports obtained through commercial channels. But in the 12th and 13th centuries many of the artisan products in particular had originally been secured as booty or represented gifts from Crusaders. The events of the 4th Crusade provide especially clear evidence of this. Unfortunately, no detailed accounts have survived but many of the collections which still exist in churches and monasteries were originally donated by persons who took part in the Crusades.

Every castle must have possessed at least a few luxury objects from the Orient and churches and monasteries were furnished with them. Altar cloths, chasubles and liturgical vessels frequently bore Arabic inscriptions or Islamic motifs. This did not seem to bother the people of the time to any great extent, perhaps because they thought that these were Hebraic symbols. The main thing was that they contributed to the solemn atmosphere.

The "reliquary trade" did unexpectedly well. Every large church and monastery of this period fought for a share of the relics and precious reliquaries stolen from the churches of the Orient and Byzantium since the reputation of the Church depended to a not insignificant extent on the value of its relics. In Halberstadt (GDR), for example, the day on which the treasures from the fourth Crusade became the property of the Church was long celebrated by a solemn procession. The fact that it originated from the plundering of a Christian city probably never occurred to anyone anymore.

Although Oriental products were so popular, local artisans were relatively slow in making the change to similar products. Silk production spread to other regions in the course of the 13th century. In the middle of the 12th century, it seems that it was still restricted to Sicily. It was from here that it spread to Central and Northern Italy, Provence and finally to Northern Germany as well. Lucca became the great centre of the silk trade but Bologna, Venice, Augsburg, Ulm and other cities also raised silkworms or produced silk fabrics.

Up to the 13th century, paper was imported from Spain and the Orient but after this date there is evidence that it was manufactured in Europe, too. From this time onwards, merchants made increasing use of paper as a writing material. At the end of the 13th century, it was being made in Genoa and Ravensburg and shortly afterwards in Bologna, Padua, Venice and other cities as well.

The Crusaders and pilgrims had observed the windmills in use in the Orient, and, in this case, it was not long before the first examples appeared in Europe. There is evidence that windmills were in use in various regions of Europe as early as the middle of the 12th century.

There was much indirect influence on the production of high-quality handmade articles, this resulting from attempts to imitate Byzantine and Oriental imports. However, this influence was often nothing more than a stimulus. After the 13th century, the cities of Northern Italy became noted for the production of high-quality woollen fabrics. The raw materials—alum, dyes and wool—were mainly imported from the Orient and Byzantium. Enamel work had been produced in Europe before the expeditions to the Orient but it was only from the 13th century that it achieved real artistic excellence, not least because of the quality of Byzantine enamel work which Europeans had learnt to appreciate. Glass production, especially in Venice, had survived the decline of Antiquity but the art of glass painting by the appropriate fusion process, the making of ground crystal dishes and other techniques date only from after the 12th century. The products of the Orient had a similar influence on the emergence of ivory carving, faience ware and the work of the gold and silversmiths.

The material production of Europe in general and of Italy in particular was stimulated in numerous ways through the contacts with Islamic Arabic and Byzantine culture. Accumulation from intermediate trade and high productivity in the crafts were two of the essential conditions for the development of that stage of history known as the Renaissance.

The utilization of the scientific and academic achievements of the Arab Islamic world took a somewhat different form.

From the 13th century, the cultivation of science and learning in Western Europe became centred in schools and universities. The most famous of these included Paris (1174/1200), Oxford (c.1170), Cambridge (1209), Naples (1224), Toulouse (1229), Montpellier (1239), Rome (1203) and others. Six universities were founded in Spain during this period and in Northern Italy a series of law schools came into being, centred on Bologna. This resulted from the prosperity of European feudal society and the growing importance of the cietis.

Under the influence of the Church and with few exceptions, theology and its philosophical consequences was the principal subject studied at the universities. Nevertheless, the natural sciences such as mathematics, physics, biology, medicine, chemistry and others were gaining in importance.

The foundations of this new interest in knowledge were provided by the teachings of Islamic Arabic and Antique authors. Translations from Arabic into Latin of the scientific and philosophical works of Greek Antiquity and the Islamic world had started to appear from the early 12th century. The translation schools were centred in Spain, Sicily and the Crusader states, Spain being the most important. The most favourable conditions existed here on account of the relatively large group of Jews and native Christians who were familiar with Hebraic, Arabic, Greek and Latin and able to make translations. One of the most outstanding of these was John of Seville, also known as John of Spain and Ibn Daud. He was a Jew who had grown up in the cultural tradition of the Omayyad empire in Spain and was a convert to Christianity. He was responsible for a large number of mathematical, astronomical, medical and astrological translations during the first half of the 12th century. A few years later, Gerard of Cremona came to the fore. He was active in Toledo in the years after 1165, probably in association with other native translators. It is said that he was responsible for seventy-one translations. It was mainly Greek authors, such as Aristotle, Euclid and Archimedes, in whom he was interested but he also translated the works of Arab Islamic scholars such as Al-Razi, Ibn Sina, Al-Kindi and others.

There was a similar situation in Southern Italy and Sicily where numerous translations were produced at the court of Frederick II.

In the Crusader states, on the other hand, the native Syrians and Jews were obviously less active in this field, at least there are not many translations which have survived. It is indeed known that pilgrims brought manuscripts back with them but it has been shown that these were translated by priests and Italians who had settled in the Crusader states, such as Stephan of Antioch and Philip of Tripoli who produced translations of medical works.

22 *Shipbuilding was a major activity in all mediaeval seaports and specialized crafts quickly developed.* (*From a relief in Sainte-Chapelle, Paris.*)

In Western Europe the number of translators living in Spain and South Italy who were able to make translations of this kind was small. Mention must be made of Adelard of Bath who had learned the Arabian language in Antioch and Toledo, and of Gerard of Cremona. There were constant laments about the difficulties of teaching and studying Arabic, Hebraic and Greek at the universities.

It is impossible to give even a list of all the translations made and a few examples have to suffice. In the fields of mathematics and astronomy, a series of works were translated which made the Indo-Arabic system of numbers known in Europe. Works by Euclid and other authors of Antiquity attracted interest, as did the works of Arab authors on algebra and trigonometry. The latter included the famous treatise by Al-Khwarizmi (from whose name the term "algorism" was derived): "al-gabr..." (hence the term "algebra") which was in use at European universities as a basic textbook on mathematics up till the 16th century. In the field of optics, an outstanding work was the "Book of Optics" by Al-Haitami (Lat. Alhazen) who examined the refraction of light in transparent media and was a source of inspiration for Roger Bacon and others. Chemistry was influenced for a long time by a series of textbooks on alchemy of Arab origin. As early as the 13th century, the works of Al-Biruni on astronomy and the calendar led to suggestions being made in Europe for the reform of the Julian Calendar. Medicine was enriched by what must be described as a flood of translations. Reference has already been made to the intermediary role of Salerno. Spain and the Crusader states followed in this tradition. It seems that in Toledo the translators specialized in medical texts. The comprehensive work by Ibn Sina, known in Europe as the "Canon of Medicine" remained a standard textbook until the 17th century. The basic compendium of medicine by Al-Razi was translated a number of times. Books on pharmacology and medicaments were widespread.

In philosophy, the translators turned their attention not only to the Antique philosophers and especially Aristotle but also to the philosophical writings of Ibn Sina (Avicenna) and Ibn Rushd (Averroes). These works exercised enduring influence on the discussions of mediaeval scholars.

As early as the middle of the 12th century, the translation of the Koran was commissioned by Petrus Venerabilis, Abbot of Cluny, following a journey to Spain. The Franciscans and Dominicans preparing for missionary work in the Orient no longer went there without a knowledge of Islam. From the 12th century, a great many Islamic Arab manuscripts were translated and many other examples could be quoted.

By way of Spain and the Norman empire in Southern Italy, this mass of learning and scientific knowledge flowed to the universities of Europe. The Crusader states, concentrating only on conquest and later after the rise of Saladin, caught up in a complicated and hopeless military situation and afflicted by major losses of territory, were unable to offer the right atmosphere for scholarly work. In addition, the native population led a separate life, quite different to the situation in Spain and Southern Italy. Nevertheless, the indirect influence of the existence of the Crusader states on the acceptance of Oriental sciences in Europe appears to have been greater than is apparent from the direct evidence.

The great universities of Southern France and Italy were not only in the vicinity of Spain and Southern Italy but were also the traditional centres of the Crusades and the trade with the Orient. There is evidence that many scholars did not keep to the "contact zone" with the Orient but went further afield. Practitioners took part as personal physicians to kings and princes in the Crusades of the 13th century and used the opportunity to extend their knowledge.

A few instances of individual careers provide an idea of the possible links and influences.

Hugo of Lucca, also known as Hugo of Bologna, was a member of a noble family and took part as a physician in a Crusade in 1218. Returning in 1221, he was appointed municipal surgeon in Bologna and set up a surgical school here, introducing a series of practical innovations. His son, a priest, was the author of a four-volume teaching manual on surgery.

Petrus of Maricourt (Petrus Peregrinus) brought knowledge of magnetism and the compass back to France from the Orient and in 1269 wrote a treatise about magnetism in which an illustration of a compass appears for the first time.

108 The cloth sewn on the flag, an embroidery on purple silk (49 × 42.5 cm), dates from the 12th century and came to Halberstadt with Bishop Konrad of Krosigk some time after 1204. It was originally used as a cover for a dish for Communion bread or a Communion chalice. Motif: Christ serving six apostles with Communion bread. The counterpiece shows Christ serving six apostles with Communion wine. Halberstadt Cathedral

109 This Demetrius reliquary of gilded silver, 10 cm high, 6 cm wide and 3 cm deep, was probably made in Salonica and came to Halberstadt along with other booty of Bishop Konrad. Halberstadt Cathedral

110 This gilded silver platen, the work of a 12th century Byzantine goldsmith, was used in the Greek Orthodox Church as a dish for Communion bread. The Bishop of Halberstadt brought it with him from Constantinople on his return from the fourth Crusade. Halberstadt Cathedral

111 The reliquary of St Demetrius (capsule reliquary) of gold, 4.7 cm in height, 3 cm wide and 1.5 cm deep, was probably made by a goldsmith of Salonica in the 10th century. The relic was kept in the capsule. The wearer of the reliquary was sure of the help of St Demetrius. Halberstadt Cathedral

112 Reliquary of St Nicholas (51 cm high). The carved wooden core, sheathed in gilded silver and ornamented with semi-precious stones, encloses the actual relic, the finger of St Nicholas. This reliquary was likewise stolen from Constantinople in 1204 and brought to Halberstadt. Halberstadt Cathedral

113 The time of the Crusades was also the golden age of chivalry. The 13th century in particular was characterized by a great variety of knightly combat and tournament clothing. Unlike the 11th century and due not least to the influence of the Orient, decorative accessories had made their appearance. Horse-cloths decorated with the rider's coat of arms, surcoats over the armour and banners were the principal characteristics. Decorations were mostly worn on festive occasions. Bibliothèque Nationale, Paris

114 The development of feudal palaces and residences in Europe continued throughout the entire period of the Crusades. These were the centres of knightly culture. It was in Falkenstein Castle that the jurist Eike of Repkow compiled the "Sachsenspiegel", a summary of feudal law, at the behest of Count Hoyer.

117 The sword was the principal weapon of attack of the mediaeval knight and the warlike symbol of his membership of a caste. Swords of all shapes and sizes were produced in an infinite variety of designs. The hardness and resilience of the blade were the criteria of quality whereas ornamentation was of secondary importance, a distinction being drawn between combat and ornamental weapons, of course. Historical Museum, Dresden

115 The Shield of Seedorf (late 12th century) is thought to have belonged to Arnold of Brienz. It is a ceremonial shield which was used by his family for many generations. It is now in the Swiss Landesmuseum in Zurich

116 The shield of the Landgrave Konrad of Thuringia (1240) features a lion as the coat of arms. The lion is of leather and is superimposed on the lindenwood shield which forms a blue background. The eyes and claws were represented by precious stones. Height 88 cm, width 72.5 cm. St Elisabeth's Church, Marburg

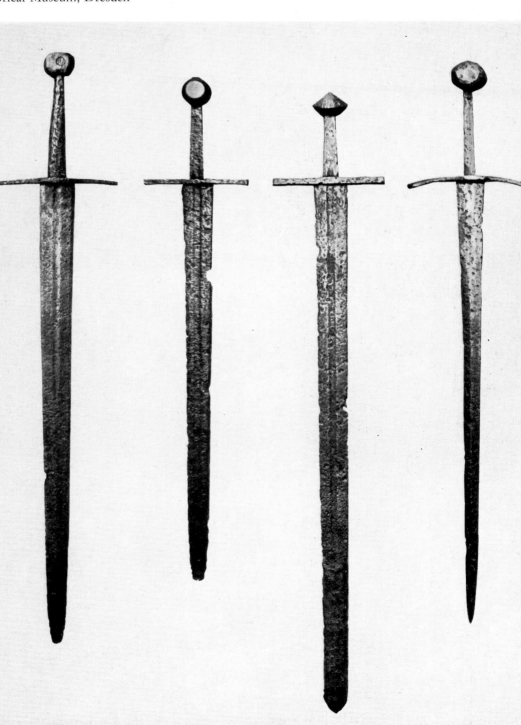

119 Ernest of Gleichen, Count of Thuringia, with his two wives, as depicted on his grave plate.

The legend which circulated after his death (1246) relates that he took part in the Crusade of 1228 and was taken captive. It was only through the love and help of a Saracen lady that he was able to regain his freedom. To keep the promise of marriage which he had given, he is said to have maintained a ménage à trois on his return home. Erfurt Cathedral

118 There is a great deal of rich and varied evidence of the golden age of feudal culture in the 12th and 13th centuries. The "Rider of Bamberg", dating from about 1230–1240 in Bamberg Cathedral, is one of the finest works of sculpture of this period. This stylized equestrian figure conveys a general impression of the features of a prince. In the historical literature on the subject, it is suggested that the artist had a definite subject in mind, perhaps King Conrad III, who died in Bamberg in 1152, or King Philip who was murdered here in 1208.

120   The effigy of Gérard de Vandémont
and his wife depicts a scene from his life—
the return from the Crusade of one believed dead. This motif is an indication of
a mood which has little in common with
the official ideology of the Crusade.
Thousands of knights never returned.

201

Leonardo Fibonacci, one of the most illustrious mathe-
maticians of the 13th century, was born in Pisa about 1180.
His father had been in charge of a Pisan trading station in
Bougie (North Africa). It was here that he learnt Arabic and
received instruction from an Arab mathematician. He then extended his knowledge of mathematics in the course of commercial journeys to Egypt, Syria, Byzantium, Sicily and Spain.
In 1202, he published his "liber abaci" (Book of the Abacus)
in which he explained the Arabic numeral system which was
soon afterwards introduced in Pisa in actual practice. In other
works, he presented the principles of Arab algebra and offered solutions to equations of the first and second degree. However, it was not in Pisa that Fibonacci was held in the greatest
esteem but at the Sicilian court of Frederick II where he was
a welcome guest.

It is obvious that only few of the men of learning of the
13th century had first-hand experience of the Islamic world.
From the 13th century onwards, the principal achievements
of Arab Islamic science and of Antique authors who had influenced the Arab scholars were known in Europe. Manuscripts of these works were kept in universities and monasteries. For the following period, there also survives a series of
examples of independent interpretations and modifications by
scholars from various European countries. Nevertheless, it
cannot be assumed from this that there was a widespread
knowledge of these works or that they had a broad influence.
Feudal society with its narrow economic basis was not in a
position to apply this knowledge on a broad scale. This is
why the process of "digestion" of these achievements continued until 1500 and later.

The extent and forms of the influence of the Crusades
and the Orient on the feudal nobility itself and especially the
knights is the subject of controversy. The age of the Crusades was simultaneously the finest hour of chivalry. These
were the centuries in which chivalry acquired its intellectual
profile. Castle architecture experienced a climax and the observance of the code of chivalry, which laid down the moral
qualities and principles of honour of the knights, was considered particularly important. Troubadours and minstrels
sung not only about the forms of courtly wooing but also
proclaimed the standards of chivalrous behaviour in general.
Some of the characteristic features of knightly ethics, such
as valour, Christian piety and so on, have already been indicated in connection with the development of the Crusade idea.
The influence of the Orient on knightly culture is evident
from the parallels between the internal developments within
the class of the feudal lords and the Crusade movement.

Despite this, the social conditions influencing the development of the knights in Europe were so different from those
of the Orient even as late as the 13th century that a closer
rapprochement was out of the question.

The intellectual level of the European feudal lords did
not approach that of their Islamic Arab counterparts nor did
they strive to attain it in their concept of the ideal knight.
Only in Spain and the Norman empire of Southern Italy did
the rulers concern themselves with scientific problems and
developments. Otherwise, the knights were practically illit-
erate and even many of the minstrels and entertainers had
to dictate their songs and epics.

A series of moral concepts are related to this, such as
valour in battle, religious piety, chivalrous behaviour towards
women, generosity towards the vanquished and others. The
Crusaders had first seen tournaments in the Orient and were
not slow in emulating them. The same applies to courtly
celebrations. Both Moslem and Christian lords cultivated the
art of chivalrous poetry and both sides presented their works
at the court of the Norman kings. Nevertheless, the points of
contact should not be overemphasized since there was much
which evidently followed an independent course and in which
knowledge of the Orient was no more than a stimulus.

Certain customs and habits, resulting from trade with
the Orient and knowledge of the life there, became established
as part of the everyday life of the knights. Bathrooms came
into use, also in the towns, toilets appeared on the scene,
beards were grown. As already indicated, residences were
characterized by a measure of Oriental luxury, although this
was scarcely comparable to that of the Arab feudal lords. In
literature, the general assumption is made that there was a
visible change in the clothing and thus in the outer appearance
of the ruling class. Women, in particular, made use of the

costly materials available. Nevertheless, even if account is taken of all this and other things, too, the influence of the Orient still remained relatively slight as a whole.

Somewhat different were the developments in the military sphere. The greatest battles and campaigns of the 12th and 13th centuries were those of the crusading armies and the armies of knights in the Crusader states. The most advanced castles were built in the Orient and were improved and extended from one decade to another. Siege techniques were also improved.

Under these conditions, the equipment of the knights underwent continuous development. Coats of mail were extended beyond the knee and were reinforced at particularly vulnerable points of the body, for instance, at the arms by iron plates. Chain-mail for horses came into use, this being designed to give greater protection against attacks by archers. All these changes were adopted in Europe, too.

The use of the tunic for the rider and a cloth for his steed, worn on top of the armour, was likewise adopted from the Orient. This was originally intended to give protection against the sun but was later regarded as a part of knightly apparel.

From the end of the 11th century, the European knights began to carry coats of arms, these also being imitated from Arab Islamic models. The point of this at first was to assist identification of the knights when they were in armour. This soon led to the development of family coats of arms and numerous symbols indicate the Orient as the beginning of this tradition.

Changes in warfare, the increased importance of archers and infantry forces, for example, resulted from experience gained in the Orient and were then employed under different conditions in the fighting of the 13th and 14th century in Europe as well.

All this seems at first to favour a positive conclusion although it is essentially a question of a sum of details, these being of a varying magnitude depending on the particular social area concerned. Some facts must not be overlooked, however. The cultural relations, links and influences were basically only concomitant phenomena of a warlike expansion. They did not reflect the intentions of the feudal forces concerned in this and thus, disregarding details, occurred more by chance on the edge of the political and military events. It would be incorrect and would obscure the nature of the Crusades if the character of this expansion would be disregarded. The fact that the Crusades in the Orient cost the lives of generations of European knights is not the main point here.

More important are the links between the feudal expansion and the cultural influence of the Orient. For Europe north of the Alps, the influence of the Orient and Byzantium remained superficial, despite the many examples of it. This was not solely on account of the different material and cultural standards of East and West but to a much greater extent because the feudal lords as a class were accidental intermediaries at most. They were in no way the exponents of Oriental civilization. This observation does not exclude the examples to the contrary already mentioned. Up to the main period of the Middle Ages if not later, the feudal expansion needed at least a minimum degree of social integration between conquerors and conquered if a genuine acceptance of the higher cultural standard of the subjugated peoples were to take place. Spain and the Norman empire in Sicily cannot be regarded as being in the same situation as the Crusader states of the Orient from this point of view.

It was a different matter as regards the relationship between expansion and acceptance of Oriental culture for the mediaeval bourgeoisie. The merchants of Northern Italy were always aliens in the Orient and in Byzantium. The elements of material civilization and culture which were adopted represented a sum total of individual achievements. In addition to the examples already mentioned, reference must also be made to the stimulus which business activities received from the Orient. Apart from the Arabic system of numbers, this included rationalized calculating methods for book-keeping and the introduction of a simplified system of payment in the shape of cheques and bills of exchange. Here, too, of course, it was the idea that mattered and not at all a question of simply adopting an existing procedure.

All these individual examples were so favourably received in the merchants' own cities that the most important spheres of social life there were given a stimulus which significantly accelerated their historical progress. The independent nature of their development did not disappear in the course of this.

The aim of this book was to examine the feudal expansions from the viewpoint of the cultural confrontation. Although they kept the whole of Western European feudal society in a state of tension for two centuries, the Crusades in the Orient were some of the most ill-advised expansions of mediaeval history. And that is stated without any desire to moralize. When it is sometimes pointed out that tens of thousands of knights had to pay for this senseless undertaking with their lives, this is true but should be a reminder that in more recent times the ordinary people had to suffer for the ambitions of conquest of the ruling class.

In addition to this basic assessment of the Crusade movement, it must be mentioned, however, that its consequence helped to shape European feudal society to a not inconsiderable extent. To be sure, the marks it left were not equally apparent in every sphere of social life and in some areas they lasted longer than in others. They were clearly reflected in knightly culture from the 11th to the 13th centuries. Like much of European intercontinental trade, the economic prosperity of Italy in the late Middle Ages would have been unthinkable without the expansion in the Orient. The colonial empires of the North Italian cities were established on the foundations created by the Crusades. Numerous points of contact were apparent as a concomitant manifestation of feudal expansion and, as individual examples, left their mark on the economy and cultural life of Europe for far longer than the actual period of the Crusades. A social synthesis of the different feudal societies did not take place, however. From a comparison of the Crusader states with the Norman empire in Southern Italy and the Christian states of Spain, it seems at first sight that the specific Crusade ideology has been exaggerated. The limits were set by the different structures of the feudal societies which, consolidated in their internal relations in each case, no longer allowed a synthesis. In this sense, the Norman empire was likewise no more than a symbiosis and indeed, from the historical viewpoint, one of only relatively short duration. It is apparent that in feudalism a social mingling of a new quality is only possible in the early feudal phase when the economic, social and cultural structure as a whole has not yet become consolidated in its internal relations.

APPENDIX

POLITICAL CHRONOLOGY

661–750   Dynasty of the Omayyads

750–1258   Caliphate of the Abbasids

755   Emirate of the Omayyads of Cordova (829 Caliphate of Cordova) founded

868–905   Rule of the Tulunids in Egypt. Egypt remains only nominally subject to the Caliphate of the Abbasids

969–1171   Rule of the Fatimid dynasty in Egypt. The nominal overlordship of the Abbasids in Egypt is ended

1016   Normans begin conquest of Southern Italy

1016   Pisa conquers Sardinia

1031   Disintegration of Omayyad Caliphate of Cordova into small kingdoms, creating favourable conditions for the continuation of the Reconquista by the small Christian kingdoms of Asturia, León, Navarre, Castile and Aragon in Northern Spain

1034   Pisa establishes trading colony in Bono (North Africa)

1054   Schism of Christian Church into Greek Orthodox and Roman Catholic Churches

1055   Seljuks capture Baghdad

1061   Beginning of Norman conquest of Sicily from Southern Italy

1064   French princes and knights capture Barbarstro in Islamic Spain

1070   Seljuks take Jerusalem from Fatimids

1071   Battle of Manzikert. Seljuks under Alp Arslan defeat Byzantine army and found the Sultanate of Rum in Asia Minor

1073–1085   Pope Gregory VII

1074   Gregory VII plans Crusade for the support of Byzantium against the Seljuks and to gain dominance of Rome over the Byzantine Church

1085   Toledo captured by Alfonso VI of Castile

1081–1118   Emperor Alexius I of Byzantium

1088–1099   Pope Urban II

1095   Council of Clermont. Pope Urban II issues call for Crusade

1096   Fatimids recapture Jerusalem from Seljuks

1096   Spring: Peasants' Crusade under Peter the Hermit; annihilated at Nicaea (6.10.1096)

1096–1099   First Crusade

1097/1098   Siege and capture of Antioch. Foundation of Principality of Antioch by Bohemund of Taranto

1097   Baldwin of Boulogne becomes lord of the Countship of Edessa

1099 (15.7.)   Capture of Jerusalem

1100   Founding of the Kingdom of Jerusalem

1101   Crushing defeat of Crusade of French, German and Lombard feudal lords in Asia Minor

1104   King Baldwin captures Acre

1105–1154   King (since 1130) Roger II of Sicily. Final Norman rule of Sicily and Southern Italy

1109   Capture of Tripoli and founding of Countship of Tripoli

1113   Beginnings of the Order of St John or the Hospitalers

1120   Beginnings of the Order of the Knights Templar

1125   Peasants' revolt in Beirut

1127–1146   Atabeg Zangi, Emir of Mosul

1137–1180   King Louis VII of France

1127/28   Zangi captures Aleppo

1131/32   First nobles' revolt in Kingdom of Jerusalem

1137–1152   King Conrad III

1139   Siege of Damascus by Zangi

1144   Zangi captures Edessa (end of Crusader state)

1146–1174   Nur ad-Din (Nureddin), ruler of Aleppo, Damascus, Mosul and Mesopotamia

1147–1149   Second Crusade (King Conrad III and Louis VII)

1147   English, Norman and German knights of the second Crusade capture Lisbon for the King of Portugal

1147   "Crusade against the Slavs". Saxon nobles attempt subjugation of West Slavs of Mecklenburg and Pomerania in the sign of the Cross

1155–1190   Frederick I Barbarossa ruler of Holy Roman Empire (Germany)

1154   Nur ad-Din (Nureddin) captures Damascus

1171   Salah ad-Din (Saladin), son of the Kurdish leader Eijub, overthrows Fatimid dynasty in Egypt (Vizier of Egypt from 1196)

1171–1250   Ayyubid dynasty in Egypt

1172   Henry the Lion leads Crusade

1185   After a long struggle, Saladin unites Egypt and the territories of Damascus, Aleppo and Mosul in a single empire

1187   Battle of Hattin. Saladin defeats army of Crusader states. Jerusalem and other important territories and cities taken from Crusaders

1184–1199   Richard Cœur de Lion king of England

1189–1192   Third Crusade (Emperor Frederick I Barbarossa, Richard Cœur de Lion of England, King Philip II Augustus of France)

1190 (10.6.)   Frederick Barbarossa drowned in the river Saleph

1190–1197   Henry VI Holy Roman Emperor

1191/92   After eventful struggles, truce between Crusaders and Saladin.

Crusader states retain only a narrow coastal strip. Not possible to recapture Jerusalem. Acre becomes capital of the kingdom

1193 Death of Saladin

1197 Crusade of Emperor Henry VI

1198–1216 Pope Innocent III

1198 Order of Teutonic Knights founded. Principal base at Acre

1202 Knights of the fourth Crusade capture Zara on the coast of Dalmatia for Venice (price for sea passage)

1202–1204 Fourth Crusade, originally planned against Egypt, was diverted to the conquest of Byzantium under the leadership of Enrico Dandolo, the Doge of Venice

1203 (17.7) Capture of Constantinople for first time

1204 (12.4.) Constantinople taken a second time and plundered

1204–1261 Founding of Latin Empire by knights of the fourth Crusade. Baldwin of Flanders becomes emperor. Dependent fiefs in Thessalonica, Athens, Thebes, Achaea, Salona. Small Byzantine realms remain: empire of Nicaea, Trebizond, despoty of Epiros

1209–1219 Albigensian Crusade. Led by Simon de Montfort on behalf of the Pope. Nominally directed against the Cathari of Southern France, the forces under his command were subsequently (up to 1229) used as an instrument by the French Crown for the subjugation of the South

1212–1250 Frederick II becomes Emperor (in 1220)

1212 Children's Crusade. Started from the Rhineland, Eastern France and Southern Lorraine. Probably a peasant movement, nominally led by children

1215 4th Lateran Council. Propaganda for the Crusade idea intensified. Appeal made to all classes and strata. Crusade tax on Church estates (20th part of income in three years)

1217–1229 Period of the fifth Crusade. Several expeditions at different times. Egypt as principal objective

1217/18 Crusade of Andrew II of Hungary to capture Acre

1219–1221 Crusade under Cardinal Pelagius to capture Damietta

1228/29 Crusade of Emperor Frederick II. Jerusalem returned to Crusader states by treaty. Frederick crowned in Jerusalem

1219 Unsuccessful attempt by St Francis of Assisi to convert Sultan Al-Kamil to Christianity

1230 Teutonic Knights begin brutal conquest of Prussia

1236 King Ferdinand III of Castile begins conquest of Cordova

1238 Valencia captured by army from kingdom of Aragon

1245 Pope Innocent IV sends Franciscan monks as missionaries under Joannes de Plano Carpini to Mongols. Negotiations carried out regarding possible alliance. Other delegations follow

1248–1254 Sixth Crusade. Louis IX of France captures Damietta, is defeated and taken prisoner at battle of Mansurah and is released for ransom money. Subsequent stay in Acre

1251 Pastoureaux uprising in North-Eastern France. Crusade sermon. Movement directed against clergy

1259 Baybars, Sultan of Egypt (from 1260) defeats Mongols and unites Egypt and Syria

1260–1277 Baybars Mameluke Sultan of Egypt

1261 With the conquest of Constantinople, Byzantium ends Latin Empire

1268 Sultan Baybars captures Jaffa and Antioch

1270 Seventh Crusade, campaign by Louis IX of France against Tunis

1289 Crusader states lose Tripoli

1291 Acre last base of Crusaders in Orient, is taken by Mamelukes (Sultan Al Ashraf). Crusaders withdraw to Cyprus

1489 Cyprus falls under Venetian rule

BIBLIOGRAPHY

The literature on this subject is almost inexhaustible. New investigations and reviews appear every year. This list cannot therefore even give an idea of the most important works and is only intended as a reference to a few introductory publications and handbooks and a few more specialized investigations.

ATIYA, A. S., *Kreuzfahrer und Kaufleute*, Stuttgart, 1964

BRADFORD, E., *Verrat am Bosporus. Die Eroberung Konstantinopels 1204*, Tübingen, 1970

BRENTJES, B., *Die Söhne Ismaels. Geschichte und Kultur der Araber*, Leipzig, 1971

DESCHAMPS, P., *Terre Sainte Romane*, Paris, 1964

DIETRICH, E., "Das Judentum im Zeitalter der Kreuzzüge." *Saeculum* 3, 1952, pp. 94–131

DURAND, W., *Das Zeitalter des Glaubens. Die Geschichte der Zivilisation*, vol. 4, Berne, 1952

EICKHOFF, E., *Seekrieg und Seepolitik zwischen Islam und Abendland. Das Mittelmeer unter byz. und arab. Hegemonie*, Berlin, 1966

ERDMANN, C., *Die Entstehung des Kreuzzugsgedankens*, Stuttgart, 1955

FEDDEN, R./THOMSON, J., *Kreuzfahrerburgen im Heiligen Land*, Wiesbaden, 1969

Geschichte der Araber. Von den Anfängen bis zur Gegenwart, vol. 1, edited by a group of authors under the chairmanship of Prof. Dr. habil. L. Rathmann, Berlin, 1961

GLOGER, B., *Kaiser, Gott und Teufel. Friedrich II von Hohenstaufen in Geschichte und Sage*, Berlin, 1970

LE GOFF, J., *La civilisation de l'occident médieval*. Paris, 1967

LE GOFF, J., "Das Hochmittelalter". *Fischer Weltgeschichte*, vol. 11, Frankfurt/Main, 1965

HAUSSIG, H.-W., *Kulturgeschichte von Byzanz*, Stuttgart, 1954

A history of the crusades, edited by K.M. Setton, 5 volumes, Philadelphia, 1955ff.

HROCHORD, VERA AND MIROSLAV, *Křižaci v Levantě*, Prague, 1975

Klassenkampf, Tradition, Sozialismus. Von den Anfängen der Geschichte des deutschen Volkes bis zur Gestaltung der entwickelten sozialistischen Gesellschaft in der Deutschen Demokratischen Republik, Berlin, 1974

KASHDAN, A. P., *Aufstieg und Untergang des Oströmischen Reiches*, Berlin, 1964

KASHDAN, A. P., *Byzanz und seine Kultur*, Berlin, 1973

KÖLLER, H./TÖPFER, B., *Frankreich. Ein historischer Abriss*, Part I, Berlin, 1969

Die Kreuzzüge in Augenzeugenberichten. Edited by R. Pernoud, German translation by H. Thurnau, Munich, 1971

LEY, H., *Studie zur Geschichte des Materialismus im Mittelalter*, Berlin, 1975

LOOS, M., *Dualist Heresy in the Middle Ages*, Prague, 1974

LÜDERS, A., *Die Kreuzzüge im Urteil syrischer and armenischer Quellen. Berliner byzantinistische Arbeiten*, vol. 24, Berlin, 1964

MAYER, H. E., *Bibliographie zur Geschichte der Kreuzzüge*, Hannover, 1960

MAYER, H. E., *Geschichte der Kreuzzüge*, Urban-Bücher der wissenschaftlichen Taschenbuchreihe, vol. 86. Stuttgart, 1965

MAZAHERI, A., *So lebten die Muselmanen im Mittelalter*, Stuttgart, 1957

MÜLLER-WIENER, W., *Burgen der Kreuzritter im Heiligen Land*, Munich/Berlin, 1966

MICCOLI, G., "La 'crociata dei fanciulli' del 1212." *Studi Medievali*, vol. 2, 1961, pp. 407–443

NORWICH, J., *The Normans in the South (1016–1130)*, London, 1967

NOTH, A., "Heiliger Krieg und Heiliger Kampf in Islam und Christentum, Beitrag zur Vorgeschichte und Geschichte der Kreuzzüge." *Bonner historische Forschungen*, vol. 28, Bonn, 1966

OSTROGORSKY, G., *Geschichte des byzantinischen Staates*, 3rd edition, Munich, 1963

PRAWER, J., *Histoire du royaume latin de Jérusalem*, Paris, 1969

PRUTZ, H., *Kulturgeschichte der Kreuzzüge*, Berlin, 1883

RICE, D. T., *Die Kunst des Islam*, Munich/Zurich, 1967

RUNCIMAN, ST., *A history of the crusades*, 3 volumes, London, 1950ff

RENOUARD, J., *Les villes d'Italie de la fin du Xe siècle au début du XIVe siècle*, Paris, 1969

SMAIL, R. C., *Crusading warfare (1097–1193.) A contribution to medieval military history* (Cambridge studies No. 53), Cambridge, 1956

THIRIET, T., *Histoire de Venise*, Paris, 1969

VERBRUGGEN, J. F., *De krijgskunst in West-Europa in de middeleeuwen (IXe tot begin XIV eeuw)*, Brussels, 1954

WAAS, A., *Geschichte der Kreuzzüge*, 2 volumes, Freiburg, 1956

WENTZLAFF-EGGEBERT, F.-W., *Kreuzzugsdichtung des Mittelalters. Studien zu ihrer Geschichte und dichterischen Wirklichkeit*, Berlin, 1960

WERNER, E., *Zwischen Canossa und Worms. Staat und Kirche 1077–1122*, Berlin, 1973

WOLFF, TH., *Die Bauernkreuzzüge des Jahres 1096. Ein Beitrag zur Geschichte des 1. Kreuzzuges*, Tübingen, 1891

WOLLSCHLÄGER, H., *Die bewaffneten Wallfahrten gen Jerusalem*, Zurich, 1973

ZABOROV, M. A., *The crusades* (in Russian), Moscow, 1956

ZABOROV, M. A., *Introduction into the historiography of the crusades* (in Russian), Moscow, 1966

SOURCES OF ILLUSTRATIONS

Lala Aufsberg, Sonthofen/Allgäu 3, 6, 18, 19, 33, 34, 35, 36, 47, 78, 80, 81, 82, 83, 104, 105

Klaus G. Beyer, Weimar: 107, 108, 110, 111, 112, 114, 119

Biblioteca Apostolica Vaticana, Archivio Fotografico, Vaticano Latino: 24, 64

Bibliothèque Nationale, Paris: 1, 4, 5, 8, 9, 16, 17, 27, 28, 49, 58, 59, 62, 106, 113

Bildarchiv Foto Marburg: 2, 7, 14, 20, 21, 22, 23, 51, 56, 60, 66, 116, 118, 120

British Museum, London: 12, 61

Burgerbibliothek, Berne: 63, 79

Deutsche Fotothek, Dresden: 13 (König), 42, 45, 46, 52, 53 (Gröber), 117

Giraudon, Paris: 50

Hochschul-Film- und Bildstelle, Martin-Luther-Universität, Halle: 32 (Lindner)

Institut für Denkmalpflege, Halle: 109

Metropolitan Museum of Art, New York, Verlagsarchiv: 10, 11

Museé de Monuments Français, Paris: 37

Museo Correr, Venice: 33

Österreichische Nationalbibliothek, Vienna: 26, 31

SCALA, Florence: 29, 30, 40, 41, 47, 57

Schweizerisches Landesmuseum, Zurich: 115

Staatliche Museen, Berlin, Münzkabinett: 84, 85, 86, 87, 88, 89, 90, 91, 92, 93, 94, 95, 96, 97, 98, 99, 100, 101, 102, 103

Stadtbibliothek, Nuremberg: 43, 44

Stiftung Preussischer Kulturbesitz, Bildarchiv, Berlin (West): 39

Universitätsbibliothek, Jena: 25

Universitätsbibliothek, Leipzig: 38

ZEFA, Düsseldorf: 15 (P. de Prins), 54 (L. Schranner)

ZODIAQVE, St Léger Vauban: 55, 65, 67, 68, 69, 70, 71, 72, 73, 74, 75, 76, 77

MAPS

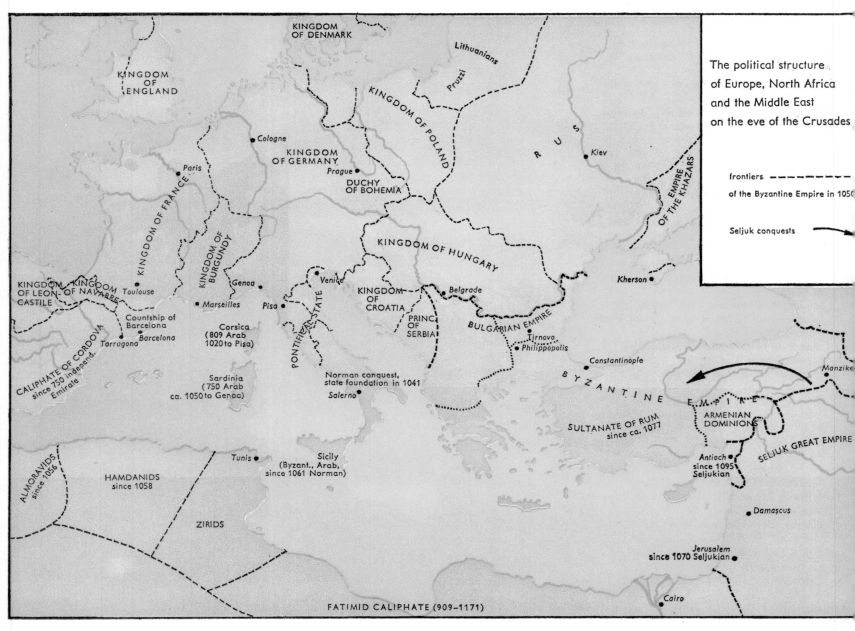

The political structure
of Europe, North Africa
and the Middle East
on the eve of the Crusades

frontiers – – – – –

of the Byzantine Empire in 1050

Seljuk conquests →

KINGDOM
OF DENMARK

Lithuanians

Pruzzi

KINGDOM OF ENGLAND

KINGDOM OF POLAND

R U S

Kiev

EMPIRE OF THE KHAZARS

Cologne

KINGDOM OF GERMANY

KINGDOM OF FRANCE

Paris

Prague

DUCHY OF BOHEMIA

KINGDOM OF HUNGARY

KINGDOM OF BURGUNDY

Genoa

Venice

KINGDOM OF CROATIA

PRINC OF SERBIA

BULGARIAN EMPIRE

Belgrade

Kherson

KINGDOM OF LEON-CASTILE

KINGDOM OF NAVARRE

Toulouse

Marseilles

Pisa

PONTIFICAL STATE

Tirnovo

Philippopolis

Constantinople

B Y Z A N T I N E

Manzike

Countship of Barcelona

Corsica
(809 Arab
1020 to Pisa)

Barcelona

Tarragona

CALIPHATE OF CORDOVA
since 750 independ.
Emirate

Sardinia
(750 Arab
ca. 1050 to Genoa)

Norman conquest,
state foundation in 1041

Salerno

E M P I R E

ARMENIAN DOMINIONS

SULTANATE OF RUM
since ca. 1077

SELJUK GREAT EMPIRE

Antioch
since 1095
Seljukian

ALMORAVIDS
since 1056

Tunis

Sicily
(Byzant., Arab,
since 1061 Norman)

HAMDANIDS
since 1058

Damascus

ZIRIDS

Jerusalem
since 1070 Seljukian

Cairo

FATIMID CALIPHATE (909–1171)

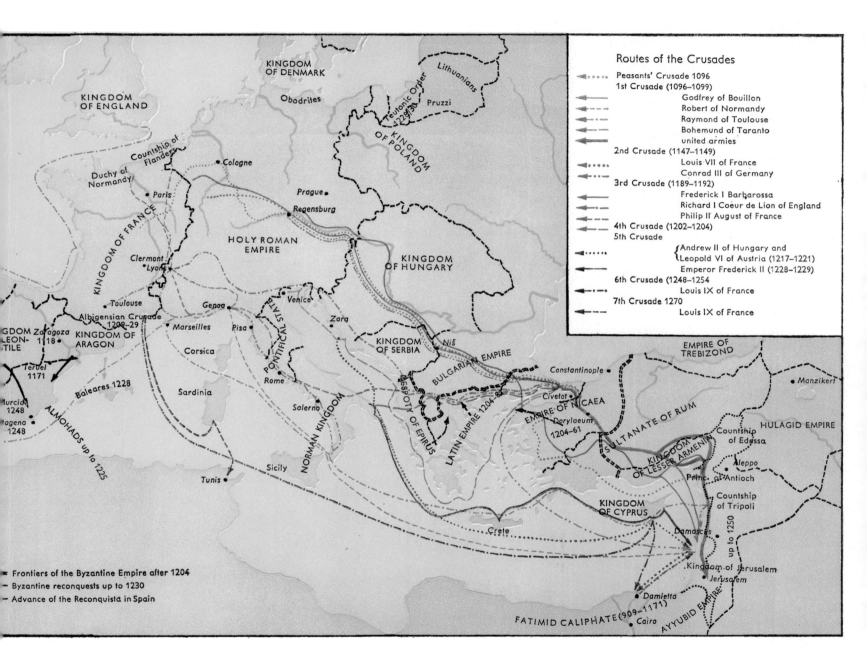

KINGDOM OF DENMARK

KINGDOM OF ENGLAND

Obodrites

Lithuanians

Teutonic Order 1225/30

Pruzzi

KINGDOM OF POLAND

Countship of Flanders

Duchy of Normandy

• Cologne

• Paris

• Prague

• Regensburg

KINGDOM OF FRANCE

HOLY ROMAN EMPIRE

KINGDOM OF HUNGARY

Clermont
Lyons

Routes of the Crusades

Peasants' Crusade 1096
1st Crusade (1096–1099)
    Godfrey of Bouillon
    Robert of Normandy
    Raymond of Toulouse
    Bohemund of Taranto
    united armies
2nd Crusade (1147–1149)
    Louis VII of France
    Conrad III of Germany
3rd Crusade (1189–1192)
    Frederick I Barbarossa
    Richard I Coeur de Lion of England
    Philip II August of France
4th Crusade (1202–1204)
5th Crusade
    Andrew II of Hungary and
    Leopold VI of Austria (1217–1221)
    Emperor Frederick II (1228–1229)
6th Crusade (1248–1254)
    Louis IX of France
7th Crusade 1270
    Louis IX of France

• Toulouse

GDOM Zaragoza
LEON- 1118
TILE

Albigensian Crusade
1209–29

KINGDOM OF ARAGON

Genoa •

Venice •

Zara •

KINGDOM OF SERBIA

Niš •

EMPIRE OF TREBIZOND

• Manzikert

• Marseilles

Pisa •

Corsica

PONTIFICAL STATES

Rome •

BULGARIAN EMPIRE

Constantinople •

Teruel
1171

Sardinia

Baleares 1228

Salerno •

NORMAN KINGDOM

DESPOTY OF EPIRUS

LATIN EMPIRE 1204

Civetot •

EMPIRE OF NICAEA

SULTANATE OF RUM

HULAGID EMPIRE

Murcia
1248

agena
1248

ALMOHADS up to 1225

Dorylaeum
1204–61

Countship
of Edessa

KINGDOM OF LESSER ARMENIA

• Aleppo

Princ. of Antioch

Tunis •

Sicily

Crete

KINGDOM OF CYPRUS

Damascus •

Countship
of Tripoli

up to 1250

Frontiers of the Byzantine Empire after 1204

Byzantine reconquests up to 1230

Advance of the Reconquista in Spain

Kingdom of Jerusalem

• Jerusalem

• Damietta

AYYUBID EMPIRE

FATIMID CALIPHATE (909–1171)

• Cairo

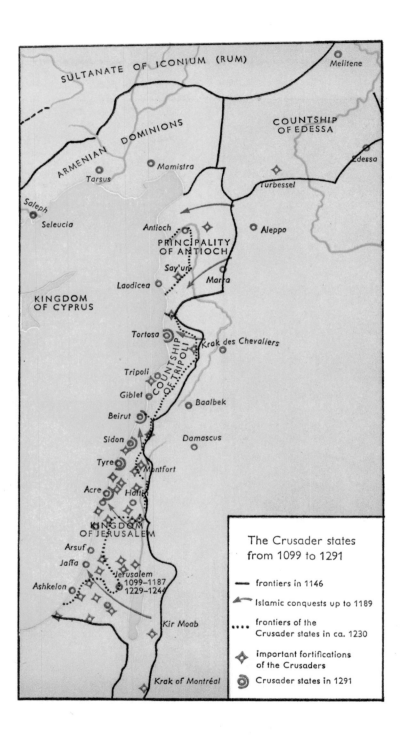

SULTANATE OF ICONIUM (RUM)

Melitene

ARMENIAN DOMINIONS

COUNTSHIP
OF EDESSA

Mamistra

Edessa

Tarsus

Turbessel

Saleph

Seleucia

Aleppo

Antioch

PRINCIPALITY
OF ANTIOCH

Say'un

Laodicea

Marra

KINGDOM
OF CYPRUS

Tortosa

Krak des Chevaliers

Tripoli

COUNTSHIP
OF TRIPOLI

Giblet

Baalbek

Beirut

Sidon

Damascus

Tyre

Montfort

Acre

Haifa

KINGDOM
OF JERUSALEM

Arsuf

Jaffa

Jerusalem
1099–1187
1229–1244

Ashkelon

Kir Moab

Krak of Montréal

The Crusader states
from 1099 to 1291

—— frontiers in 1146

→ Islamic conquests up to 1189

···· frontiers of the
Crusader states in ca. 1230

✦ important fortifications
of the Crusaders

◎ Crusader states in 1291

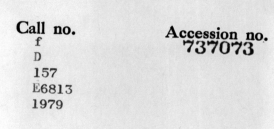